1860 CENSUS

CABELL COUNTY
WEST VIRGINIA

Carrie Eldridge

Heritage Books
2024

HERITAGE BOOKS

AN IMPRINT OF HERITAGE BOOKS, INC.

Books, CDs, and more—Worldwide

For our listing of thousands of titles see our website
at
www.HeritageBooks.com

Published 2024 by
HERITAGE BOOKS, INC.
Publishing Division
5810 Ruatan Street
Berwyn Heights, MD 20740

Heritage Books by the author:

1860 Census, Cabell County, West Virginia

An Atlas of Appalachian Trails to the Ohio River

An Atlas of German Migration and America

An Atlas of Northern Trails Westward from New England

An Atlas of Settlement between the Appalachian Mountains and the Mississippi/Missouri Valleys: 1760–1880

An Atlas of the Southern Trails to the Mississippi

An Atlas of Trails West of the Mississippi River

Cabell County's Empire for Freedom

Cabell County, Virginia/West Virginia, Superior Court Records, 1843–1848

Etna Iron Works: Ledger Book - Expense Records, 1876–1878 (Final Ledger), Lawrence County, Ohio

Looking at the Personal Diaries of William F. Dusenberry of Bloomingdale, (Cabell County), Virginia/West Virginia, 1855 and 1856, Plus Parts of 1862, 1869, 1870, and 1871

Minute Books: Cabell County, [West] Virginia Minute Book 1, 1809–1815

Miscellaneous Cabell County, West Virginia Records: Order Book Overseers of the Poor, 1814–1861; Fee Book, 1826–1839; 1857–1859 (Rule Book); Cabell Land for Tax Purposes, 1861–1865

Nicholas County, Kentucky Property Tax Lists, 1800–1811 with Indexes to Deed Books A & B (2), and C

Nicholas County, Kentucky Records: Stray Book 1, 1805–1811; Stray Book 2, 1813–1819; Stray Book 3, 1820–1870; and Execution Book A, 1801–1878

On the Frontier of Virginia and North Carolina

Owen County, Kentucky Stray Books 1 & 2: 1819–1830, 1830–1864

Torn Apart: How Cabell Countians Fought the Civil War

International Standard Book Number
Paperbound: 978-0-7884-2870-8

CONTENTS

1860 CENSUS DISTRICTS

    BARBOURSVILLE
    GUYANDOTTE
    McCOMAS
    CARROLL
    UNION

1870 CENSUS DISTRICTS

    BARBOURSVILLE
    GUYANDOTTE
    McCOMAS
    GRANT(formerly Carroll)
    UNION

1970 CENSUS DISTRICTS

    BARBOURSVILLE
    GUYANDOTTE
    McCOMAS
    GRANT
    UNION
    GIDEON (from Guyandotte)
    KYLE(from Guyandotte)

Square Miles	1809	1820	1842	1867	1895
CABELL	2109	1229	721	282	282
LOGAN		880			
WAYNE			508		
LINCOLN				439	
MINGO					424

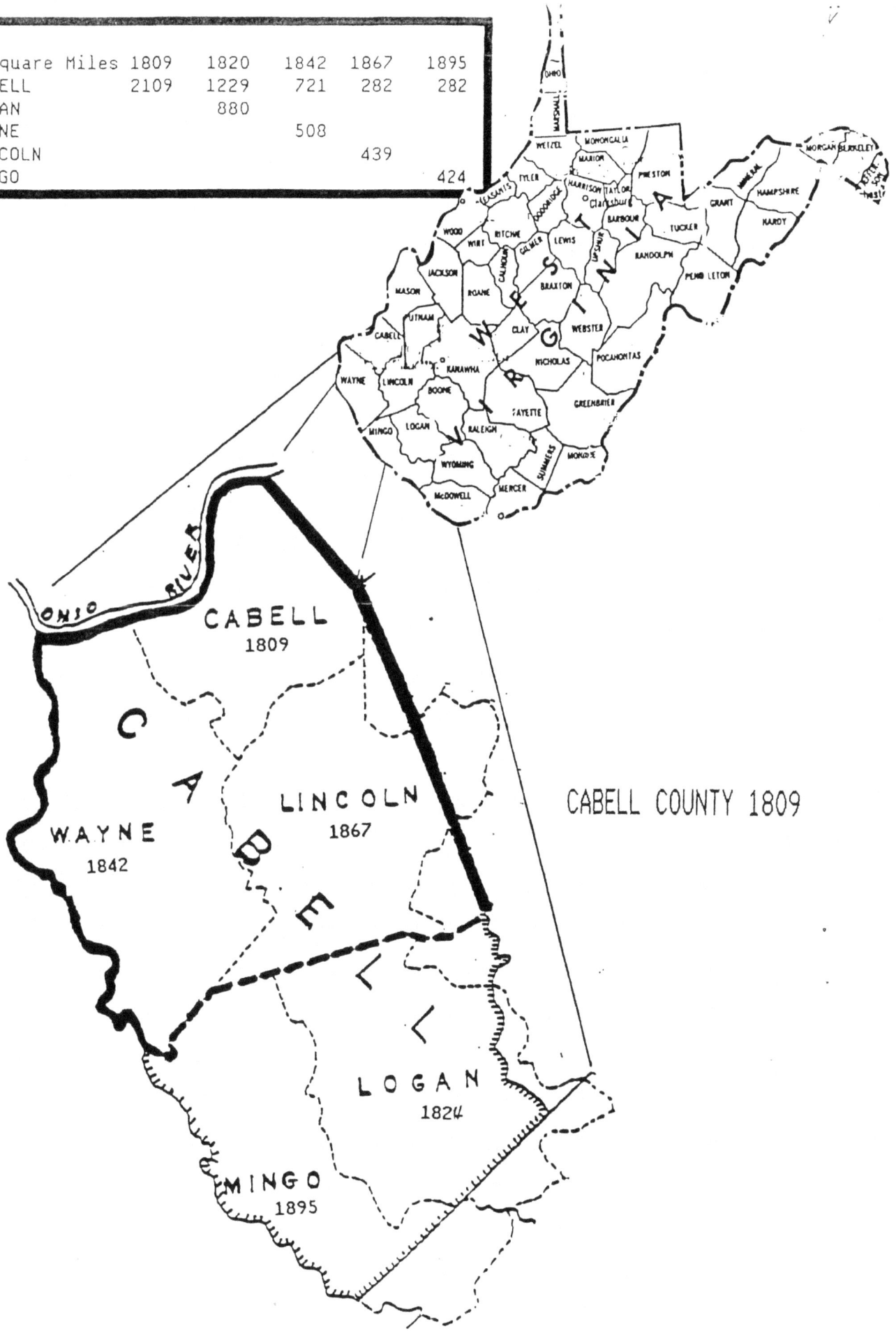

CABELL COUNTY 1809

OHIO RIVER

CABELL
1809

WAYNE
1842

C A B E L L

LINCOLN
1867

LOGAN
1824

MINGO
1895

CENSUS MISTAKES

REMEMBER.......
      Each person who handles the information can make a mistake, so be alert for misinformation.

1. Informant: not necessarily giving personal information.
      inlaws, older children, neighbors ????
2. Informant may wish to give false information.
      wants to be older or younger
3. Enumerator: Misunderstands. Informant is illiterate,
      and enumerator is a poor speller or writer.
4. Copyist: All original lists were entered onto one master.
      He could not read original or made spelling errors.

ALL THESE MISTAKES HAVE TAKEN PLACE BEFORE MICROFILMING.
NEXT A WELL MEANING GENEALOGIST COPIES THE RECORDS.

5. Poor microfilm copy.
      illegible, spotted
6. Transcriber misreads microfilm.
7. Transcriber mistypes information.
8. Transcription is retyped by another party
      with more mistakes.

EXAMPLE
      John Drown mother lives with him. His wife gives the information. The enumerator is hard of hearing and the copyist cannot read the enumerators hand writing.

      Correct information: Sarah Drown age 51 born TN (old NC)
      Given information: Sary Drown age 61 born NC
           (she was borned during the first year Indian War)
      Recorded information:Mary Drown age 61 born NC
      Copied information: Mary Brown age 61 born NC

At this point the information was microfilmed and YOU are still trying to figure out who the heck is Mary Brown.

ALWAYS COMPARE ANY TYPED CENSUS WITH THE ORIGINAL MICROFILM AND ADD A PRAYER THAT THE ORIGINAL INFORMATIION IS CORRECT, BUT ASSUME THAT AT LEAST ONE MISTAKE HASE BEEN MADE.

DISTRICT DIVISIONS

CABELL COUNTY

VIRGINIA

1860

OHIO

GUYANDOTTE

BARBOURSVILLE

UNION

CABELL

McCOMAS

PRESENT COUNTY LINE →

LINCOLN

CARROLL

PORTERSVILLE

HAMLIN

GRIFFITHSVILLE

GARRETTS BEND

McCORKLE

BRANCHLAND

MIDKIFF

RANGER

SPURLOCKVILLE

MANN KNOB

HARTS

FERRELLSBURG

TRACE FORK

MIDDLE FORK

GUYANDOTTE RIVER

MUD RIVER

GUYAN CREEK

SPURLOCK CK

GWINN

MILLERS PORT

PERRY CK

BRIAN CRK

PARKERS

HOWELLS MILL

YATES CROSSING

MUD

McCOMAS

HAZLETT FK

COX LANDING

GUYANDOTTE CK

DAVIS CK

BIG TEN CK

HERD

GREEN RIDGE

SALT

FOUR POLE

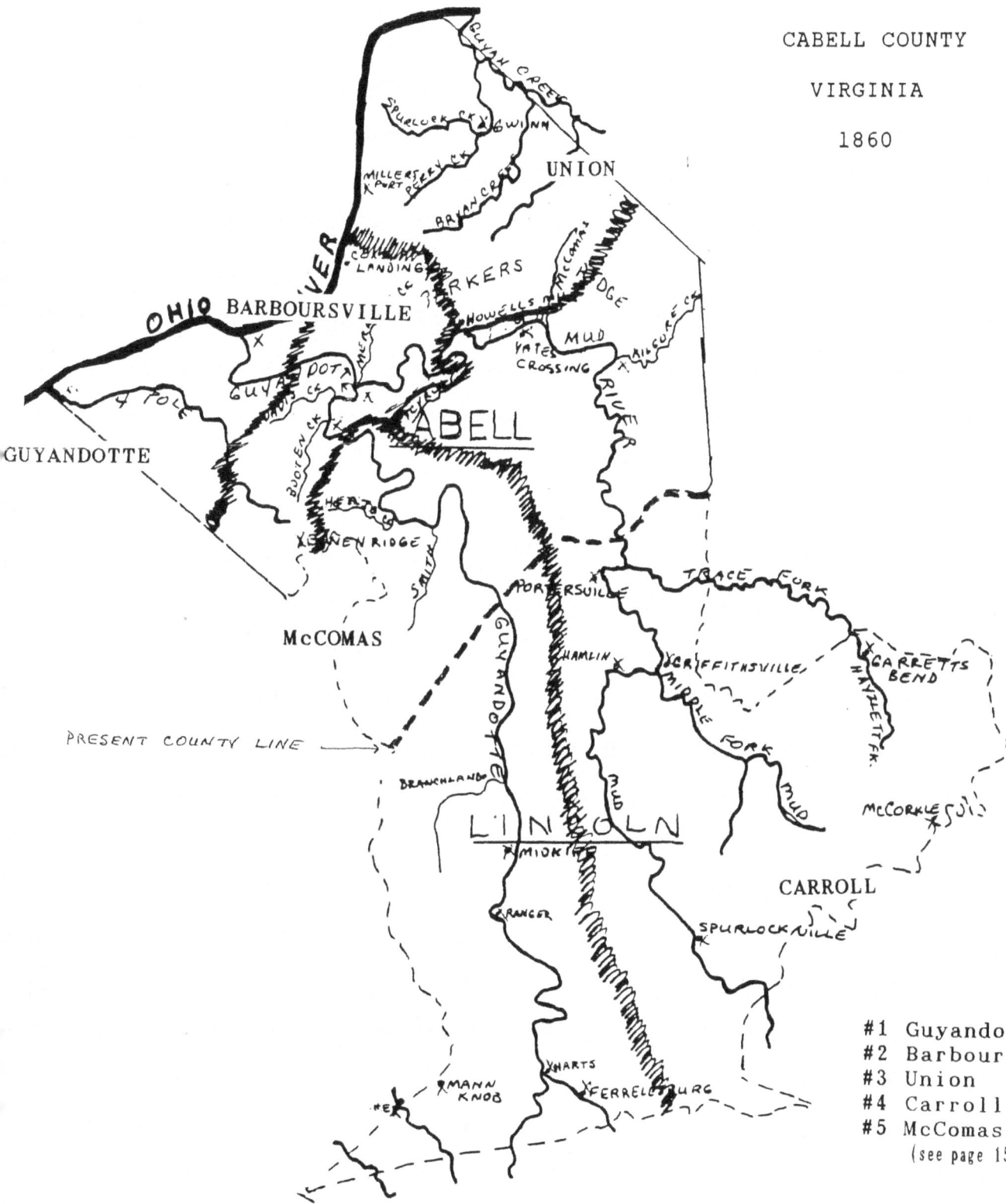

#1 Guyandotte
#2 Barboursville
#3 Union
#4 Carroll
#5 McComas
(see page 150)

CENSUS ODDITIES

Each census has pecularities and oddities that identify it from each other census. These differences are usually made by the original census enumerator and may include odd spellings, abbreviations, pecular numbering or any number of other oddities.

In the 1860 census, the chief enumerator was --Miller one of the local post masters. Either he or one of his deputies made all the entries for Cabell County because the handwriting is similiar.

Some of the oddities of this census:
1. William is almost always abbrieviated Wm.
   Samuel is also abbrieviated Saml.
2. Initials are often given for head of household.
3. Ownership of slaves is identified, but their names are not given.
4. Household numbers are continuous for the entire county.
5. Districts were divided into post office areas.

1-1		BARBOURSVILLE DIST.

JONES
- William E. 37m VA tailor
- Mary J. 37f
- Clayton 13m
- Enos K. 6m
- Florence M. 4f

2-2
DUNDASS
- Ann 55f VA
- Maria 21f
- Lucy 17f
- Sarah 14f
- Thomas 12m

3-3
WINGO
- A.W. 40m VA carpenter
- Sarah S. 33f
- Mary E. 14f
- Francis 12f
- Ann Eliza 10f
- Georgia 8f
- Henry 4m
- Charles 6m
- Josephine 2f

4-4
CHURCH
- Octavius 48m ENG gent.
- Margaret 41f VA
- John W. 18m
- Henry L. 14m
- George 12m
- Francis 10m
- Octavius 3m

TURNER
- Susan S. 18f

5-5
HATFIELD
- Thomas 58m VA shoemaker
- Susan H. 41f
- Jane H. 23f
- Joseph 17m lab
- Albert 3m
- William J. 1m

5-5 HATFIELD (con't)
WYLIE
- Joseph 22m lab

6-6
HARSHBARGER
- David 48m VA hotel
- Mary Jane 41f
- Peter 19m lab
- Ellen 13f
- Henry 10m
- p2 George 8m
- Alice 6m
- Mary 4m
- Ira 2m

McGINNIS
- Ira 27m

7-7
FREUTEL
- Julius 34m HAN butcher
- Sophia 35f HAN
- Christian 8m PA
- Mary 6f PA
- Henry 4m VA
- William 2m
- Alexander H. 2/12m

COOK
- Eliza 21f dom

FREUTEL
- Catherine M. 67f HAN

8-8
SALMON
- Joel K. 30m NY merchant
- Martha A. 23f VA
- Albert E. 3m
- Stephen J. 1m

9-9
BAUMGARDNER
- John B. 34m VA labor
- Louisa C. 31f
- Lawrence K. 10m
- William L. 8m
- Charles A. 6m
- Cora V. 3f

10-10
  SAMUELS
    Lafayette   31m VA labor
    Frances   28f OH
    Emma   8f VA
    John E.   3m
    Mary E.   1m
11-11
  MILLER
    George F.   42m WIRT merch.
    Mary   33f VA
    Christian S. 15m
    Hannah C.   13f
    George   12m
    Wm. C.   4m
    Mary M.   2f
12-12
  THOMPSON
    Matthew   40m VA merchant
    Elizabeth   45f
  McCARTY
    Sarah   80f
  PAINE
    John   17m ENG
13-13
  LLOYD
    John   39m VA shoemaker
    Urania   35f OH
    Fidelia   14f VA
    Jane A.   12f
14-14
  ALLEN
    R.B.   36m SCOT timb.
    Frances   32f
    America   14f IN
    Jennie B.   12f
  HOLDERBY
    America   50f KY
15-15
  SAMUELS
    H.J.   34m VA lawyer
    Rebecca A. 32f PA
    Sarah F.   10m VA
    Ceres B.   6f

15-15 SAMUELS (con't)
    Nettlesia   1f
16-16
  HATFIELD
    J.T.   28m VA hotel
    Malinda   32f
    Effie Afton 4f
    Millard F. 3m
    Margaret   2f
  HATFIELD
    Frances   28f VA seamtress
  CRUMBY
    Elizabeth   15f   domestic
  BOGGESS
    George W.   25m   dentist
17-17
  FARRELL
    Francis M. 33m VA tailor
    Elizabeth   28f
    Virginia   11f
    William F. 9m
    Mary C.   7f
    Lawrence H. 3m
18-18
  MATHER
    O.W.   38m VA tailor
    Augusta   33f
    Lelia A.   15f
    Valcolon W 12m
    Rocksalina 9f
    Hally   5m
    Hizzie   3f
19-19
  LAIDLEY
    Albert   35m VA lawyer
    Vesta   35f
    Alberta   13f
    John   10m
  JOHNSON
    Nancy   17f   dom
20-20
  HARRISON
    Greenville 44m VA blacksmith
    Emily   38f

20-20 HARRISON (con't)
    Ellen   7f
    Leander   3m
    HARRISON
    Rachel   64f
    JUSTICE
    P.V.   25m OH blacksm
    PINE
    William   18m VA apprentice
    BUTCHER
    America   21f VA
    HARRISON
    Polly   25f VA
21-21
    DERTON
    John   41m VA ferryman
    Louisa   39f
    Phillip   19m
    Eliza J.   15f
    William D.   13m
    Louisa A.   8f
    Thomas   5m
    Henry J.   1m
22-22
    FELIX
    James   52m SWI surveyor
    Julia   46f SWI
    Arnold   16m   lab
    Warren   15m
23-23
    McKENDREE
    Ariana   55f VA hotel
    Mary   17f
    Lucinda   15f
    Elvira   12f
    SMITH
    Mary A.   10f
    WILLIAMS
    John   21m   lab
    CAMPBELL
    Elizabeth 64f
    KRAUS
    Walter   27m PRU Gent.

23-23 McKENDREE (con't)
    ALFORD
    John   35m VA constable
    LONG
    Charles   24m PRU farmer
24-24
    KYLE
    Thomas   64m VA gunsmith
    Sarah   24f
    Melitta   20f
    Teresa   18f
    Edgar   6m
25-25
    MILLS
    John   43m VA cooper
    Mary   45f MD
    William   20m VA
    John O.   16m
26-26
    HIBBINS
    John T.   37m VA wheelwright
    Attimus   35f
    Sarah I.   12f
    Eddie   8m
    Mary   6f
    Henry B.   3m
    Valcolon   8/12m
27-27
    LUSHER
    Johnson   40m VA gent.
    Lucy   31f
    Scott   14m
    George   2m
    Henry J.   2/12m
28-28
    SHELTON
    Thomas   31m VA carpenter
    Eliza   26f
    Walter   9m
    Amelia   5f
    Charles   4m
    Francis   1m

29-29
   LATTIN
      Charles   51m CT surveyor
      Jane A.   48f NY
      David C.S. 21m VA blacksmith
      Charles A. 15m VA

30-30
   SHELTON
      Anthony   65m VA jailor
      Margaret   50f
      John   28m
j   CREMANS
a   Luther   22m   lab
i   HARRIS
l   Matthias   24m   lab
   PEYTON
      Daniel   36m   lab

31-31
   FRELWILER
      George W. 35m VA carpenter
      Matilda   28f
      John W.   9m
      George   7m
      Catherine 1f

32-32
   WADE
      Saml.   31m VA carpenter
      Emily   27f
      Fenton   7f
      Charles   5m
      Asa N.   1m
   CONNER
      Amanda   24f   dom

33-33
   SAMUELS
      John   69m VA lawyer
      Alexander H. 30m   clerk
      America   19f

34-34
   THORNBURG
      Moses   30m VA dpty CC
clerk
      Mary   24f

35-35
   DERTON
      Elizabeth   74f VA (insane)

36-36
   MOORE
      W.B.   40m VA sheriff
      John Thos. 12m
      Charles   10m
      Mary E.   9f
      George   7m
      Eliza   5f

37-37
   MOORE
      Mary   67f VA

38-38
   BAUM
      George   53m FRA labor
      Barbary   53f

39-39
   WHITTEN
      L.T.   41m VA carpenter
      Emelilne   40f
      Elizabeth 19f KY
      Mary M.   18f KY
      Hetty   15f VA
      William W. 12m
      Thomas M. 9m
      Cire   8/12f
   VERTIGANS
      Edward   21m ENG teacher

40-40
   FETTER
      H.A.   31m NC saddler
      Louisa   29f
      Virginia   3f VA
      Attumas   2f VA

41-41
   PROCTOR
      George   40m SCT tailor
      Margaret   40f
      Agnes   22f
      Margaret   19f
      James   18m   gent.
      Ellen   15f

41-41 PROCTOR (con't)
    John   12m
    Mary   8f VA
    George   5m VA
42-42
FEAZEL
    Wm.E.   30m VA constable
    Amasetta 23f
    Virginia 8f
    Alice   5f
    Frank   2m
    Wm.E.   2/12m
PERRY
    Margaret 17f   dom
43-43
HOLDRYDE
    Peter   30m VA carpntr
    Susan   28f
    Anna   4f
    Robert 2m
44-44
SHIPE
    Charles 24m VA labor
    Ellen   23f
    Wm.A. 3m
    Mary E. 11/12f
BUTCHER
    Rachel 60f
45-45
MERRITT
    Wm.   47m VA stonems
    Deborah 44f
    Theresa 17f
    Henry 15m
    Phillip 13m
    Walter 9m
    Theodore 6m
CONNER
    Hetty   48f
46-46
MOREY
    Frank   44m ME currier
    Eliza   47f MA
    Anna   15f

46-46 MOREY (con't)
    Julia   13f
    Cynthia 12f
    Frances 11f
47-47
EGGERS
    Wm.   50m KY shoemaker
    Catherine 50f IRE
FERGUSON
    Ann   14f VA
48-48
BUTCHER
    James 33m VA labor
    Margery 23f IRE
    Rachel A. 1/12f VA
STANLEY
    Sarah 23f VA domestic
49-
50-49
ANDERSON
    Nancy 20f VA m laundress
    Edmund 1m   m
51-50
SHELTON
    Monroe 23m VA labor
    Eliza 19f
    Mary E. 2f
    Jefferson 3/12m
52-51
DERTON
    Harrison 37m VA labor
    Ann   25f
    Mary A. 8f
    Isabella 1f
53-52
WESTHOFF
    Arnold 41m PRU tanner
    Josephine 30f PRU
    Anna   8f VA
    Joseph 6m
    Edward 3m

54-53
  BECKER
    Albert   48m GER tanner
    Mildred   40f VA
    Joanna   16f
    Frederick   14m
    Matilda   12f
    Thomas   9m
    Wilhelmina 7f
    Albert   4m
    George   9/12m
55-54
  WOOD
    H.H.   44m VA CCClerk
    Margaret   33f
    Frances   11f
    Mary E.   8f
    Laura A.   5/12f
56-55
  DERTON
    Wm.   30m VA labor
    Mary   25f
    Charles   1m
57-56
  MAUPIN
    H.B.   43m VA doctor
    Lucinda   22f
    Socrates   2m
    Margaret E. 1f
58-57
  MILLER
    John G.   51m WIRT merch
    Eveline   28f VA
    Frances   12f
    George H.   8m
    Claudius   5m
    Frank   5/12m
    Henry   5/12m
  MILLER
    Sigismund   54m WIRT merch
  STOWATER
    Caroline   15f WIRT dom

59-58
  MILLER
    Wm.C.   51m OH merchant
    Eliza   44f KY
    Eugenia   23f VA
    Charles   21m   clerk
    Frank G.   16m
    John W.   14m
    Joseph   11m
    Florence   5f
  THACKETON
    B.H.   33m VA teacher
                (select school)
60-
61-59
  THORNBURG
    Thomas T.   44m VA merch
    Mary L.   21f
    Ellen   17f
    John S.   16m
    George E.   14m
    Maggie L.   3f
62-
63-60
  MERRITT
    John   32m VA farmer
    George   8m
    Virginia   6f
    Susan   4f
    John   3m
  DUNDAS
    Frances   27f
  SHEFF
    Wm.P.   56m   miller

end Barboursville

  Cabell CH District (not town)
64-61
  ALEGO
    Wm.D.   27m KY teacher
    Amasetta   19f VA
    Beverly J. 1m

65-62
CHILDERS

Saml. A.	44m	VA	farmer	
Catherine	40f			
Sarah E.	19f			
Wm.S.	17m		farmer	
George W.	16m			
Henry	15m			
John M.	14m			
Philip	12m			
Charles T.	11m			
James	10m			
Conwelsey	9m			
Jasper	3m			
Newton	3m			

66-63
McCOMAS

Wm.	66m	VA	farmer
Sarah	48f		
Irene O.	17f		

67-64
MORRIS

James R.	30m	VA	farmer
Helen M.	30f		
Joseph W.	11m		
Albert A.	9m		
Walter T.	5m		
Sarah	3f		
Frances	2f		
Eugene J.	6/12m		

68-65
WARD

Thomas	39m	VA	labor
Cynthia	39f		
Eliza A.	15f		
John H.	13m		
Patrick	10m		
William	9m		
Jasper W.	8m		
Walter	6m		
Mary F.	3f		

69-66
McLEESE

Patrick	54m	IRE	farmer
Mary Ann	61f	IRE	

MONTGOMERY

Alexander	41m	IRE	farmer

ADKINS

Clara	15f	VA	dom

70-67
CHILDERS

A.M.	34m	VA	farmer
Elizabeth	29f		
Mary J.	10f		
Almeda J.	8f		
Alexander	6m		
Louisa	4f		

71-68
McKANNON

Matthew	60m	PA	stmason
Rebecca	41f	VA	

TAYLOR

William	13m	

WHEELER

Joseph B.	34m		labor

72-69
KNIGHT

John	27m	VA	farmer
Margaret	25f		
Frances J.	2f		

73-70
NICELY

James	30m	VA	farmer
Sarah	27f		
Sarah	13f		
Haney	10m		
Henry	9m		
Albert	8m		
Emily J.	7f		
William	5m		
Mary H.	4f		

74-71
BLAKE

Isaac	24m	VA	farmer
Mary A.	22f		

8

74-71 BLAKE (con't)		
Anna	3f	
Emma	1f	
FERGUSON		
Elizabeth	15f	
75-72		
BLAKE		
Sarah	57f VA	
76-73		
CHILDERS		
Green A.	32m VA farmer	
Mary	28f	
Elizabeth	7f	
Mary M.	5f	
Geneva	1f	
77-74		
NEWMAN		
Alexander	59m NC farmer	
Bettie	47f VA	
Emily	22f	
Alexander	18m	labor
Joseph	14m	
78-75		
CHILDERS		
Benjamin S.	26m VA farmer	
Malvina	22f	
79-76		
NEWMAN		
Winston	31m VA labor	
Sarah	26f	
Emily	2f	
80-77		
GIBSON		
James	47m VA labor	
Frances	47f	
Mary	20f	
Amanda	18f	
Cynthia	16f	
Matilda	14f	
81-78		
MEADOWS		
James	29m VA farmer	
Emily	28f	
James A.	6m	

81-78 MEADOWS (con't)		
Henry	3m	
Mary E.	1f	
82-79		
DOLAN		
George	27m VA ferrym	
Elletha	32f	
Rebecca	7f	
Martha	3f	
SMITH		
W.W.	26m	labor
DOLAN		
Joanna	6f	
83-80		
MAYS		
Hamilton	40m VA farmer	
Nancy	39f	
Elizabeth	14f	
John	12m	
Catherine	11f	
Matilda	10m	
Hezekiah	9m	
Ezekiel	8m	
Sarah A.	7f	
Julia	6f	
Nicholas	3m	
Emma	1f	
BEECH		
Saml.	22m labor	
84-81		
EARLS		
Permelia	52f VA	
David	20m	labor
John	18m	
James	15m	
85-82		
BUKEY		
Rodolphus	34m VA farmer	
Eveline	38f	
Rebecca	8f	
Preston M.	4m	
COX		
Sarah	18f	
Emily	17f	

86-83
  MAYS
    John D.   28m VA farmer
    Eliza   16f
87-84
  DUNDAS
    Thomas   26m VA farmer
    Martha J.   25f
    Virginia   1f
88-85
  MERRITT
    William M.   33m VA farmer
    Mary M.   25f
    Olga   4f
    Cassius H.   2m
    Joseph   3/12m
89-86
  ROSE
    Enoch   52m VA cooper
    Elizabeth   42f
    Charles H.   5m
    Sarah A.   4f
    Eliza J.   2f
90-87
  MERRITT
    Melcher   50m VA farmer
    Mary   53f
    Mahala   29f
    Joseph   24m   farmer
    Harriett   22f
    Nancy J.   19f
    Thomas   16m   farmer
    Emma   12f
    Martha (J/G)   10f
    George W.   4m
91-88
  DILLON
    John L.   37m VA raftsman
    Ruth   32f
    Luvender   6f
    Julius   5m
    Orinda   3f
    Mary J.   2f

92-89
  BRYANT
    Dennis O.   43m VA shoemk
    Malinda   36f
    Jane A.   15f
    Marion   13m
    Alice   12f
    Thomas H.   10m
    Seibert   9m
    Virginia   7f
    John L.   2m
93-90
  DICK
    A.J.   32m VA farmer
    Cynthia   29f
    Anna E.   8f
    Morris F.   4m
    Henry   3m
94-91
  CYRUS
    Joseph   35m VA farmer
    Sarah E.   3f
95-92
  SEAMONDS
    A.J.   30m VA farmer
    Mary   32f OH
    Henrietta   7f VA
    Albert G.J.   3m
  LETCHER
    John   3/12m
  MANN
    Catherine   35f OH
  SEAMONDS
    Charles   26m VA labor
96-93
  MAYS
    Charles   47m VA labor
    Alnna   45f
    America   18f
    Joseph   15m
    Elizabeth   9f
    Charles   7m
    Frances   4f
    Ellen   1f

97-94
- BIAS
  - Berry   35m VA farmer
  - Sarah   25f
  - Charles L.   7m
  - Andrew   4m
  - Emerine   3f
  - Mary A.   2f
- COLLINS
  - Mary   25f
  - William   3m
- BIAS
  - James R.   80m   farmer

98-95
- BIAS
  - R.S.   38m VA farmer
  - Sarah   33f
  - Margaret   10f
  - Saml. A.   6m
  - Augusta   5f
  - Arabella   4f
  - John   2m
  - America   2/12f
- BIAS
  - Emily   25f

99-96
- HERENKOLH   (Russia&Prussia)
  - Albert   30m RUS farmer
  - Louisa   28f   VA
  - Charles   2m
- FULLER
  - Sarah   9f
- HERINKOLH
  - Helen   65f PRU
- KRAUS
  - Anna   61f PRU
- TELGINER
  - Emile   27m PRU cabnetmk

100-97
- YATES
  - Wm.P.   74m VA farmer
  - Elizabeth   64f
  - Wm.Jr.   22m   farmer

101-98
- SEAMONDS
  - Wm.R.   51m VA farmer
  - Nancy   50f
  - Elizabeth   23f
  - Peyton   17m
  - America S.   16f
  - Nancy   13f
- BAKER
  - Henry   11m
- DUNDASS
  - James   23m
  - Eliza   19f

102-99
- ARTHUR
  - Sanders   41m VA boatbld
  - Elizabeth   40f
  - James   16m   labor
  - Sarah   14f
  - Thomas   11m
  - Emma   9f
  - Eliza   8f
  - America   6/12f

103-100
- COWAN
  - James   38m VA labor
  - Sarah   34f
  - Thomas J.   15m   OH
  - Mary S.   3f   VA

104-101
- CHILDERS
  - Thomas A.   40m VA farmer
  - Elizabeth   88f
  - Thomas   11m
  - Wm.   7m
  - Ellenor   5f
  - George   4m
  - Benton   4/12m
- BIAS
  - Miram   35f

105-102
- HENSLEY
  - Saml.   26m VA farmer
  - Hannah   27f

105-102 HENSLEY con't)

Mary E.	4f	
Wm.W.	3m	
Lorie A.	9/12f	

BALSER (Baker ?)

Albert	10m	

106-103 SHELTON

James	24m VA farmer	
America	19f	
Albert G.	3m	

107-104 FERGUSON

Jesse	45m VA labor	
Hannah	44f	
Polly	16f	
Malinda	7f	
Joseph	5m	
Catherine	3f	

108-105 LUCAS

George	53m VA labor	
Phoebe	27f	
William	17m	labor
James J.	12m	
Gordon	9m	

LUCAS

Sarah	28f	
Cynthia A.	1f	

109-106 JEFFERSON

John W.	28m VA farmer	
Angelina	25f	
Albert G.	3m	
William R.	1m	

110-107 KYLE

Saml.	23m VA labor	
Missouri	22f	
George	3m	
Adaline	6/12f	

111-108 KYLE

Peter	21m VA labor	
Margaret	19f KY	
Samuel	1m VA	

112-109 WOODYARD

Sandford	22m VA labor	
Rebecca	19f	

113-110 GRIMES

George	46m VA farmer	
Harriett	38f	
Wm.H.	14m	
Martha	7f	
Roberta	5f	
George F.	4m	
Robert	1m	

114-111 EDENS

James	30m VA farmer	
Harriett	23f OH	
Wm.D.	5m VA	
Melvin	3m	
Emma J.	2f	

115-112 RODGERS

Wm.S.	45m VA farmer	
Isabella	35f	
George	18m	farmer
Wilson	17m	farmer
Thomas M.	15m	
Mary E.	13f	
Cynthia	11f	
Wm.L.	5m	

WINTZ

Thomas N.	15m	
William	13m	
Mary	11f	
Pompey	9m	

116-113 SWANN

Levin	46m VA farmer	
Susan	44f	

12

116-113 SWANN (con't)			
Shelley	17m		
John R.	15m		
Martha	14f		
Joseph W.	10m		
Cynthia	6f		
James H.	4m		
Emanuel	1m		
SEAMONDS			
Alfred	27m	VA	surveyor
117-114			
KEYSER			
Ephraim	34m	VA	farmer
Eliza	32f		
Hugh	12m		
Thomas	10m		
William	8m		
Ephraim	4m		
George	2m		
Malinda	1f		
SNELL			
Julia	25f		
KEYSER			
George	21m		labor
HENSLEY			
Bird	20m		labor
118-115			
ROFFE			
Joseph W.	47m	VA	farmer
Rebecca	42f		
Thomas J.	22m		student
Wm.D.	20m		
Lucretia	16f		
Charles P.	13m		
Letha T.	8f		
Joseph W.	6m		
Eva A.	4f		
Carolina D.	2f		
119-116			
FIELDER			
William	28m	VA	laobr
Siporah	30f		
Julia A.	6f		
Emily A.	4f		

119-116 FILEDER (CON'T)			
James A.	2m		
Mary A.	2/12f		
TURLEY			
Patsey	76f		pauper
WILLIAMS			
Spencer	16m		labor
FERGUSON			
Cynthia	20f		dom
120-117			
BARNETT			
Thomas	42m		
Nancy	35f		
Mary A.	5f		
121-118			
DAVIS			
Benjamin S.	46m	VA	farmer
Harriett	45f		
Wm.W.	20m		
John S.	16m		
Albert G.	14m		
Mary H.	12f		
Elizabeth	10f		
Benjamin S.	5/12m		
SMITH			
William	7m		
DEAN			
Saml.	20m		labor
122-119			
McCOMAS			
John	21m	VA	labor
Eliza	23f		
Lelia F.	9/12f		
123-120			
KEYSER			
David	40m	VA	farmer
Valeria	36f		
Wm.W.	14m		
Emeline	12f		
Patrick H.	10m		
John	8m		
David	6m		
Albert	4m		
Oscar	6/12m		

123-120 KEYSER(con't)
  HENSLEY
    Virginia   21f   dom
124-121
  COOK
    Thomas   36m VA farmer
    Louisa   32f
    Martha   8f
  BOWLIN
    Benjamin   15m
    John B.   25m   labor
125-122
  TULEY
    Tandy   44m VA farmer
    Cynthia   36f
  MORRISON
    Venalla   30f
    George W.   5m
    David H.   2m
126-123
  EGGERS
    Joseph   21m VA labor
    Mary   19f
    Wilbert   3/12m
127-124
  YATES
    E.W.   40m VA farmer
    Mildred   43f
    Granville   19m   labor
    Wm.H.   15m
    Warner W.   15m
    Elijah M.   14m
128-125
  HATFIELD
    D.K.   21m VA labor
    America   22f
    Martha   1f
  BALL
    Hugh M.   25m   labor
  SCITEZ
    Thomas   21m   labor

129-126
  BAUMGARDNER
    James   53m VA farmer
    Elizabeth   41f
    Henrietta   20f
    Arminta   18f
    Henry J.   16m
    John A.   14m
    Wm.J.   12m
    Welcome A.   10m
    George F.   8m
    Sarah E.   6f
    Millard   2/12m
  JOY
    James   22m   labor
130-127
  McVICKERS
    Archibald   48m VA farmer
    Permelia   48f
    Almira   18f
    John   14m
    James   14m
    Matilda   8f
131-128
  BRYANT
    W.G.   45m SC teacher
    Elizabeth   47f   VA
  WILLIAMS
    Jane   14m
132-129
  CYRUS
    Sarah   60f VA
    Matilda   22f
    William H.   20m   farmer
    Mary   17f
133-130
  CHAPMAN
    Henry W.   40m VA labor
    Mary A.   36f
    John M.   17m   labor
    Susan E.   16f
    Lewis H.   14m
    Mary M.   12f
    Pocahontas   10f

133-130 CHAPMAN (con't)

Eliza	8f	
Francis V.	7f	
James J.	5m	
Peter	3m	
Franklin M.	2/12m	

CHAPMAN

Elizabeth	86f	VA

WOODEN

John H.	40m	

134-131

LONG

Wm.H.	41m	VA labor
Emily J.	40f	
James S.	9m	
Betsey	4f	
Sarah B.	3f	
Wm. M.	6/12m	

135-132

COX

James O.	35m	VA mercht
Margaret	32f	
Geneva C.	9f	
Georgia H.	6f	
Cora S.	2f	

136-133

HARVEY

Calvery	35m	VA labor
America	30f	
John W.	13m	
Elizabeth	11f	
Octavia	9f	
Mary E.	7f	
Florence	2f	

137-134

BILLUPS

R.A.	33m	VA farmer
Huldah	32f	
James B.	12m	
Robert H.	10m	
Adalaide	8f	
Charles A.	6m	
Elliott T.	3m	
John W.	1m	

138-135

KELLY

Saml.	26m	VA labor
Elizabeth	24f	

139-136

BLAKE

Pennill	55m	VA farmer
Nancy	34f	
Frederick	15m	
Mary	13f	
Margaret	11f	
James	9m	
Anselon	7m	
Sarah C.	6f	
Preston	4m	
Thomas	2m	

140-137

MESSINGER

William	43m	VA labor
Nancy	42f	
Isaac	20m	labor
Emily	15f	
Marvin	13m	
Albert	11m	
William	6m	

141-138

BIAS

Linsey	21m	VA labor
Martha	20f	
Matilda	5/12f	

142-139

LATIMORE

Robert	40m	Atlantic Ocean plasterer
Olive	21f	OH
James M.	19m	PA plastr
Thompson J.	12m	OH
Sarah J.	10f	
Simeon	2m	VA

143-140

DIAL

Elisha	35m	VA farmer
John	37m	

143-140 DIAL (con't)

Nancy	70f
Nancy Jr.	31f

PAINE

Mary	12f

144-141

CHAPMAN

Wm.	48m	VA	labor
Elizabeth	42f		
Henry J.	15m		
John G.	13m		
Elijah	11m		
Sally H.	9f		
Ellen	7f		
Olivia	5f		
Martha	1f		

145-142

SWITZER

Jonathan	30m	VA	sawyer
Ellen	31f		
Rufus P.	4m		
E.C.R.	2m		
Vara A.	6/12f		

PEYTON

Francis	20f	domestic

146-143

McKENDREE

A.F.	55m	VA	farmer
Catherine	42f		
Saml.	20m		labor
Charles	17m		
Frances	15f		
Robert	13m		
William	11m		
Susan	9f		
Emily	7f		
Melitta	6f		
Rebecca	2/12f		

LAWTER

Michael	75m	pauper

147-144

SANDERS

Frank	32m	VA	farmer
Margaret	18f		

148-145

HOWELL

John H.	27m	VA	farmer

JORDAN

Peter	50m	labor
Ann	35f	
William	12m	
Charles	9m	
Peter	7m	
Frances	5f	
Margaret	6/12f	

HOWELL

Mary E.	7f

149-146

LUSHER

Margaret	36f	VA
Sarah J.	17f	
James M.	15m	
Mary L.	13f	
Toliver	11m	
Matthew J.	7m	

HODGE

Charles	22m

150-147

MARTIN

Andrew	40m	VA	farmer
Eliza	37f		
Romaine	12f		
George A.	9m		
Frances	7f		
William	5m		
John	3m		
Ida	1f		

151-148

PEYTON

S.M.	67f	VA
John W.	40m	doctor
Thomas	9m	
Frank	7m	

WATSON

Virginia	45f	
Mary	22f	LA

16

152-149
SWEATLAND
    I. V.   40m VA farmer
    Martha   37f
    John S.   16m   farmer
    Mary   14f
    Anna   12f
    Margaret   8f KY
    Caroline   5f KY
    Louis R.   1m KY
CROOKS
    Abraham   20m KY labor
GRIFFITH
    Milton   14m KY
153-150
NEWMAN
    Joseph   57m NC farmer
    Mary   30f VA
    Cyrus P.   22m   farmer
    Malinda S.   18f
    Joseph A.   15m
    Sylvanus T.   12m
    Charles A.   9m
154-151
CYRUS
    Elijah   41m VA farmer
    Margaret   34m
    Mary E.   14f
    John E.   13m
    William T.   9m
    Lucinda   7f
    James N.   5m
    Sarah A.   3f
    Joseph W.   1m
155-152
NEWMAN
    Morris   32m VA labor
    Elizabeth   28f
    William F.   8m
    Frances A.   5f
    Beatrice M.   4f
    Isabella H.   1f

156-153
DUNDASS
    John   32m VA labor
    Mary   26f
157-154
TURLEY
    Jonathan   34m VA farmer
    Elizabeth   28f
    Frances   7f
    Anna   5f
    Eliza   3f
McCOMAS
    Perry   16m   labor
158-155
TURLEY
    Elijah   37m VA farmer
    Agnes   34f
    John   5m
    William   3m
    Thomas   1m
159-156
MORRISON
    Frances   50f VA
    Allen   22m   farmer
    Mary   17f
    Henry   15m
    Frances   13f
    Telitha   9f
160-157
ARTHUR
    Isaac   47m VA farmer
    Julia   25f
    Ambrose A.   13m
    Telitha   10f
    Lycingus   3m
    Mary J.   2f
161-158
ARTHUR
    Thomas   71m VA farmer
    Elizabeth   51f
    Lafayette   14m
TEMPLETON
    Matilda   16f

162-159
   ARTHUR
      John M.   42m VA farmer
      Sarah A.   41f
      Wm.S.   17m   labor
      John   14m
      Mary M.   13f
      Ann   8f
      Isaac   4m
      Albert   3/12m
   COLLINS
      Permelia   6f
163-160
   ARTHUR
      James   45m VA farmer
      Elizabeth   40f
      Ann M.   19f
      Lewis T.   13m
      James C.   9m
      Eliza J.   7f
164-161
   PEYTON
      Alexander   34m VA farmer
      Pelina   23f
      Isabella   2f
      Fianna   1f
165-162
   BLAKE
      Jeremiah   66m VA farmer
      Margaret   60f
   MILLER
      Polly   44f
   BLAKE
      Margaret   98f VA
   ARTHUR
      Clarissa   18f
166-163
   POTEET
      H.C.   30m VA merchant
      Amanda   24f
      Frances B.   4f
      William A.   2m

167-164
   STRUPE
      William   68m VA farmer
      Frances   20f
      Wm.H.   2m
   ADAMS
      Thomas   13m
   WINTZ
      Lewis   20m
168-165
   CLARK
      Ervin   27m VA farmer
      Catherine   24f
      Angelia   9/12f
169-166
   COLLINS
      Charles   68m VA farmer
      Mary   33f
      Mortimer   11m
      Hester Ann   9f
      Salome   6f
      Charles G.   3m
      Henry A.   4/12m
170-167
   COLLINS
      Wm.   74m VA farmer
      Zitthia   51f NY
      Nathan   21m VA
      Patience   17f
      Adam   12m
      Christopher 10m
      Enoch   5m
      Lafayette   9m
171-168
   HERALD
      William   58m TN farmer
      Nancy   39f VA
   ELKINS
      Amanda   18f
   BIAS
      Matilda   58f

172-169
  BIAS
    Wm.E.   28m VA farmer
    Elizabeth   26f
    Larkin   8m
    Nancy M.   6f
    Andrea   4f
    Lucinda   2f
  BURNS
    John   15m
173-170
  WINTZ
    Joseph   65m VA farmer
    Mary   60f
    Betsy   27f
    John   25m
  HOWARD
    John   30m
174-171
  JOY
    Thomas   54m VA farmer
    Mary   50f
    Elleanor   23f
    Sarah   19m
    Elizabeth   17f
    Thomas   15m
    Victoria   12f
  WINTERS
    Danl.   32m   labor
175-172
  FRANCE
    William H.   40m VA farmer
    Patience   39f OH
    Isaac M.   16m   labor
    Wm.H.   14m OH
    Sarah   12f
    Phoebe   10f
    Mary E.   8f
    Nancy A.   7f
    Matilda J.   6f
    George W.   4m VA
    Lucretia   3f
    Thomas J.   1m

176-173
  COX
    A.J.   45m VA farmer
    Mary A.   38f
    Henrietta H. 17f
    Sarah J.   15f
    Elizabeth   11f
    America M.   9f
    Eliza   7f
    Jennette   5f
    James A.   3m
177-174
  COX
    Wm.   71m VA farmer
    Sarah   65f
    Joseph   21m   farmer
  JOY
    Amy   20f
178-175
  COX
    John A.   30m VA farmer
    Adala   27f OH
    William T.   7m
    Sarah   5f
    Mary A.   2f VA
    Albert E.   4/12m
179-176
  WOODYARD
    Wm.C.   34m VA farmer
    Tabitha   56f
180-177
  WOOD
    Nancy   55f VA
    John G.   33m   labor
    George   15m
181-178
  KYLE
    John   60m VA labor
    Sarah   17f
    Rebecca   15f
    Anna   11f

182-179
FERGUSON
Wm.	40m VA labor
Polly	56f
Leonard	6m

183-
184-180
WINTZ
| Jacob | 80m PA |

185-181
FERGUSON
Joseph	50m VA farmer
Sarah	51f OH
Levina	24f VA
Cynthia	22f
James	19m labor
Atha F.	16f
Eveline	12f
Jessee	10m
George	6m

PERRY
| Hannah | 22f |
| Telitha | 5f |

FERGUSON
| Sarah A. | 6f |

186-182
PULLEY
| David | 52m OH collier |
| Lemanda | 26f |

187-
188-183
PULLEY
Wm.	40m NC farmer
Julia A.	35f
John	14m
Melissa	12f
Rebecca	10f
William	7m
David	4m

189-184
JEFFERSON
Henry	38m VA farmer
Mary A.	25f
Mahala	12f

189-184 JEFFERSON (con't)
Saml.W.	9m
Wm.H.	7m
Elizabeth	5f
Malinda	3f
Marinda R.	1f

KYLE
| Margaret | 18f |

190-185
JEFFERSON
Henry Sr.	79m VA gunsmith
Elizabeth	76f
Jackson	36m labor
America	29f
Mary E.	2/12f

191-186
FERGUSON
James	45m VA labor
Martha	49f
Jessee	15m
Eliza	14f
Elizabeth	12f
Martha	10f
James H.	8m
Jackson	7m
Mahala	5f

192-187
METZNER
| Frank | 54m BOH blacksm |
| Matilda | |

193-188
FERGUSON
Sarah	84f PA
Sarah Jr.	33f VA
Mary	18f

194-189
PERRY
| Richard | 70m NC farmer |
| Anna | 60f PA |

HAGELY
Ariadna	27f Va
Henry	23m farmer
Harrison	21m farmer

194-189 PERRY (con't)
   HAGELY (con't)
      Joseph   17m   farmer
      Lucinda   1f
195-190
   HAGELY
      Peter   36m VA farmer
      Mary   30f
      Polly   13f
      Peter   12m
      Hannah   10f
      Elizabeth 7f
      Sarah   4f
      Mahala   1f
   HAGELY
      Polly   32f
196-
197-191
   KNIGHT
      Anselom 38m VA farmer
      Matilda 32f
      Leonard 15m
      Harriett 12f
      Catherine 10f
      Abner   9m
      Mary   7f
      Sarah   4f
      Wm. H.   1m
198-192
   KNIGHT
      Abner P. 23m VA farmer
      Caroline 22f
      Wm.A.   1m
   NEWMAN
      Lucinda 14f
199-193
   CORNELL
      Martin   52m NY farmer
      Amy M. 50f
      Louisa   48f
200-194
   WINTERS
      Esther   56f VA
      Mary   19f

200-194 WINTERS (con't)
      Lemmel 16m   labor
   WINTERS
      Elizabeth 52f
201-195
   SCARBERRY
      Joseph   25m OH farmer
      Hester   22f
      John   4m
      Malinda 1f
202-
203-196
   ANSEL
      Martin   76m VA farmer
      Hannah   66f
      Catherine 26f
      Malachi 24m   farmer
      Abraham 22m   sawyer
      Sarah   19f
      Mahala   18f
204-197
   COLVIN
      Wm.   22m OH farmer
      Rachel   23f
      Elizabeth 6f VA
      Jackson   4m OH
      Solomon   3m
205-198
   COLVIN
      Jackson   26m VA farmer
      Elizabeth 24f OH
      Elizabeth 3f VA
      William   1m
   PETERSON
      Frances   10f OH
206-199
   DUNE
      Solomon   52m OH farmer
      Margaret 44f
      Margaret J. 15f
      Wm.H.   13m
      Sarah   10f
      Mary   8f

206-199 DUNE (con't)
    Solomon   5m
    Lewellyn   1f
207-200
  DUNE
    John   32m OH labor
    Lydia   24f
    Solomon   7m
    Charles   6m VA
    Margaret   4f
    Jackson   2m OH
208-201
  KNIGHT
    George   46m NC farmer
    Mary   46f VA
    Sarah   24f
    John   21m   cooper
    Parthenia 18f
    George   16m   farmer
    Margaret 10f
    Alvin   6m
    Eliza   4f
  CASEY
    Elisha   15m
209-202
  WINTERS
    G.W.   24m VA farmer
    Mary   23f
    William   1m
210-203
  LESAGE
    Francis   24m NY cooper
    Mary   18f VA
    Zelia   4/12f
    Henrietta 8f
211-204
  BLAKE
    Isaac   47m VA farmer
    Joanna   40f
    John M.(?) 19m   labor
    Christian S.17m   labor
    Albert   16m   labor
    Jeremiah 14m
    Sarah   9f

211-204 BLAKE (con't)
    John   7m
    Dolph   5m
    Elizabeth 3f
    Louisana 3/12f
  SASSON
    Catherine 27f SWI dom
    Charles   6m
    George   3m
212-205
  LESAGE
    Julius   49m FRA farmer
    Mary   56f
    Joseph   22m PA
213-206
  JEFFERSON
    Thomas   40m VA farmer
    Thenia   30f
    Elizabeth 18f
    Malinda 12f
    Louis   10m
    Nancy   4f
    Mary   1f
214-207
  KNIGHT
    James   73m NC farmer
    Anna   60f VA
    Harriett 20f
    Abner   25m   farmer
215-208
  HAGELY
    Joseph   45m VA farmer
    Louisa   30f
    Polly   13f
    Joseph   12m
    George   10m
    Louisa   7f
    James   5m
    Melcher   3m
    Elizabeth 1f
216-209
  HALL
    Nehemiah 28m OH farmer
    Mahala   22f

216-209 HALL (con't)
    Warren   2m
    Augusta   1f   VA
217-210
  ANSEL
    Martin   37m VA farmer
    Nancy   35f
    Jessee   6m
    Albert   4m
218-211
  ANSEL
    Michael   44m VA farmer
    Elizabeth   33f
    Susan   11f
    Harvey   11m
  PERRY
    Malachi   22m   labor
219-212
  KNIGHT
    Henry   54m NC farmer
    Margaret   48f VA
    Parthenia   22f
    William   20m
    Nimrod   18m
    Lafayette   15m
    Catherine   13f
    Sarah   11f
    Henrietta   2f
    Amasetta   2f
  JEFFERSON
    Joseph   21m
220-213
  COLLINS
    Nathaniel   29m VA labor
    Mary J.   22f
    Greenville   1m
221-214
  McCUNE
    Benjamin   34m VA carptr
    Sarah   30f
    Julia   10f
    John   8m
    Frank   6m
    Charles   4m

221-214 McCUNE (con't)
    Lawrence   2m
    Benjamin   1/2m
  KEYTON
    Harriett   30f   dom
  MATHER
    John   17m   carptr
222-215
  WARD
    John Jr.   39m VA labor
    Joanna   35f
    Mary   8f
    Eliza   6f
    William   5m
    Elizabeth   3f
    Henry   1m
  WARD
    John Sr.   66m   labor
    David   27m   labor
223-216
  BAUMGARDNER
    John   51m VA farmer
    Malinda   40f
    Armana   21f
    John P.   19m   farmer
    Margaret   16f
    William   13m
    Fredrick   10m
    Emma   9m
    Mary   5f
    Frank   3m
224-
225-217
  SMITH
    Charles   26m GER labor
    Elizabeth   26f   VA
    William   6m
    Sarah   3f
    Sarah   11f
226-218
  RICHARDS
    Hez.   29m VA farmer
    Ann   29f

226-218 RICHARDS (con't)
 STEELE
 Thomas 25m
 Samuel 19m
227-219
 SHELTON
 H.W. 42m VA farmer
 Sarah C. 40f
 Henrietta 17f
 John W. 15m
 Henry 13m
 Sarah 11f
 Percilla 9f
 Madison 7m
 Ada 3f
228-220
 CONNER
 Wm.W. 28m VA farmer
 Louisa 24f
 Charles 3m
 John W. 2m
 CONNER
 Amasetta 18f
229-221
 CHAPMAN
 Willis 21m VA labor
 Missouri 17f
230-222
 THORNBURG
 John W. 27m VA farmer
 Emily 26f
 Mary 6f
 Willis 5m
 Claudius 3m
 Anna 1f
 Emma 1/12f
 THORNBURG
 Mary M. 67f
 CONNER
 America 23f dom
 EVERETT
 James 37m farmer
 Elizabeth 4f

230-222 THORNBURG (con't)
 BAUM
 John 18m FRA labor
231-223
 GRIFFIN
 Elizabeth 44f VA
 Mary H. 19f
 William 12m
 Sarah 7f
 Cora 4f
 John 2m
 ROBERTS
 Mary S. 27f dom
232-224
 EDEN
 Edward 44m B VA farmer
 Mary Jane 42f B
 Lucy Ann 21f B
 William 19m B farmer
 Martha 17f B
 John 15m B
 Virginia 12f B
 Sarah 8f B
 Benjamin 6m B
 Mary 3f B
 Henry 1f B
233-225
 HOLLENBACK
 Lorenzo 30m VA timber
 Martha 28f
 Mary 3f
 Rachel 3/12f
234-226
 DILLON
 Rece W. 30m VA timber
 Adalaid 19f
 Sarah 1f
 DILLON
 Marlin 72m labor
 Lucy 62f
 RAY
 Lemuel 20m laobr
 BLANKENSHIP
 Marlin 14m

235-227
  WALKER
    James H.   38m VA farmer
    Adalea   33f
    James   12m
    Martha   10f
    Sarah   5f
    Henry   4m
    Adalea   1f
  BARNETT
    Sylvester   14m
    John C.   12m
236-228
  DAVIS
    Wm.G.   49m VA farmer
    Paulina   43f
  HUGHES
    Margaret   23f
    Mary   19f
    Lorenzo   16m   labor
    Ralph   13m
    Jeremiah   12m
237-229
  HENSLEY
    Saml.   57m VA farmer
    Parthenia   57f
    Washington   30m   labor
    Philly   24m
    Mary   18f
    Lucy   14f
  PRICE
    James A.   10m
238-230
  HENSLEY
    John L.   32m VA farmer
    Susan   31f
    Rufus   10m
    Isabella   5f
    Georgia   4f
    Charles   3m
    Susan   2f

239-231
  KNIGHT
    Matthew   45m KY farmer
    Nancy   49f VA
    Wayne   21m   labor
    Mary   19f
    James   18m   labor
    William   15m
    Alvin S.   10m
240-232
  MORRISON
    Henry   29m VA farmer
    Malinda   27f
    Charles   3m
    Frank   2m
    Elizabeth   1f
241-233
  COOK
    James   40m VA labor
    Julius   11m IN
    Thomas   10m
    James M.   7m VA
    Susan   3f
    Mary   1f
242-234
  MORRISON
    Patrick   69m TN farmer
    Anna   24f VA
  DAVIS
    Matilda   35
    Edny   3f
    Cortez   2m
    Willie   2/12f
  SCALES
    John   50m   labor
243-235
  STANLEY
    Joseph   38m VA farmer
    Cynthia   36f OH
    Saml.   14m VA
    Margaret   12f
    Adaline   10f
    Sarah   7f
    James   5m

243-235 STANLEY (con't)

Isadora	1f		
BEECH			
Walden	50m	VA	shoemk

244-236

LOVE			
P.E.	27m	VA	farmer
Ann	26f		
Charles	6m		
John	4m		
Conwesley	1m		
SHEFF			
Daniel	21m	⸱labor	
POOR			
Susan	16f	dom	

245-237

HENSLEY			
A.J.	26m	VA	farmer
Amanda	17f		

246-238

McLEARY			
Robert	25m	VA	farmer
Frances	27f		
James	18m	farmer	
Isaac	16m	farmer	
Mary	14f		
McCOMAS			
Peyton	17m	labor	

247-239

RAINS			
Lewis	23m	VA	labor
Eliza	22f		
James	6m		
Albert	3m		
Mary	2f		

248-240

SMITH			
Eveline	38f	VA	
Marcus	17m		
Mary	3f		

249-

250-241

SWANN			
Benjamin	27m	VA	blacksm
Louisa	27f		
Frances	6f		
Emily	4f		
Charlotte	1f		
HATFIELD			
Amasetta	22f		

251-242

LLOYD			
R.J.	37m	VA	miller
Elizabeth	30f		
William	11m		
George	9m		
Susan	7f		
John	5m		
Sarah	4f		
Robert	1/12m		

252-243

CAIN			
Martin	38m	IRE	labor
Mary	34f		
Ann	10f		
Thomas	7m	IN	
Bryant	5m	VA	
Michael	2m		
William	1m		

253-244

SMITH			
Harvey	38m	VA	Sawyer
Sarah	37f		
John	9m		
Francis	3m		
SMITH			
David F.	32m	shoemk	

254-

255-245

WILLIAMS			
Wm.	54m	VA	labor
Nancy	44f		
Elizabeth	20f		
Mary	18f		
America	12f		

255-245 WILLIAMS (con't)

    Mariam   11f
    Cynthia   7f

256-246

  HOLLENBACK

    F.P.   25m VA timber
    Adaline   37f OH
    Mary   2f VA
    Alphonso   1m

  NEWMAN

    Harvey   51m NC labor
    Albert   21m VA labor

257-247

  BLUME

    E.W.   37m NC farmer
    Eveline   28f VA
    George   6m
    Ada   4f
    Albert   2m

258-248

  WEBB

    John   23m OH labor
    Julia   21f
    George   8/12m VA

259-249

  HANDLEY

    Sampson   59m VA blacksm
    Susan   56f
    Mary   24f
    Martha   19f

  McCOMAS

    Andrew   9m

  RECE

    Elizabeth   5f

260-250

  HERNDON

    James   48m VA farmer
    Adaline   44f
    John W.   11m
    James F.   8m
    Mordica   6m
    Charles   2m

261-251

  RECE

    John B.   40m VA farmer
    Mary   78f

  HATTON

    Sylvester   17m   labor

262-252

  FRANCE

    James   25m VA farmer
    Ann   35f
    Julia   21f
    Benjamin   16m   laobr

263-253

  ELMORE

    Wm.   26m VA farmer
    Joanna   19f
    Rhoda   3f
    Edward   2m
    Jefferson   1m

264-254

  CUSTIS

    Mary   49f VA

  SMITH

    Elizabeth   24f KY
    John C.   21m
    Jane   17f

  SMITH

    Mary   90f SC pauper

  PEYTON

    Perry   36m VA labor

265-255

  WILLIAMS

    George W.   31m VA farmer
    Elizabeth   19f
    Lily   2f
    David   9/12m

  SHOWANS

    Presley   22m   farmer

266-256

  BIAS

    Daniel   52m VA farmer
    Jennetta   52f
    Julia   21f
    Thomas   18m   farmer

266-256 BIAS (con't)

Sarah	16f	
Daniel B.	15m	
Jennetta	13f	
Ruth	11f	
Cordelia	9f	

267-257

BIAS

David H.	27m	VA farmer
Sarah	21f	
Elizabeth	2f	
Adolphus	1m	

ADAMS

Elizabeth	14f	

268-258

GIBSON

Wm.	25m	VA labor
Melissa	24f	
Marion	4m	
Isabella	2f	
Randolph	1m	

MAYS

Emily	18f	

269-259

SMITH

Jacob M.	36m	VA farmer
Elizabeth	35f	
William	15m	
Mary	14f	
Sarah	12f	
Martha	10f	
Henry	8m	
Eliza	7f	
Burwell	5m	
James	4m	
Angelina	1f	

SMITH

Jacob	87m	pauper

MATTHEWS

John	25m	labor

270-260

SMITH

Viola	67f	VA
Joanna	25f	

270-260 SMITH (con't)

Viola	21f	

ADKINS

Calvery	13m	

271-261

ROBERTS

Mary	52f	KY
Rebecca	27f	VA
Mary E.	25f	
Sarah J.	21f	

272-262

BUTCHER

T. J.	26m	VA farmer
Susan	18f	
Matthew	10/12m	

RAINS

Wm.	15m	

273-263

STANLEY

David	27m	VA farmer
Adaline	23f	
Emma	3f	
Jasper	2m	
Edney	1f	
Lucinda	8/12f	

274-264

SMITH

Amborse	29m	VA farmer
Telitha	31f	
Emma	7f	
Sarah	5f	
Randolph	3m	
Mary	2f	

275-265

SAMMONS

Rolin	27m	KY labor
Lucinda	28f	IL
Henry	5m	VA
Nancy	4f	
Lawrence	1m	

276-266

NIPPS

Saml.	25m	VA labor
Anna	28f	

276-266 NIPPS (con't)

Morris	4m	
James	1m	

277-267

RODGERS

Fenton	21m	VA labor
Amanda	24f	

278-268

CHILDERS

M.M.	35m	VA farmer
Catherine	29f	
John	9m	
Spencer	8m	
Amanda	6f	
James	4m	

CHILDERS

Nancy	59f

279-269

PORTER

Alexander	49m	VA farmer
Harriett	46f	
Frances	22f	
Cynthia	20f	
Tabitha	18f	
John	15m	
Elvira	13f	
Elisha	10m	
Patrick	7m	

280-270

KING

Sampson	29m	VA farmer
Mary	24f	
Wm. H.	5m	
Martha	2f	
Elizabeth	7/12f	

281-271

COLLINS

John	64m	VA farmer
Nancy	58f	
Addison	17m	labor
Jennie	15f	
Hezekiah	13m	
Clarrissa	12f	
Thomas	9m	

282-272

KIRK

John	35m	VA farmer
Jemimah	33f	
Emerine	11f	
Sarah	9f	
William	6m	
James	4m	
Martha	3f	
Mary	2f	

283-273

ROSS

Robert	45m	OH farmer
Elizabeth	46f	VA
George	18m	
Hugh	16m	
Jane	14f	
Nancy	10f	
Robert	9m	

284-274

GILL

Joseph	58m	ENG civ eng
Mary A.	44f	
George	18m	farmer
Charles	13m	
John	11m	VA
Sarah	9f	
Henry	6m	
Thomas	4m	

285-275

JIMESON

Joseph	35m	VA farmer
Malinda	29f	
Hannah		
Susan	10f	
James	6m	
Benjamin	4/12m	

CANN

Charles	26m	FRA merchant

APPLE

A. N.	18m	PA clerk

FREUTEL

William	18m	PA labor

29

286-276
  HENRY
    Lewis   25m GER farmer
    Jerusha 22f VA
    Joseph   1m
287-277
  HENSLEY
    John   49m VA farmer
    Malinda 47f
    Virginia 22f
    Missouri 21f
    Elizabeth 18f
    David   16m   labor
    Ephraim 11m
    John   9m
  McCORKLE
    George   19m   labor
288-278
  BUTCHER
    Matthew 47m VA farmer
    Lucinda 47f
    Martin   19m
    Julia   17f
    John   16m
  STANLEY
    Sarah   22f
    Mary   3f
  PEYTON
    Lewis   9m
    Lucinda 7f
289-279
  THOMPSON
    Carrie   46f VA
    Isaac   25m   labor
    Jemimah 22f
    Mary   18f
    John   13m
    Mary   1f
290-280
  PEYTON
    Elisha   29m VA farmer
    John   55m
    Mildred 50f

291-281
  MOSS
    V. R.   28m VA doctor
    Mary   22f
  MOSS
    Mary   70f
292-282
  THOMPSON
    Wm.   44m VA farmer
    Martha 38f
    John T. 17m   farmer
    Nancy A. 15f
    Wm. S. 10m
    Elizabeth 8f
    Stanhope 5m
    James   2m
    Lawson 3/12m
293-283
  BECKETT
    Lewis   31m VA farmer
    Susan   25f
    Charles 5m
    Francis M. 3m
    Wm. L. 1m
294-284
  HATFIELD
    Moses   37m VA farmer
    Permiah 39f
    Martha 15f
    Lucinda 13f
    Albert   11m
    Joseph   8m
    Adam   6m
    James   3m
    Emily   3/12f
295-285
  ABBOTT
    James   35m VA labor
    Polly   25f
    Martha 3f
    Margaret 6/12f
296-

297-286

HATFIELD

A. L.	45m VA farmer	
Frances	42f	
Benjamin	20m	labor
Phoebe	14f	
Lucretia	10f	
Joseph	7m	
Jefferson	4m	

298-287

HARLER

Charles	30m VA farmer
Mildred	41f
Elizabeth	19f

SMITH

Cynthia	6f

299-288

TEAL

Saml .	48m VA farmer	
Elizabeth	44f	
Wm. J.	21m	farmer
John W.	19m	farmer
Jacob	16m	farmer
Lerissa	14f	
Adam	12m	
Phillip	11m	
Elizabeth	8f	
Lorri	6f	

300-289

BIAS

Rolin	66m VA farmer	
Martha	39f	
William	17m	labor
Drucilla	16f	
Adalaide	12f	
Elizabeth	9f	
Catherine	2f	

301-290

ROBERTS

Richard	22m VA labor
Emily	19f

302-291

PAINE

Simeon	40m VA farmer
Frances	40f
Eliza	20f
Elizabeth	5f
Simeon	9/12m

303-292

TASSON

John	32m HOL plaster
Cynthia	23f VA
Rebecca	6f
Mary	4f

304-293

GUE

Linsey	46m VA farmer	
Nancy	42f	
Presley	21m	farmer
James H.	20m	farmer
Saml. D.	15m	
Powhatan	13m	
Lucy	10f	
Mary	9f	
Amelia	5f	

PARSONS

James	18m	labor

304-294

HOLDRYDE

Sarah	60f VA
Olivia	40f
Lizzie	37f
Mary	28f
Lewis	25m
Virginia	16f

HOLDRYDE

James	70m	pauper

306-295

TURLEY

Sarah	64f VA	
Eliza	25f	
Joseph	21m	farmer

DUNE

William	9m
Elizabeth	5f

307-296
    WILSON
        A. L.   43m OH farmer
        Mary   37f VA
        Eliza   21f
        Lemuel   20m   farmer
        Elizabeth   18f
        Frances   16f
        John   14m
        Emily   12f
        Ellen   10f
        Malinda   5f
        Georgia   3f
        Hester   2/12f
    WILSON
        Harvey   17m   labor
    SANDRIDGE
        Justin   80f
308-297
    McCORKLE
        A. M.   53m VA doctor
        Elleanor   40f
        Phoebe   28f
        Effie   6f
        Ida   4f
        G.W.S.   2m
    HANDLEY
        Lycingus   17m   clerk
        Olga   14f
        Samuel   10m
309-298
    CLARK
        Elizabeth   50f VA
        Charles R.   25m   farmer
    BUCKINGHAM
        Elisha   57m   brmason
310-299
    BURNS
        Andrew   53m VA farmer
        Mariam   46f
        Jane   8f
        Charles   7f

311-300
    BOWEN
        Jefferson   25m VA farmer
        Angeline   25f
        Isabella   5f
        Paulina   3f
        Lemuel   1m
312-301
    CREMEANS
        Durgan   26m VA labor
        Rose   23f
        James   2m
        Sarah   9/12f
    CREMEANS
        Miama   45f
313-302
    SARGENT
        David   28m VA farmer
        Hannah   23f
        Sarah   4f
314-303
    DROWN
        Benjamin   36m VA farmer
        Martha   18f
        Luke   12m
        John   10m
        Rufus   9m
        Elizabeth   7f
        George   6m
        Henry   4m
315-304
    SMITH
        Henry   28m VA farmer
        Sinia   29f
        Zachariah   12m KY
        Noah   4m VA
        Eliza   1f
316-305
    DROWN
        George A.   38m VA farmer
        Sarah   34f OH
    COCKE
        John   8m ENG

32

317-306
    ELMORE
        Edward   57m VA farmer
        Rhoda   57f
    BLANKENSHIP
        Ariana   13f
318-307
    BRADSHAW
        Cynthia   38f VA
        William   14m
        Allen   12m
        Mary H.   8f
        Greenville 5m
319-308
    DeBOY
        John   52m VA farmer
        Polly   50f
        Julia   23f
        Elizabeth   19f
        John   17m   farmer
        Margaret   15f
        Mahala   13f
320-309
    CARSON
        Wm. A.   37m VA cooper
        Nancy   37f
        Rachel   11f
        Nancy   9f KY
        Joanna   8f KY
        Wm.   6m KY
        Saml.   4m KY
        John   1m KY
321-310
    ADKINS
        Benjamin   28m VA farmer
        Nancy   25f
        Amos   3m
        Paralee   2f
        Arnold   8/12m
322-311
    CHILDERS
        Royal   54m VA farmer
        Nancy   56f
        Sarah   18f

322-311 CHILDERS (con't)
        Royal   16m   farmer
    KEENE
        Eliza   45f VA teacher
323-312
    CHILDERS
        Wm. L.   33m VA farmer
        Elizabeth   32f
        Mary F.   20f
        Joseph B.   9m
        Colonel   7m
        Nancy   4f
        Albert   2m
        Greenville 5/12m
324-313
    SIMMONS
        Conwesley   35m VA farmer
        Elizabeth   35f
        Mary F.   20f
        Sampson S. 17m   farmer
    SHOEMAKER
        Charles   23m   labor
    POINDEXTER
        James   22m   labor
    LOVE
        Margaret   19f
    SMITH
        Lucy   7f
    JEWELL
        Gottier   17m   labor
    HOUCHINS
        Rebecca   22f   dom
    ROBERTS
        Eveline   21f   dom
325-314
    SCALES
        Thomas   47m VA farmer
        Ruth   45f
        John   13m
        Conwesley   10m
        Peter   7m
        Rebecca   5f
        Albert G.   2m

325-314 SCALES (con't)
    JEWELL

Mott	22m	labor
Abagail	21f	

326-315
    HENSLEY

Byrd	50m	VA farmer
Nancy	50f	
William	21m	IL
Mary	19f	IL
Sarah	16f	IL
Columbus	12m	VA
Salina	9f	
Emma	5m	

327-316
    BRAMLET

Wm. C.	35m	VA farmer
Armilda	30f	
Eliza	9f	
Josephine	5f	
Eugenia	3f	

328-317
    SWANN

Josiah	64m	VA farmer
Rachel	46f	
Thomas	17m	farmer
Cynthia	15f	
Sarah	12f	
George	10m	
Joseph	7m	

329-318
    DUSENBERRY

Wm. F.	32m	NY dentist
Cynthia	31f	
Susie	12f	
Caleb C.	7m	
Sarah	5f	VA
Jessie	3f	

330-319
    DUSENBERRY

Susan	50f	NY
Ann B.	50f	
Robert F.	22m	farmer
Samuel	17m	farmer

330-319 DUSENBERRY (con't)

Charles O.	30m	jeweler
Anna	20f	
Wm.C.	1m	VA

    McKIBBY

Harriet	55f	NY

331-320
    MORRIS

Charles	40m	VA farmer
Martha	40f	
Ellen	18f	
John	15m	
Thomas	13m	
Edney	11f	
Ida	5f	
Charles	1m	

    CAIN

Michael	30m	IRE labor

    HESSIAN

Patrick	32m	IRE labor

332-321
    CARPENTER

Perry	26m	VA labor
Mahala	23f	
Malinda	10/12f	

333-322
    SWANN

John K.	48m	VA farmer
Nancy B.	45f	
Elizabeth	26f	
Hester	21f	
Nancy	18f	
Enoch	16m	farmer
William	15m	
Reason	13m	
McHearston	12m	
Joseph	5m	

334-323
    SWANN

Calvary	40m	VA farmer
Emily	41f	
Josiah	19m	farmer
Henry C.	16m	farmer
Mary	13f	

34

334-323 SWANN (con't)

Calvery	12m		
Benjamin	10m		
John	8m		
Edith	6f		
Richard A.	4m		
Daniel W.	3m		
Jerome S.	1m	MO	

335-324
THURSTON

Clark	49m	VT	farmer
Eveline	38f	VA	
Charles	11m		
Mary	7f		
Alexander	5m		
Emily	1f		

336-325
LUNCEFORD

Richard	38m	OH	farmer
Nancy	30f	VA	
Mary	12f		
John H.	10m		
Calvery	8m		
Emily	6f		
Elijah	2m		
Elijah Sr.	22m	OH	labor

PEYTON

Mary J.	22f	VA
Mary	60f	
Allen	1m	

337-326
DEAN

George	30m	VA	labor
Catherine	30f	OH	
Samuel	12m		
Stephen	9m	KY	
Sarah	8f	VA	
George	4m		
Margaret	6/12f		

338-327
WEBB

Alexander Jr.	30m	VA	labor
Roxana	25f	OH	

338-327 WEBB (con't)

James	11m	VA
William	8m	

339-328
UNDERWOOD

E. M.	40m	TN	carptr
Cynthia	40f	VA	
John	21m		labor
Jane	8f		
Emma	3f		

340-329
SMITH

John	38m	VA labor
Mary A.	22f	
Eliza	9f	
Charles	7m	
Catherine	5f	
James H.	2m	
Martin	6/12m	

341-330
GWINN

Andrew Jr.	28m	VA farmer
Harriett	28f	
Charles	3m	
William	1m	

342-331
SEXTON

John	58m	VA farmer
Horatio	16m	
Henry	14m	
James F.	10m	

SEXTON

Elizabeth	76f

343-332
EVERETT

Sarah	65f	VA
Polly	43f	
Saml.	41m	farmer
Peter R.	30m	farmer

CARTER

Andrew	30m	labor

344-333
  TAYLOR
    Henry   21m VA labor
    Catherine   19f
    William   1m
345-334
  WEIGER
    Lewis   45m GER miller
    Mary   35f GER
    Susan   8f VA
    Lewis   3m
    Frank   11/12m
  RHODE
    Sarah   16f
346-335
  WEBB
    Stephen   30m VA labor
    Sarah   40f
  DEAN
    Samuel   18m   laobr
347-336
  WEBB
    Alexander Sr. 60m VA labor
    Peggy   50f
    Nancy   19f OH
    David   18m   labor
    Margaret   16f
348-337
  MYERS
    Charles   38m   farmer
              b (Schaumberg Lippi)
    Martha   26f VA
    Mary   5f
    Charles   4m
    Augusta   2f
  SMALLRIDGE
    Mary   21f
349-338
  STOWATER
    Anthony   40m BOH farmer
    Louisa   41f SAX
    Henry   2m VA
  BAKER
    Matilda   9f SAX

350-339
  BERRY
    Philo B.   33m OH farmer
    Mary   25f
    John   11m
    Letitia   5f VA
    Corila   4f
    Mary   2f
351-340
  MILLER
    Charles W.   39m SAX farmer
    Caroline   38f
    Lenora   16f
    Caroline   8f
    Rosamond   4f VA
    Isabella   1f VA
352-341
  HENRICH
    Charles   41m SAX farmer
    Wilhelmine 33f
    Theodore   14m
    Amelia   12f
    Augusta   8f
353-342
  TONEY
    Joel   33m VA farmer
    Edney   25f
    Lucinda   8f
    Hester   3f
    Nancy   2f
  TONEY
    Betsey   60f
354-343
  SCHULTZ
    Joseph   62m SAX farmer
    Rosa   44f FRA
    Jacob   15m
    William   9m
355-344
  DIEHL
    Lewis   39m PRU farmer
    Rosa   38f HAN
    Lewis   9m PA

355-344 DIELH (con't)
　　Albert　　　7m
　　Robert　　　1/12m　VA
356-345
　GIBHEART
　　John　　　60m BOH farmer
　　Eliza　　　38f
　　John　　　13m
　　Mary　　　6f
357-346
　STOWATER
　　Frank　　　42m BOH farmer
　　Christiana　32f　SAX
358-347
　BICKER
　　Henry　　　38m BAV farmer
　　Joanna　　50f　PRU
359-348
　SMITH
　　Frank　　　32m SAX farmer
　　Anna　　　32f　SAX
　　Mary　　　3f　VA
360-349
　MECKL
　　George　　62m BOH farmer
　　Agnes　　　23f
　　Julia　　　2f　VA
　　Bertha　　　3/12f
　GOLDEN
　　Gustave　　40m SWI labor
361-350
　KORN
　　David　　　60m PRU sheperd
362-351
　McGINNIS
　　John B.　　60m VA teacher
　　Joan　　　37f　OH
　　Charlotte　9f　VA
363-352
　JEWELL
　　Benjamin R.　60m NY farmer
　　Perses　　　44f　OH

364-353
　MARSTON
　　Henry　　　59m ENG farmer
　　Hannah　　57f
365-354
　BEXFIELD
　　Richard　　34m ENG farmer
　　Mary　　　33f　VA
　　Joseph　　9m
　　James　　　6m
366-355
　HOUCHINS
　　Clarissa　48f　VA
　　William　19m　　labor
367-356
　GILL
　　Joseph　　23m ENG farmer
　　Frances　30f　VA
　　Emily　　　3/12f
　PAINE
　　Julia　　　16f　　　dom
368-357
　CREMEANS
　　Elizabeth　80f　VA
　　Polly　　　30f
　HOLLY
　　Marietta　11f
　　Francis M.　9m
369-358
　WITCHER
　　Stephen　60m B VA farmer
　　Annie　　70f　B
370-359
　LEONARD
　　Rufus　　55m VA brickms
　　Mary　　56f
　WINTZ
　　Elizabeth　80f
371-360
　HINCHMAN
　　William　60m VA farmer
　　Elizabeth　47f
　　Louis S.　21m　　farmer
　　John W.　19m　　farmer

371-360 HINCHMAN (con't)
    Adam   17m   farmer
    Susannah   16f
    Wesley   15m
372-361
  NEWMAN
    Russell   60m VA farmer
    Eliza   26f
    Addison   24m   farmer
    Amanda   21f
    Milton   19m   farmer
    Edney Ann 14f
373-362
  DOLEN
    John   55m VA farmer
    Julia   50f
    Daniel   30m   farmer
    Frances   17f
    Eliza   16f
  DOLEN
    James   25m   farmer
    Sarah   19f
    John   2/12m

374-363
  ROFFE
    Charles L. 52m VA farmer
    Mary   32f
    Ida   4f
    Ann   2f
    Cornelia 1f
  DICK
    Mary   21f
  SWEATLAND
    Wm. A.   30m VA merchant
  SHELTON
    Susan   66f
    Nancy   47f
    Charles J. 27m   farmer

END BARBOURSVILLE DISTRICT

GUYANDOTTE DISTRICT (town)
skips number (375-364)
376-365

THORNBURG

H. M.	26m VA farmer	
Barbary	27f	
Walter	5m	
Isabella	3f	
Benton	2m	

THORNBURG

John	33m MD doctor	

FANDRY

Joseph	22m VA labor	

DAVIS

Mary	25f	dom

377-366

ONG

Isaac	43m VA tailor	
Susan	38f	
John	21m	clerk
Albina	19f	teacher
Ernest	15m	
Augusta	12f	
Isaac B.	7m	
Joseph R.	4/12m	

CAMPBELL

James	35m OH tailor	

378-367

WOLCOTT

A. S.	51m OH wharf mas	
Susan H.	41f	
Cordelia	20f VA	
Bryon A.	17m	labor
Robert B.	15m	
Ellen T.	13f	
William W.	11m	
Laura A.	9f	
Cassius C.	7m	
George F.	5m	
Addie A.	2f	

379-368

RUSSELL

S. M.	50m VA minister
Dollie	44f

379-368 RUSSELL (con't)

M. M.	23f	
St. M. E.	21m	merchant
Mary A.	12f	

380-369

HOFFMAN

P. H.	36m VA minister
Penelope	33f KY

HUNTER

Margaret	13f VA

381-370

DUSENBERRY

J. T.	41m NY merchant
Louisa	32f VA
Frances F.	8m
Theodore	6m
James B.	4m
Mary E.	1f

382-371

HILTBURNER

Jacob	44m PA tinner	
Mary	35f	
Stephen	18m	tinner
William	11m VA	
Virginia	6f	
Ezra	3m	
Hiram	1m	

ARTHUR

Mary	20f	dom

383-372

MAYS

Elisha	37m VA barber
Eliza	26f OH
Wm. E.	2m VA

384-373

SMITH

E. A.	29m VA merchant
Josephine	24f
Mary P.	3f
Edward E.	5/12m

385-374

SCOTT

Sandford W.	23m Va blacksm
Mary J.	24f

385-374 SCOTT (con't)
    Edward E.   1m
  LARKIN
    Thomas   19m   blacksm
  WINDEN
    James   23m   labor
386-375
  CHAPMAN
    A. P.   33m VA merchant
    Mary   25f
    Anna   2/12f
387-376
  BEEKMAN
    Lewis   44m BAV mercht
    Pauline   32f FRA
    Ellen V.   5f VA
    Betty A.   3f
    Samuel M.   3/12m
388-377
  EMSHEIMER
    Joseph   24m FRA merchant
    Fanny S.   22f BAV
    Jacob   23m FRA shoemkr
    Emanuel   15m FRA
389-378
  McMAHAN
    Wayne   50m VA bridge keepr
    John   26m   tobaccoist
    Amasetta   10f
    George W.   7m
  NIFFIN
    Melissa   20f   dom
390-
391-379
  SUMMERSON
    Charles   30m Va tobaccoist
    Emma   23f
    Richard   1m
392-380
  CLARK
    Lyman   49m VT st mason
    Julia   29f ME
    Roland   18m   farmer
    George   10m

392-380 CLARK (con't)
    Frederick   6m VA
    Elizabeth   3f
    Lorenzo D.   7/12m
393-381
  PETERS
    Lewis   31m VA painter
    Virginia   28f
    Richard   9m
    Mary   5f
    James   1m
  HAYSLIP
    Carey   18m   painter
  GARDNER
    Elizabeth   47f
394-382
  DOWTHIT(Douthit)
    Wm.   50m VA merchant
    Charlotte   40f
    Wm.H.   19m   labor
    John L.   17m   labor
    Mary A.   13
    Edward   11m
    Columbia   8f
    Richard H.   6m
    Clarence   2m
395-383
  DUPINE
    Francis   40m FRA shoemkr
    Louisa   38f FRA
396-384
  MOORE
    F. M.   39m TN silversm
    Amanda   36f VA
    Salina   16f
    Sarah   13f
    James   9m
    Alice   7f
    John   4m
    Harriett   3f
    Albert G.   2/12m

397-385
  WARREN
    George W.   28m NY grocer
    Caroline   26f
    Angelina   2f VA
  WARREN
    G.D.   29m NY lawyer
    Chancey   18m   labor
  WHITE
    Caroline C. 51f PA

398-386
  HITE
    John W.   57m VA broker
    Malinda   53f
    Victoria   21f
    Adalaide   18f
    Catherine A. 14f
  HITE
    Sarah   76f
  McMAHAN
    Nancy   72f NC

399-387
  MASON
    George W.   38m OH lawyer
    Salina   27f VA
    John H.   5m
    Mary   3f
    George   1m NB

400-388
  MILLER
    H. H.   46m VA merchant
    Eliza   42f
    Leonora   19f MO
    Belle   12f VA
    Edward   10m
    Cora   4f
  CHAPMAN
    Frances   70f

401-389
  RICKETTS
    Elijah   66m MD farmer
    Eleanor   60f
    Virginia   35f
    Albert G.   15m

401-389 RICKETS (con't)
    Lucian C.   14m
    George H.   12m
    Edwin   10m
    Girard B.   6m
    Charles H.   4m
    Sarah E.   2f

402-390
  HITE
    John B.   55m VA tanner
                & currier
    Elizabeth   43f CAN
    Elizabeth   22f VA
    Sarah   21f
    John B.   3m
    Martha   1f
  HITE
    Eliza   35f

403-391
  HAZELTINE
    Kendale   57m VT farmer
    Jane   60f NH
  REED
    Sophia   35f VT
  GOULD
    Hannah   60f VA

404-392
  HATFIELD
    Alexander   30m VA shoemkr
    Diana   29f
    Alice   2m OH

405-393
  SCOTT
    Sanford   55m VA blacksm
    Sarah   50f
    Alizira   23f
    Harvey   18m   painter
    Eliza   16f
    Virginia   11f
    Charles   9m

406-394
  HITE
    Wm.   52m VA gentleman
    Mary   44f

406-394 HITE (con't)

| Malinda | 18f |
| Virginia | 14f |

SMITH

| Joseph | 40m M VA labor |

407-395

GREGG

James H.	27m VA carpenter
Jane E.	26f
Sarah E.	2/12f

408-396

AYERS

Wm.	29m VA engineer
Hannah	21f
James H.	5m
John M.	3m
Alice A.	1f

409-397

AYERS

Mahlon	59m VA sawyer
Sarah	52f
John	21m	sawyer

410-398

PRICE

Joseph	45m WALES miller
Minerva	35f KY
George L.	11m KY

411-399

BRAMER

Clark K.	29m OH painter
Melilta	23f VA
Victoria	5f

412-400

WELLINGTON

Erastus	67m CN carptr
Charlotte	58f
James W.	24m VA carptr
Sarah	21f
Lucinda	17f
Zach.Taylor	13m

413-401

WELLINGTON

| Erastus Jr. | 29m VA carptr |
| Frances | 20f |

413-401 WELLINGTON (con't)

| Nanthaniel | 1m |

EMMONS

| Cyrus | 18m | carptr |

414-402

WELLINGTON

Noadiah	30m VA carptr
Elizabeth	26f
Charlotte	4f
Sarah	8/12f

415-403

WOOD

J. E.	38m NY plaster
Ann J.	32f VA
Cora J.	13f
Alfred	8m
Alzada	5f
Texana	3f
Ada B.	3/12f

416-404

FLOWERS

E. H.	43m KY engineer
Ellen F.	45f OH
Eliza	16f
Marcellus	10m VA
Rosetta	5f

CHAPDU

| Peter | 80m St.Domingo |
| | Saddler |

(see Gallia Co.OH)

417-405

PARKER

Greenville	51m MA Lawyer
Eliza A.	51f ME
Emily T.	21f MA
Eliza G.	19f MA

418-406

CARROLL

Thomas	42m IRE hotel
Mary	25f	hotel
McHenry	15m MD
Margaret	12f
Austin	10m VA
Catherine	4f

418-406 CARROLL (con't)
    Caroline   3f
  FEE
    Ann   22f IRE
419-407
  SEDINGER
    Lewis   47m PA shoemkr
    Rebecca   45f
    James   22m OH plaster
    Rachel   20f
    Margaret   13f
    Frank   7m VA
    Henry   5m VA
    Charles   1m
420-408
  KEENAN
    A. J.   41m VA saddlr
    Sarah   26f
    Newton   16m   labor
    Sanford C.   7m
    Sarah C.   4f
  TINVEY
    Sarah   70f
421-409
  SPURLOCK
    M. J.   40m VA merchant
    Rebecca E.   36f
    Josephus   9m
422-410
  SMITH
    Percival   63m OH retired
            merchant
    Mary A.   57f VA
    Richard P.   26m   gentleman
    Percival S.   22m   clerk
  CHAPMAN
    George   83m   farmer
    Elizabeth   73f
  PREBLE
    Ulysus   26m VA minister
423-411
  STONE
    Grace   64f VA
    Susan W.   32f

423-411 STONE (con't)
    Elizabeth   26f   teacher
  FREEMAN
    Agnes   13f M   dom
  VANDIVER
    J.H.   42m KY stage agt
    R. P.   9m VA
    Ann G.   6f
424-412
  RODGERS
    William C.   31m NY owns livery
    Emeretta   26f VA
    Kate   3f
    Susan   1f
425-413
  WALTON
    E. H.   40m VA merchant
    Susan   45f
    W. W.   15m
    Mary   12f
426-414
  ONG
    John   67m VA butcher
    Margaret   62f
  JEWELL
    Catherine   24f   seamtress
    Helen   18f   seamtress
  ROBERTS
    Sarah   17f   domestic
  PARKINS
    Cynthia   13f
427-415
  WOLCOTT
    L. M.   32m OH merchant
    Mary C.   24f NY
    Peter C.   4m NY
  KISE
    Harriett   18f VA dom
428-416
  EVERETT
    H. C.   30m VA merchant
    Kate L.   20f IL
    Ellen V.   2f VA
    Mary   5/12f

429-417
  MOLESWORTH
    W. W.   29m OH dentist
                    & doctor
    Cecelia R. 26f OH
    Cicero   3m OH
  MATHUS
    Sarah   22f OH dom

430-418
  MOORE
    Orren   38m ME gentleman
    Sarah   28f KY
    Frank B.   5m VA
    Cyrus S.   2m
    Wm. P.   2/12m

431-419
  SMITH
    D. D.   57m OH merchant
    Elleanor C. 46f
    Whitcomb 27m   merchant
    Sarah J.   25f VA
    William   23m   carpntr
    Mary   20f
    Dudley J. 18m   clerk
    Abraham 16m
    Rebecca   14f
    Georgia   12f

432-420
  HAYSLIP
    T. J.   52m VA teacher
    Mary   52f OH
    James   25m   stage dr
    Samuel   21m   clerk
    Lewellyn 15f VA
    Thomas J. 12m
    R.H. S.   9m

433-421
  HAMBURGER
    Joseph   40m AUS labor
    Henrietta 27f
    Caroline 7f PA
    Mary   4m VA
    Lewis   2m

434-

435-422
  BLANPED (Blanssed)
    Elisha   26m OH saddler
    Isabella 21f
    Mary E.   3f   VA
    Elisha   1m

436-423
  BIERLY (Burley)
    Joseph   42m VA wagon mkr
    Sarah M. 36f
    Eliza   16f
    Saml.   14m
    John D.   10m
    Tucker   8m

437-424
  ARTHUR
    Wm.   27m VA labor
    Martha   25f OH
    Lucetta   8f VA
    Virginia 5f
    Bedford 4m
    Martha   4/12f
  KNIGHT
    Ellen   25f   dom
    Mary   4f
    Sarah   6/12f

438-425
  DOTSON
    Jessee   35m VA pilot(river)
    Lucetta   32f
    Mary A.   12f
    Wm.E.   10m
    Amanda   6f
    Milton   4m
    Charles   2m
    Henry   2/12m
  ARTHUR
    Letitia   19m   dom

439-426
  WRIGHT
    Nancy   58f
    Mary   17f
    James   23m   carpntr
    Frances   23f

440-427
  DEITZ
    Hugo   35m Hess Darmstaad
                            carptr
    Minerva   23f ME
    Charlotte 5f VA
    Wm. C.   3m
    George   2/12m
    Henry   2/12m
  MAGNUS
    JoAnna E. 56f Hess Darm
  BOYD
    Nancy   22f KY   dom
441-428
  HILMAN
    William   62m VA shoemkr
    Nancy   61f
  ARTHUR
    Agnes   16f   dom
442-429
  DOTSON
    Thomas   25m VA carpntr
    Sarah   28f OH
    Elizabeth 3f VA
443-430
  GASNER
    George   45m GER labor
    Mary   36f ENG
    Harrietta 18f VA
    Victoria 7f
    John H.   5m
    Mary S.   1f
444-431
  CLARK
    Silas   37m ME druggist
    Martha   28f VA
    Robert   7m
    Alexander 5m
    Clarence 8/12m
445-432
  ELZEY
    James   54m CN labor
    Sarah   41f NJ

445-432 ELZEY (con't)
    Eliza   19f NY
    Charles W. 17m   labor
446-433
  LETULLE
    Nancy   49f VA
    Lenora   21f
    Victora   19f
    Sarah   17f
    Lewis   14m
    Josephine 12f
    James L. 10m
    Margaret 6f
447-434
  DEITZ
    Otto   39m Hesse Darm
                     labor
    Rosanna 24f VA
    Charles   4m
448-435
  DEITZ
    John K.   25m Hesse Darmstaad
                    blacksm
    Elizabeth 25f KY
    Levina   5f
    Mary E.   3f
    Lewellyn 1f
449-436
  PETERMAN
    Ralph   45m KY labor
    Frances   27f VA
    Jacob   8m KY
    William   4m
    Isadore   1f
450-437
  STEWART
    Burgess   43m VA stone mason
    Maria   38f OH
    Hamilton 12m VA
    Mary   8f
    Daniel E. 6m
    Viola A.   4f
    Fletcher 1m

450-437 STEWART (con't)
NODDLE
Abraham 27m OH blacksm
McKINLEY
M. M. 25m VA coach mkr
EVICKS
William 16m blacksm
451-438
McGINNIS
A. B. 31m VA doctor
Elizabeth 19f
MAUPIN
R. W. 11m
452-439
PETIT
Hugh B. 49m VA cooper
Frances 49f
Frances 20f
Wm. E. 18m labor
Noah C. 16m
John A. 13m
Julia 9f
Durasia 8f
453-440
EVERETT
John Sr. 72m VA farmer
Hannah 50f NY
RUSSELL
Romaine 20f VA
John 16m
454-441
SMITH
Austin 47m OH teamstr
Nancy 45f VA
Amanda 18f OH
Charles E. 10m
Lewellyn 6f VA
Henry S. 1m
455-442
BAKER
J. C. 44m VA carpntr
Catherine E. 35f
Preston 15m TN
Zora 6f VA

456-443
SHOMBURG
John B. 37m FRA carpntr
Mary 38f ENG
George 8m ENG
457-444
WHITE
Albert 30m VA pilot(river)
Mary 25f
Susan G. 1f
MATHER
Julia 54f
Eliza 19f
Amasetta 15f
458-445
HUXOM
Henry 31m ENG stone mas
Sarah 28f
Elizabeth 7f FRA
Charlotte 4f VA
Florence 8/12f
459-446
TURNER
Leonard 35m VA teamstr
Elizabeth 24f
America 2f
Joseph 8/12m
460-447
CARTER
Henry 39m MA carpntr
Mary E. 32f
Mary A. 17f
Charles 13m VA
James 11m
Martha 8f
Lewellyn 6f
Elleaner 3f
Sarah 1f
461-448
WHITE
John 29m VA butcher
Lucy 23f
Martha M. 4f
Mary 2f

461-448 WHITE (con't)
    Alice J.   16f
462-449
  FLOWERS
    Alfred   49m VA millwrght
    Sarah   49f KY
    Nathaniel   22m OH carpntr
    Thaddeus   20m   engineer
    Ezra   18m   labor
    Melissa   16f
    Josephine   14f
    Alonza   11m VA
    Lewellyn   9f
    James   6m
463-450
  BROWN
    Wm.   47m NC farmer
    Elizabeth   37f
    Charles   12m
    Wm.   9m OH
    Henry   6m VA
464-451
  CHAPDU
    Martha   39f OH
    James   14m
    Nathan   9m VA
465-452
  MONROE
    Thomas H.   42m VA ministr
    Margaret   36f
    John E.   16m
    James H.   14m
    Wm.M.   12m
    Watson   10m
    Charles A.   7m
    Sarah E.   1f
  MORRIS
    Elizabeth   21f
466-453
  NESMITH
    John   55m VA miller
    Susan   42f
    Wm. W.   22m   miller
    Eliza J.   21f

466-453 NESMITH (con't)
    Robert A.   19m   farmer
    Charles D.   18m   clerk
  EVANS
    Laura   24f OH dom
    Frank   7m
467-454
  BAUMGARDNER
    Jacob   66m VA gentlmn
    Mary   68f
    Rebecca   29f
    Henry W.   28m   hotel propri
    James M.   26m   hotel propri
    Mildred   18f
H TAYLOR
O   Frances   13f
T HOLDERBY
E   G. W.   22m   merchnt
L ROUSE
    James H.   25m OH doctor
  DAVIDSON
    Alex   47m ENG clerk
  LOUCHINE
H   Sol.   22m OH silversm
O BENT(Burt)
T   J. M.   21m VA teacher
E THOMPSON
L   John   28m   pilot
  REYNOLDS
    L. M.   50m   ostler
  PAINE
    Anna   19f
468-
469-455
  RUSSELL
    A. G.   35m VA pilot
    Sarah   30f
    Laura   4f
    Charles   4/12m
470-456
  MITCHELL
    Wm.   41m VA carpntr
    Elizabeth   44f
    John   13m

470-456 MITCHELL (con't)
      Lucy   11f
      Wm. H.   5m
      Nancy J.   3f
471-457
  HITE
      Frank   40m VA carpntr
      Mary   35f OH
      Frances   13f VA
      Edgar   10m
      Gertrude   4f
      Henry Clay 2m
472-458
  DEITZ
      Rodolphus 45m Hesse Darm.
                      carpntr
      Maria   24f MA
      Mary   10f VA
      Ola   8f
      Allen   1m

end town of Guyandotte
Guyandotte Post Office
473-459
  BUFFINGTON
      J. H.   30m VA farmer
      Columbia   29f
      George W.   9m
      Wm. H.   4m
474-460
  BUFFINGTON
      P. C.   45m VA farmer
      Eliza J.   45f
      Willie A.   16f
      Eugenia J. 14f
      E. C. S.   12m
  STANDARD
      Henry   11m TX
475-461
  BUFFINGTON
      Nancy   66f NC
  DIOME
      Dilsey   66f M VA

476-462
  HAGEN
      Wm. H.   37m VA farmer
      Mary J.   36f
      Nannie   10f
      James W.   7m
      Imogene   3f
      Peter B.   1m
477-463
  BUFFINGTON
      John   27m VA farmer
      Maria   24f
      Columbia   1f
478-464
  BOYD
      Claiborne 27m KY labor
      Minerva   23f
      Lucilla   9/12f VA
479-465
  WINN
      Juda   57f VA
      George W. 27m   labor
      Elizabeth 14f OH
      Robert   24m KY
      Elizabeth 21f OH
      Parks   1m VA
480-466
  BOYD
      Joseph   75m VA labor
      Sarah   40f
      Sarah   22f
      Nancy   20f
      Polly   16f
      Susan   11f
      James   8m
481-467
  SHY
      Edward   74m VA labor
      Elizabeth 65f
      Mahala   25f
482-468
  PLYBON
      Jacob   56m VA labor
      Polly   55f

48

482-486 PLYBON (con't)
```
     John         28m      labor
     Eliza        18f
     Elizabeth    15f
```
483-469
SHY
```
     Benjamin     32m Va farmer
     Mary         25f
     Edgar        5m
     Mary E.      1f
```
484-470
LAIDLEY
```
     John         69m VA lawyer
     Mary         59f
     Eliza        23f
     William S.   21m      farmer
     George       19m      farmer
     Helen        17f
```
HITE
```
     Isabella     38f
```
485--471
BROWN
```
     Edmund       65m M VA labor
     Lucinda      55f  B
```
486-472
HARRISON
```
     Otis         33m  Va farmer
     Ruth F.      28f  OH
     Lucien       5m VA
     Eugenia      4f
     Orren B.     2m
```
487-473
PAINE
```
     William      75m VA doctor
     Henry        38m      Carpntr
     Olivia       30f
     Emma         12f
     Eliza        10f
     Charles      8m
     Mary         6f
     Frances      3f
     George W.    1m
```

488-474
WOOD
```
     James        26m VA labor
     Louisa       22f  KY
     Malinda      2f
     James        1m
```
489-475
RUSSELL
```
     George W.    26m KY  labor
     Melissa      23f
     Charles      2m MI
     Georgia      5/12 VA
```
490-476
HERMAN
```
     George       40m GER labor
     Matilda      37f  VA
     John         10m
     Samuel       3m
     Frederick    2/12m
```
RIPLING
```
     John W.      12m
```
491-477
CUNNINGHAM
```
     Isaac        27m VA Wagon mkr
     Harriett     25f
     Elizabeth    5f
     Georgia A.   7f
     Kate         10/12f
```
492-478
WINN
```
     Emos         30m VA labor
     Elizabeth    25f
     John W.      6m
     Emma L.      4f
     William E.   1m
```
493-479
STEWART
```
     James        42m VA Stone msn
     Sarah        28f
     Isaac F.     20m KY brick msn
     Hansford     17m  farmer
     Joseph       14m
     Columbia     12f
     James B.     1m VA
```

493-479 STEWART (con't)
   JONES
     Elizabeth 18f OH dom
494-480
  WARD
    Adaline   36f VA
    Charles W. 14m
    William   12m
    Elizabeth 11f
495-481
  MAYO
    Joseph   26m VA labor
    Maria   26f
    Charles   8/12m
496-482
  BROWN
    John R.   25m VA ministr
    Mary W.   22f
    Henry B.   3m
497-483
  HARDEN
    John   49m VA farmer
    Pheobe   40f
    Thomas   19m   labor
    Henry   15m
    Creed   13m
    Fenten   10m
    Sydney   8m
    Belle   4f
    Willard   2m
498-484
  PORTER
    Cummings 23m VA labor
    Priscilla   16f KY
499-485
  RECE
    John C.   42m VA minstr
    Margaret   36f
    Andrew G. 3m
    Emma V.   2/12
  SEAMONDS
    William   21m   labor

500-486
  McGINNIS
    A. A.   61m VA farmer
    Eliza   63f
    John W.   24m   farmer
    Sarah   20f
    Henry H.   17m   farmer
  MAUPIN
    America   34f
    Margaret   13f
    Allen   10m
    Leonidas   8m
    Henry B.   6m
    Sarah   3f
    John   1m
501-487
  EVERETT
    T.W.   39m VA farmer
    Elizabeth 36f
    John T.   15m
    Virginia   14f
    William W. 12m KY
    Clayton   11m
    George S.   7m
    Mary F.   6f
    Emily C.   6f
    Laber T.   4m
  POWERS
    Thomas   75m M VA labor
502-488
  SHOEMAKER
    James H.   35m VA r. pilot
    Martha   25f
    Joanna   9f
    James   7m
    George   5m
    Sarah   2f
503-489
  BURKS
    Luther   49m VA farmer
    Martha   36f
    Lewis   20m   farmer
    Charles   18m   farmer
    Bluford   16m   farmer

503-489 BURKS (con't)

Martha	14f	
Emma	12f	
George	8m	
Phoebe	6m	
Cassie	3f	

504-490

POAGE

James H.	43m KY farmer	
Sarah	33f VA	
James E.	7m KY	
John B.	5m	
Anna M.	1f VA	

GALLAGHER

Sarah	66f PA	
John	23m VA farmer	

POLLARD

J.C.	20m KY labor

505-491

JOHNSON

William L.	39m VA carpntr
Susan L.	32f OH
Frederick	11m VA
Marcellus	9m
James	7m
Mary	5f

506-492

BEUHRING

F.D.	31m VA farmer
Fanny	22f
Emma	1f

RAY

Levina	16m OH dom

TOPPING

Andrew	34m ENG labor

WARD

Rundle	28m OH labor

HERM

George	21m PA labor

RODGERS

John	20m OH labor

ROW

Uriah	18m OH labor

506-492 BEUHRING (con't)

WILSON

George	39m M VA labor

507-493

BAILEY

Lemuel	66m VA labor
Nancy	50f
Paulina	16f KY
Polly A.	13f
George W.	12m

508-

509-494

McCULLOUGH

P.H.	44m PA doctor
Rachel	38f MD
Isadora	18f OH
Julius	16m VA
Emma	8m
Bob	6m
Frank	3m

HOTCHKISS

Mary	18f OH

510-495

RIGGS

James	24m VA labor
Amanda	22f OH
Greenville	2m VA
Mary	1f

511-496

SHY

Edward	28m VA farmer
Abagail	28f
Eustassis	5m
Marcellus	4m
Franklin	3m
Cenna	1f
Henry	1/12m

512-497

SHY

H.W.	26m VA labor
Josephine	23f
Edney	10/12m

513-498
  LOVEJOY
    Daniel   44m MD farmer
    Jenetta   40f
    John   38m
  HOLLENBECK
    Elleanor   75f VA
514-499
  HARRISON
    William   57m VA labor
    Sarina   50f
    Catherine 26f
    William   23m labor
    Henry   21m labor
    James S.   17m labor
    Columbia 14f
    Salina R. 11f
515-500
  STARK
    John   30m GER Vine Dress
    Emma   25f VA
    John   2m
  APPERSON
    James   8m
    Ann   5f
516-
517-501
  BEST
    William   39m GER Vine Dress
    Elizabeth 38f
    Carrie   12f
    Mary   9f OH
    John   5m VA
    Elizabeth 2f
518-502
  ROSS
    David   35m VA labor.
    Jane   29f OH
    William D. 8m
    Amasetta 4m
    Mary E.   2f
    Isaac   1m VA
  ROSS
    Polly   58f

519-503
  ADAMS
    John Q.   59m VA farmer
    Sarah A. 44f OH
    Jordan   44m VA labor
  ELKINS
    Levina   17f
  JUDA
    John   3m OH
520-504
  ROBERTS
    Patterson 38m VA labor
    Jennetta 29f
    Elizabeth J. 10f
    Felicia H. 8f
    John   6m
    Sylvania 4f
    James H. 1m
521-505
  ROBERTS
    James M. 42m VA farmer
    Sarah L. 36f
    James   14m
    John W. 12m
    William 10m
    Emma J. 7f
    Julia A. 3f
  ADAMS
    Julia   24f
522-506
  SULLIVAN
    Henry   35m KY labor
    Catherine 35f VA
    Alonzo C. 10m
    Daniel   9m
    Melissa 5f
    Martha   4f
    Elizabeth 3f
    Henry M. 1m
    Mary J.   7f
523-507
  ROBERTS
    Marion   33m Va labor
    William D. 4m

52

523-507 ROBERTS (con't)
  BOOTEN
    Elizabeth   65f
524-508
  BAILEY
    Elijah   28m KY labor
    Mary A.   37f NC
    James D.   4m KY
    Nancy J.   2f VA
  PIGG
    Louisa   18f IL
    William   13m IL
    John C   9m VA
525-509
  PUCKETT
    John   26m KY labor
    Patsey   18f
    Nancy E.   1f
526-510
  EARLES
    David   27m VA farmer
    Cecelia   26f
    Charles H.   4/12m
  DILLON
    Squire   22m VA labor
527-511
  THORNBURG (Shonburg)
    David W.   46m MD farmer
    Joanna   34f VA
    Rachel   7f
  THORNTON
    John C.   24m labor
528-512
  ALLEN
    James   33m OH farmer
    Elizabeth   31f VA
    Saml. V   6m
    Virginia   4f
    Willie B.   9/12f
529-513
  STONEBRAKER
    William   23m KY labor
    Susan   22f

529-513 STONEBRAKER (con't)
    Mary   2f
    Henry J.   6/12m VA
530-514
  KELLY
    Jackson   23m VA labor
    Jane   23f
    Joseph   5/12m
531-515
  TRENT
    John   28m VA
    Margaret   29f
    Eliza   5f
    Eddie   3m
    John   1m
    Willie V.   11f
    Egbert   16m   labor
532-516
  McCONNELL
    William   39m VA farmer
    Mary A.   28f
    Mary A.   9f
    Letitia   7f OH
    Eliza C.   5f VA
    Albert T.   2m
    James R.   1/12m
533-517
  JOHNSON
    Saml.   48m PA. farmer
    Eliza   33f VA
    Napoleon   18m   farmer
    Frances   14f
    Martha E.   13f
    Emily   12f
    Abner   10m
    Albert   8m
    Benjamin   6m
    Saml. W.   2m
  FISHER
    John A.   22m   labor
534-518
  REYNOLDS
    Robert   33m VA farmer
    Frances   24f

534-518 REYNOLDS (con't)
    Eliza   4f
    DILLON
      William F. 24m labor
535-519
  McLARY
    David   44m PA carpenter
    Mary   33f
    Jane   16f VA
    Nancy   12f
    Barbary   8f
    Alice   2f
536-520
  JOHNSON
    Alex.   54m PA farmer
    Nancy   46f
    Saml.   26m   labor
    Louisa J.   24f
    David   22m   farmer
    Anna   20f
    Josephine 18f VA
    Nancy   16f
    Rachel   14f
    Armstead   13m
    Henry C.   12m
    Joseph   9m
    Martha E.   7f
    Marcella   4f
537-521
  JOHNSTON
    James   74m IRE farmer
    Sarah J.   35f VA
    Martha H. 25f
    John L.   32m   farmer
    Mary J.   26f KY
    POAGE
    Marcella   30f VA
    Alberta   1f
    KYLE
    Eliza   15f OH
    Wm.H.   14m
    MORRIS
    James   22m VA labor

538-522
  PINE
    Alex.   60m VA
    Julia   57f
    Mary   21f
    Chloe   16f
    Rufus   14m
539-523
  PINE
    Floyd   33m VA farmer
    Virginia   30f
    Hester Ann 10f
    Mary J.   9f
    Laura A.   5f
    Martha F.   2f
540-524
  WALKER
    Wm.   23m VA teamstr
    Elizabeth 18f
    Mary V.   1f
541-525
  THORNBURG
    James L.   24m VA farmer
    Virginia F. 21f
    Charles   1m
542-526
  BROWN
    John F.   25m NC farmer
    Eliza A.   23f VA
    John   2m
    Mary   8/12f
543-527
  BELLAMY
    E.   47m VA farmer
    Samuel   16m
    Melissa J. 15f
    Nelsina   14f
    Armstead   9m
    John M.   7m
544-528
  PINE
    Overton   30 m VA farmer
    Nancy E.   20f
    Elizabeth 4f

54

544-528 PINE (con't)
   James E.   2m
   Emma   1/12f
545-529
  MATTHEWS
   Saml.   40m MD blacksm
   Mary J.   34f OH
   William   12m
   Martha   8f
   Alice   2f
   Saml.   5/12m
546-530
  HUFFMAN
   Wm.   50m VA farmer
   Catherine   47f
   James   24m   labor
   Andrew   15m
   Thomas   9m
547-531
  STILL
   E. H.   36m VA farmer
   Margaret   30f
   Mary   6f
   Sarah E.   4f
   John W.   2m
   Martha J.   2/12f
  STILL
   George W.   25m   labor
  INSCO
   James   24m   labor
548-532
  FRAMPTON
   David   27m OH farmer
   Clara   22f
  WALKER
   Matthew   20m VA labor
  NEWTON
   Thomas   19m VA labor
549-533
  SUITER
   Jacob   38m OH tanner
   Caroline   37f VA
   Sarah A.   14f OH
   Saml.   13m

549-533 SUITER (con't)
   Ella   6f VA
   Tennessee   1f
  NEWTON
   Sylvester   24m   labor
550-534
  WILLIAMS
   Wm.   55m CN farmer
   Rebecca   46f NY
  PEARSON
   Frances   27f KY
  PAINE
   Laura   16f KY
  WILLIAMS
   Arthur   25m OH farmer
   Eliza   25f
   Frances B.   2f VA
551-535
  WALKER
   Saml.   44m OH farmer
   Jane E.   38f
   John W.   17m VA labor
   Eliza   6f
   Martha   4f
   Saml.   1m
552-536
  KELLY
   Stephen   55m KY farmer
   Hester A.   49f VA
   Charles   15m
   James D.   13m
  McCORMICK
   Walstein   11m
553-537
  HULL
   Martin   73m NJ farmer
   Ann   45f PA
   Eliza   19f VA
   Harriett   16f
   Matilda   14f
   Bartholomew 10m
   Columbus   8m
  REED
   Judson   25m PA stonemsn

554-538
HULL

John	29m	VA farmer
Virginia	33f	
William M.	8m	
Salome	4f	
Anna P.	1f	

555-539
HUGHES

R. B.	35m	VA cooper
Julia	29f	
Cora S.	9f	
James D.	4m	

CHILDS

Phoebe	60f

556-540
BAILEY

Anderson	32m	VA farmer
Amanda	25f	
Overton	5m	
Martha	3f	
Clotilda	6/12f	

557-541
DUDDING

B.A.	35m	VA cooper
Martha A.	19f	

558-
559-542
OHI

John	27m	VA blacksmith
Elizabeth	21f	
Catherine	2f	
Martha	4/12f	

560-543
RATCLIFF

Jane	37f OH	
Nancy	21f	
Matilda	18f	
James	16m	labor
Ephraim	14m VA	
Squire	11m	
Alice	9f	IA
William	6m	
George	1m VA	

561-544
MEDLIN

Henry	53m	PRU farmer
Dorathea	53f	
John	23m	farmer
Borino	20m	
Herminia	15f	

562-545
ALLEN

John W.	65m	VA farmer
Nancy	55f	
Saml.	24m	OH labor
Runnell	23m	OH labor
Henry	18m	OH labor

563-546
ALLEN

William	35m	OH farmer
Matilda	34f	
Mary J.	13f	VA
William	10m	
Missouri	7f	
Cyrus	4m	
Irving	2m	
Sarah	1f	

564-547
PORTER

Anna	58f	VA
Sarah	30f	
Catherine	23f	
Joseph	16m	labor
Alonzo	12m	
Mary	8f	

565-548
SULLIVAN

James	45m	VA farmer
Elizabeth	45f	
Mary	14f	

566-549
BIAS

James A.	30m	VA farmer
Elizabeth	26f	
Lily A.	5/12f	

WILKES

James	75m	labor

56

567-550
PATTERSON

Berry	37m	VA	farmer
Nancy	32f		
John D.	8m	OH	
Robert T.	6m	VA	
Sarah M.	3f		
Nancy A.	1f		

568-551
WILKES

Burwell	40m	VA	farmer
Barbary	40f		
James	22m		labor
George W.	19m		labor
Mary	17f		
Sarah	12f		
Alexander	10m		
Nathan	7m		
Albert	5m		
Henry	2m		

569-552
BAILEY

Lemuel	65m	VA	labor
Nancy	55f		
Paulina	16f		
Polly	13f		
George W.	12m		

570-553
SMITH

William	34m	ENG	cooper
Lucy	29f	VA	
Thomas	10m		
William	8m		
Daniel	4m		
Robert	2m		
John J.	3/12m		

571-554
NELSON

A. B.	35m	OH	farmer
Elizabeth	34f		
John H.	16m		labor
Middleton	10m		
Lewis	8m	KY	

NELSON 571-554 (con't)

Arthur P.	6m	OH
James T.	3m	VA
Andrew J.	6/12	

572-555
ELKINS

Wm.	48m	VA	farmer
Elilzabeth	41f		
James	18m		labor
Alexander	14m		
Amanda	9f		
Augustus	6m		
Sanford	3m		

573-556
HATTON

Solomon	54m	VA	farmer
Mary H.	33f		
Lucretia	13f		
Hester	12f		
Wm.H.	10m		
Edmund	7m		
Polemus	4m		
Sanford	2m		

574-557
SIMMONS

Adam	55m	VA	farmer
Delilah	53f		
Joseph	24m		farmer
Robert	22m		farmer
Henry A.	20m		farmer
Nathaniel	15m		
Joel	13m		

THOMPSON

Mary A.	18f	
Martha J.	15f	

575-
576-558
PORTER

Zephemiah	65m	OH	labor
Mary J.	39f	IN	
Benjamin F.	9m	KY	
Mary C.	5f	OH	
Nancy	2f	VA	

576-558 PORTER (con't)
    DUNCAN
      Rebecca   16f
577-559
   BIAS
      James S.   36m VA farmer
      Sarah   28f
      Emily   12f
      Wm. H.   8m
      George W. 7/12m
    NOWELL
      Thomas   18m   labor
578-560
    THOMPSON
      Gilmore   25m VA farmer
      Lucinda   25f
    THOMPSON
      Mary J.   58f
579-561
    THOMPSON
      Virginia   50f VA
      Thomas   21m   labor
      Lucetta   19f
      Maria   17f
    THOMPSON
      Charles   30m M VA gentlem
580-562
   ADKINS
      Jeremiah   33m VA farmer
      Elizabeth 26f OH
      Aaron   9m VA
      Georgia   6f
      Thomas   4m
      Ephraim   1m
581-563
   BURKS
      Wm.   26m KY labor
      Catherine 28f OH
      Jefferson   5m VA
      Greenville 5m
      Columbia   2f
      Eliza G.   10/12f
      Lucinda   10/12f

581-563 BURKS (con't)
    McFARLAND
      James   30m   labor
    BLANKENSHIP
      Salome   13f
582-564
   JARROLD
      Ambrose   28m VA farmer
      Mary E.   21f
583-565
   FLOWERS
      John K.   43m VA farmer
      Mildred   40f
      George W. 20m   labor
      Frederick   17m   labor
      Eliza   15f
      Louisa   12f
      Alice   10f
      Herminia   8f
      John A.   6m
      James   4m
      Emeretta   2f
584-566
   PLYBON
      John   47m VA farmer
      Irene   33f
      Louis   17m   farmer
      Calvery   13m
      Mary   8f
      Elizabeth   2f
      Alfred   6/12m
585-567
   EAVES
      Thomas   26m VA farmer
      Eliza   20f
      Matilda   3f
      James F.   1m
586-568
    BLANKENSHIP
      Samuel   63m VA labor
      Lalila   45f
      John T.   15m
      Saml. J.   13m
      George   12m

586-568 BLAKENSHIP (con't)

Wm.J.	10m	
Rece	8m	
Girard	6m	
Lucy	2f	
Frances	9/12f	

587-569

OWEN

Henry T.	55m VA farmer	
Elizabeth	32f	
George L.	4m	

588-570

OWEN

Eppie	55m VA farmer	
Saluda	54f	
Jordan	23m	farmer
James	21m	farmer
Edmund	15m	
Mary J.	2f	

589-571

PLYBON

James C.	25m VA farmer	
Emily	24f OH	
Lucian	4/12m VA	
Evermont	4/12m	

590-572

EAVES

Thomas	59m MD shoemkr	
Eliza	50f VA	
James F.	20m	farmer
Alex. H.	17m	farmer
Martha J.	16f	
Sarah A.	9f	

591-

592-573

DAVIS

Greenville	40m VA farmer	
Isabella	32f	
Victor	9m	
Lewellyn	7f	
Florence	5f	
Georgia	3f	
Albert	1m	

593-574

CHATTERTON

George	46m VA farmer	
Rocksalina	34f	
Henry	11m	
Mary	10f	
Richard	6m	
Amanda	1f	

594-575

RAY

Wm.	50m VA farmer	
Emily	49f	
Lemuel	20m	farmer
Albert	16m	farmer
America	14f	
Virginia	12f	
Emily	10f	
Jefferson	8m	
Marcellus	7m	

595-576

BARBOUR

Robert	30m VA constbl	
Mary	31f	
Alvin	6m	
Janthe	2f	
Linsey	3/12m	

596-577

RAY

Isaiah	52m VA farmer	
Lucy	38f	
Joseph	16m	
Benjamin	14m	
Susan	13f	
Eglantine	12f	
Mary A.	8f	
Eliza	6f	
Millard	4m	
Sarah	2f	

597-578

STEPHENSON

Mark	65m VA farmer	
Mary	38f	
Georgia	14f	
Charles	12m	

597-578 STEPHENSON (con't)

William	10m	
Thomas	6m	
Ellen	4f	
Sydney	2m	
Helen	5/12m	

598-579

GRAHAM

Jonas	53m VA farmer	
Mary	50f	
Marion	20m OH farmer	
Jefferson	20m	farmer
Virginia	13f VA	

SMITH

Thomas	30m OH labor	

599-580

STEPHENSON

Joseph	26m VA farmer	
Amanda	25f	
Aetna	3f	
Joseph	1m	
St.Luke	2/12m	

STEPHENSON

Elizabeth	40f

600-581

CARTER

Hiram	60m VA farmer
Nancy	60f

601-582

CARTER

James	26m VA farmer
Eliza	30f
Geneva	3f
Thornton	1m

COOK

Abner	27m	labor

602-583

TOPPING

Levi	37m VA labor
Catherine	24f
America	7f
Cassius	4m

603-584

BLANKENSHIP

Permelia	53f VA
Jesse	19m farmer
Henry	16m farmer

604-585

HEARD

Wm.	43m NJ labor
Sarah	34f TN
Israel	15m IL
Mary	11f IL
Cornelia	10f VA
Caroline	7f
Ella V.	6f
Willie J.	4f
Mary L.	1f

605-586

TOPPING

Wm.	62m ENG farmer
Elizabeth	57f VA
William	20m
Mary	16f
Almedia	12f

606-587

McCORKLE

James	39m OH farmer
Sarah	39f KY
Mary J.	18f OH
Catherine	16f OH
Lafayette	13m VA
Sarah	11f
Louisa	9f
James	8m
Frederick	5m
Ariana	2f
Olive	2/12f

607-

608-588

STEPHENSON

Caleb	40m Va farmer
Mary	35f
Lafayette	8m
Columbia	6f
Margaret	4f

60

609-589
SULLIVAN
Jacob	32m VA farmer
Amanda	22f
Louisa	4f
David	1m

610-590
GILES
John	30m VA labor
America	27f
Ann	1f

SULLIVAN
| Ellen | 5f (next door ?) |

611-591
STEPHENSON
J. M.	25m VA stonemsn
Harriett	27f
Emaretta	9/12f

612-592
STEPHENSON
Wm.	64m VA farmer
Mary E.	60f
Saml. P.	19m farmer
Sylvester J.	14m

613-593
STEPHENSON
Wm. M.	29m VA farmer
Martha	23f
Addison	4m
Ebba	1m

614-594
BATES
| A .J. | 27m VA farmer |
| Olivia | 18f |

BATES
Nancy	65f KY
Susan	21f
Ellen	20f

615-595
STEPHENSON
Gilbert	40m VA cooper
America	38f
Newell	9m

615-595 STEPHENSON (con't)
Louis	6m KY
Leonard	5m KY
Lucy	3f VA
Amanda	3/12f

616-596
WORKMAN
Squire	54m VA farmer
Nancy	54f
Jasper	23m labor
Peterson	16m
Thomas	14m
Dryden	12m
Amanda	11f

617-597
WORKMAN
| Marion | 23m VA farmer |
| Caroline | 22f |

618-598
STEPHENSON
Henry	30m VA farmer
Helena	30f
Eugenia	6f
Edney	4f
A. B.	1m

619-599
TOPPING
John	35m VA farmer
Chloe	33f
Henry	11m
Adalaide	8f
Frank	7m
Amanda	5f
Lucy	3f IN
Leander	2/12 VA

620-600
KELLER
Adam	55m GER shoemkr
Nancy	50f VA
John	23m farmer
Mary	21f
Thomas	19m labor
Rhoda	17f
Theresa	13f

620-600 KELLER (con't)

Edward	10m		
Henry	6m		
Lucy	4f		

KELLER

Albert	27m		farmer
Adaline	26f		

621-601

MILLER

Henry	60m	VA	farmer
Susan	55f		
Abagail	28f	OH	
Margaret	17f	VA	
Georgia	12f		

IZE

Elizabeth	65f	VA	

622-602

DUNFIELD

Lewis	30m	OH	farmer
Rebecca	23f	VA	
Sarah	3f	OH	
Elvira	1f	OH	

623-603

ROBERTS

George W.	32m	VA	farmer
Mary	21f		
Sarah	3f		
Allen	1m		

624-604

DAVIS

Mary	70f	VA	
Elizabeth	34f		

625-

626-605

TURNER

N. S.	36m	VA	farmer
Cerilda	34f		
Henry B.	3m		

627-606

TURNER

Thomas	41m	VA	farmer
Susan	42f	OH	
Albert	16m	VA	farmer
Victor	12m		

627-606 TURNER (con't)

Lyman	10m		
Sinora	8f		

628-607

CRUMP

Isaac	37m	OH	farmer
Nancy	27f		
Mary	9f	VA	
Martha	4f		
Elizabeth	1f		

GRATTON

Jefferson	20m		labor

EAVES

John	23m		labor

HUGHES

Jane	20f		domestic

629-608

DUNKLE

Daniel	50m	VA	farmer
Eliza	45f		
James	22m		farmer
Theodore	17m		farmer
Lucy	15f		
Alexander	12m		

630-609

DILLON

Wm. J.	40m	VA	farmer
Julia	30f		
George	14m		
Lucy	12f		
Elizabeth	9f		

631-

632-610

FERGUSON

D. P.	43m	VA	merchnt
Susan	30f		
William	21m		carpntr
Julius	15m		
Monroe	6m		
Ellen	4f		
Helen	1f		

DILLON

Benjamin	27m		labor

633-611
  HOWARD
    Aaron   35m VA labor
    Lydia   37f
    Daniel   16m   labor
    Francis J. 14f WI
    William   12m KY
    Susan   10f OH
    Edward   7m
    Hugh   5m
    David   3m
    Margaret   1f VA
634-612
  ARTHUR
    Lewis S.   66m VA farmer
    Lucy   53f
    Eliza   22f
    Temperance 21f
    Lenora   19f
    Wm. J.   26m
635-613
  SHOWANS
    Abagail   63f VA
    Mary M.   17f
    Saml.   14m
636-614
  BLAKE
    Miles   43m VA cooper
    Martha   35f
    Miles L.   19m   cooper
    Frances   15f
    Mary   14f
    Amasetta   12f
    Alice   4f
    Charles   2m
  IMANION
    Emily   14f
637-615
  MORRIS
    Wm.   42m VA farmer
    Nancy   48f
    Lucetta   17f

638-616
  MORRIS
    Eaton   50m Va farmer
    Lucy   39f
    Thomas   19m   labor
    Henry   16m   labor
    Fanny   15f
    George   11m
    Sarah   8f
639-617
  CAMPBELL
    George   59m VA farmer
    Letitia   60f
    Letitia Jr. 20f
    George W.   14m
  ROBINSON
    Mary A.   6f
  MORRIS
    James   21m   labor
640-618
  WORKMAN
    Newton   26m VA farmer
    Sarah   21f
    Theresa   1f
  THOMPSON
    A. J.   19m   labor
641-619
  WILSON
    James   47m VA farmer
    Sarah   41f
    Charles   18m   farmer
    Elizabeth   17f
    Nancy   13f
    James M.   8m
    John T.   5m
  BLACKWOOD
    Robert   26m   labor
  PUGH
    Jessee   40m GER labor
642-620
  FULLER
    Achilles   45m VA farmer
    Elizabeth   43f

642-620 FULLER (con't)

Eliza	17f	
Albert	16m	farmer

643-621

WINTZ

John P.	21m VA	farmer
Mary	19f	
Anna Cora	2f	

644-622

POTEET

Skelton	54m VA	farmer
Martha	51f	
Clementine	26m	farmer
James	22m	farmer
Susan	16f	
John L.	13m	

645-623

DAVIS

Harrison	47m VA	farmer
Louisa	28f	
Henderson	12m	
Paul	8m	
William	6m	
Drucilla	4f	
Missouri	2f	

DRAKE

Frances	13f

646-624

WRIGHT

Edward	49m VA	farmer
Elizabeth	45f	
Wm. O.	23m	farmer
Richard C.	21m	farmer
James H.	19m	farmer
Drucilla	17f	
Sarah E.	15f	
Lucy	11f	
Albert W.	8m	
Harriet	6f	

HOLDERBY

Edward	16m
Henry	14m

647-625

DAVIS

Wesley	26m VA	farmer
Josephine	24f	
Wm. H.	4m	
Albion	2m	

648-626

DAVIS

Lockie	46f VA	
Christopher	16m	labor
Mary A.	10f	
Cynthia	6f	
Oscar	3m	

649-627

BATES

Grism	30m KY
Julia	32f VA
Georgia	8f
Peter	5m
Andrew	2m

650-628

WENTZ

William	51m VA	farmer
Matilda	48f	
America	21f	
Mary	19f	
Louisa	15f	
Henry C.	13m	
Alexander	11m	
William	9m	

651-629

WOOD

Thomas H.	51m MA	carpntr
Mary A.	29f NY	
Mary J.	14f LA	
Thomas	12m LA	
Lucy	9f VA	
William	7m	
Alfred	5m	
Francis	3m	
Levacia	1f	

64

652-630
  McGINNIS
    Achilles   34m VA carpntr
    Miriam   24f
    Lucian   6m
    Allen   1m
653-631
  FULLER
    Sylvester   67m RI farmer
    Sarah L.   64f VA
    Edmund   40m OH farmer
    Jasper   17m VA farmer
    Wm. S.   8m
    James H.   3m MO
654-632
  COOK
    Solomon   31m VA farmer
    Elizabeth   30f
    John W.   10m
    Henry J.   6m
    Eliza   4f
655-633
  THOMPSON
    Ahart O.   50m VA labor
    Harriett   46f
    Emily   19f
    James   17m   labor
    Milton   10m
    Adaline   8f
656-634
  DUNKLE
    Henry C.   23m VA farmer
    Catherine   18f
657-635
  COOK
    Abner   60m VA farmer
    Mary   38f
    Mary   25f
    Abner Jr.   22m   labor
    Nancy   17f
    Catherine   15f
    Eliza   12f
    Jennie   9f

657-632 COOK (con't)
    Henry   7m
    George   6m
658-636
  EVERETT
    Charles T.   30m VA farmer
    Rebecca   23f OH
    George F.   2m VA
  FRAMPTON
    Isaac   17m OH farmer
  MOORE
    Elizabeth   11f VA
  CLARK
    Robert   22m ME labor
659-637
  CLARK
    Daniel   47m VA farmer
    Rachel   23f
    Harvey   21m   labor
    Eveline   20f
    David   18m   labor
    William   13m
    Taylor   11m
660-638
  WOODYARD
    Presley   35m VA farmer
    Eliza   23f
    William R.   4m
661-639
  HOLDERBY
    Susan   50f VA
    Dudley D.   31m   farmer
    Robert S.   25m   farmer
662-640
  EVERETT
    John S.   37m VA farmer
    Emily   23f OH
    Louisa   11f VA
    Sarah   5f
    Peter   1m

663-641
  HALEY

Mary	38f	B	VA
Hannah	13f	B	
Sarah	11f	B	
Melissa	8f	B	
Lewellyn	8f	B	
Priscilla	5f	B	
Frances	2f	B	

  HALEY

Delphia	65f	B

664-642
  JENKINS

Anderson	85m	VA	farmer
Telitha	40f		
Eliza	16f		
Emily	14f		
John	11m		
William	9m		
Bailey	3m		

665-643
  HENSLEY

F. G.	36m	VA	farmer
Dicey	37f		
Parthenia	13f		
Dicey	12f		
Coleman	9m		
Anderson	8m		
Samanthia	7f		
Wesley	5m		
John	2m		
Edith	1f		

666-644
  COOK

Matthew	36m	ENG teachr
Frances	35f	S.America
Frances	8f	VA
Florence	5f	

  FULLER

John	23m	farmer
Sarah	19f	
Mary	7/12f	

end Guyandotte Post Office

Falls Mills Post Office
667-645
   TURLEY

Emberson	54m	VA	farmer
Mary	54f		
Susan	18f		
Amasetta	15f		
Floyd	12m		
Emberson	10m		
Saml.	8m		

   CONNELL

Jane	43f
Malaria	8f

   COLLINS

Wm.	25m
Zedic	3f

668-646
   FRY

John G.	42m	VA	farmer
Elizabeth	34f		
Mary	12f		
Sethe	10f		

669-647
   McCOMAS

Elisha	34m	VA	farmer
Rocksalina	22f		
Minerva	4f		
Mary	3f		

670-
671-648
   MILLER

Joycey	42f	VA
Frederick	15m	
Gebring	12m	
Jacob	9m	
James	2m	

672-649
   CREMEANS

James	25m	VA	labor
Elizabeth	22f		
David	3m		
James	8/12m		

673-650
   FIELDER

John	36m	VA labor	
Eliza	26f		
Mary	12f		
Murray	12m	idiot	
Martha	8f		
John	6m		
Jane	4f		

674-
675-651
   MIDKIFF

Spencer	21m	VA	farmer
Julia	20f		
Albert	8/12m		

676-652
   SMITH

John	37m	VA	farmer
Patsey	28f		
Emma	12f		
Wm.	10m		
Elizabeth	9f		
James	7m		
Jackson	5m		
Benjamin	3m		

677-653
   CREMEANS

Amasa	29m	VA labor
Margaret	18f	

678-654
   BOOTHE

John	34m	VA labor
Edith	36f	
Nancy	11f	
James	9m	
Elias	4m	

679-655
   BOOTHE

Nathan	28m	VA farmer
Mildred	26f	
James	8m	
Wm. E.	8m	
John	6m	
Julia	4m	

679-655 BOOTH (con't)
    Charles   2m
    Alexander   6/12m
680-656
  BOOTHE
    Saml.   69m VA farmer
    Rachel   65f
    Artemisia   38f
    James   35m   labor
    Martha   23f
    Ballard   22m   labor
    William   15m
    Nancy   9f
681-657
  WAUGH
    Charles   29m OH farmer
    Louara   22f VA
    Hiram   2/12m
  CREMEANS
    Nancy   34f
    George   5m
    Wilson   2m
  CREMEANS
    Susan   22f
682-658
  PAINE
    Jessee   44m VA farmer
    Mildred   36f
    Matilda   8f
    Sarah   3f
683-659
  MIDKIFF
    Louis   52m VA farmer
    Elizabeth   51f
    Harriett   20f
    Adaline   18f
    Sarah   15f
    Solomon   14m
    Mary   11f
    James   15m

684-660
  MIDKIFF
    John   24m VA farmer
    Mary   22f
    Josephine   1f
685-661
  McCOMAS
    Alexander   44m VA farmer
    Julia   35f
    Andrew   13m
    Susan   8m
    John   6m
    Mary   4f
    Vitura   8/12f
  ADKINS
    Cerilda   20f
686-662
  McCOMAS
    John   71m VA farmer
    Mary   64f
    Minerva   41f
687-663
  McCOMAS
    James M.   32m VA farmer
    Susan   24f
    Eliza   4f
    Minerva   2f
    Juda   6/12f
688-664
  PEYTON
    John   46m Va farmer
    Juda   41f
    Wm. H.   17m
    John   9m
    Louisa   7f
689-665
  LUCAS
    David   24m VA farmer
    Sarah   22f
    Chloe   4f
    Mary   2f

690-666
  JACK
    John   54m PA miner
    Levina   52f VA
    Mary E.   26f OH
  PORTER
    James   37m VA labor
691-667
  PORTER
    Lewis   23m VA labor
    Eliza   23f
    John   2m
692-668
  NANCE
    Clement   37m OH labor
    Martha   26f VA
    Ellen   5f
    Eliza   3f
    Angelina   1f
  ELKINS
    Christiana   24f
693-669
  CHAPMAN
    Julia   53f VA
    James B.   26m KY farmer
  LUSHER
    Francis   3f VA
    Elizabeth   2f
694-670
  ADKINS
    Wm.   65m VA farmer
    Elizabeth   64f
    Thomas   26m   labor
695-671
  ADKINS
    Anderson   32m VA farmer
    Sarah   27f
    Jessee   7m
    Jackson   5m
    Polly   4f
    Randolph   9/12m

696-672
  ADKINS
    Matthew   24m VA labor
    America   26f
    Blackburn   3m
697-673
  ADKINS
    Elliott   35m KY farmer
    Rebecca   28f VA
    Thomas   5m
    Napoleon   3m
    Cynthia   9/12f
698-674
  LUCAS
    Rebecca   40f VA
    William   23m   farmer
    Mary   20f
    Saml.   16m   farmer
    Martha   13f
    John   10m
    Marion   1m
699-
700-675
  HARLESS
    James   24m Va farmer
    Sarah   31f
    Nancy   5f
    Wm.R.   2m
    Malinda   1f
    Eliza   5/12f
701-676
  HARLESS
    Wm.R.   45m VA farmer
    Nancy   45f
    Polly   22f
    John   20m   farmer
    Jasper   13m
    Joseph   12m
    Rebecca   10f
    Cynthia   8f
    Martha   10/12f

702-677
  ADKINS

Wm. D.	31m	VA	farmer
Anna	45f		
Icob	14m		
Letha	13f		
Elizabeth	10f		
William	9m		
Sarah	4f		

703-678
  ADKINS

Perry G.	24m	VA	farmer
Lucinda	23f		
Naria	3/12f		

704-679
  CHAPMAN

John	37m	VA	farmer
Malvina	28f		
Almeda	7f		
Andrew	4m		
Alice	2f		
Elisha	8/12m		

  TERRY

Elizabeth	17f		dom

  McCOMAS

Elisha	66m		farmer

705-679
  DIAL

John	47m	NC	farmer
Caroline	37f	VA	
James	18m		farmer
Elizabeth	16f		
William	14m		
Juda	12f		
John	10m		
Edward	8m		
Mary	6f		
Catherine	4f		

  DIAL

Mary A.	89f	NC

  HAYNER

Lewis	27m	VA	labor
Maria	18f	OH	

706-681
  STAFFORD

Wm.	35m	VA	labor
Celicia	25f		
Jackson	4m	MO	
Elizbeth	2f	MO	

707-682
  WATSON

Alexander	32m	KY	farmer
Sarah	25f	VA	
Wm. L.	5m		
Nancy J.	4f		
Mary A.	1f		

  DAVIS

John	22m		labor

708-683
  HUNTER

Saml.	74m	VA	blacksm
Margaret	74f		

  PORTER

John	25m		farmer
Sarah	25f		
William	8m		
Polly	7f		
Levina	5f		
Jackson	3m		
John L.	1m		

709-684
  ADKINS

Parker	50m	VA	farmer
Cynthia	46f		
Sylvester	18m		labor
Merritt	15m		
Mary	15f		
Lucy	10f		
Hiram	6m		
John L.	3m		

710-685
  PORTER

William	28m	VA	farmer
Lucinda	27f		
Margaret	11f		
James	9m		
Saml.	7m		

70

710-685 PORTER (con't)			
Nancy	4f		
Elijah	2m		
711-686			
DAVIS			
J. M. C.	33m	VA farmer	
Eliza	24f		
Nephremes	7m		
Marcellus	5m		
Artenus	3m		
Eugenia	2f		
DAVIS			
Sarah	74f		
HOLT			
Minerva	16f	dom	
SADDLER			
John	9m		
712-687			
MOORE			
Alexander	29m	VA	
Rachel	33f	KY	
Corbin	11m		
Elizabeth	8f		
Margaret	5f		
Emerine	3f		
713-688			
BAKER			
Guy	24m	VA farmer	
Polly	18f		
714-689			
PARSONS			
George W.	53m	VA farmer	
Sarah	44f		
John	18m		
George	15m	labor	
Francis	14m		
Julila	11f		
Edward	9m		
Lorenzo	5m		
James	1m		
715-			

716-690			
McNEELY			
Benjamin	33m	VA farmer	
Rebecca	26f	KY	
Malinda	9f		
CLAY			
Matilda	19f		
717-691			
CRUMB			
Daniel	30m	KY farmer	
Rhoda	30f		
George W.	10m	VA	
Polly	8f		
Maria	6f		
Elizia	3f		
718-692			
TURLEY			
Obidiah	23m	VA farmer	
Rebecca	19f		
James	2m		
719-693			
BAKER			
George	45m	VA	
Jane	35 f	KY	
John	13m		
Wm. W.	11m		
Amanda	7f		
Araminta	4f		
Jackson	2m		
720-694			
ADKINS			
John T.	44m	VA farmer	
Nancy	45f		
Joseph	20m		
721-695			
MENARY			
Mitchell	33m	VA	farmer
Elizabeth	29f		
Victora	10f	KY	
John	8m		
Eliza	6f		
Elijah	3m		
Andrew	4/12m	VA	

722-696
    BOWLIN
        John W.   32m KY carpentr
        Louisa   26f
        Mary   9f
        Andrew   7m
        William   4m
        Elisha M.   1m VA
723-697
    HARRIS
        Saml.   62m VA labor
        Nancy   60f
        John   24m KY
        Sarah   17f VA
        Wm. H.   1m
724-
725-698
    ROY
        James H.   19m VA labor
        Victoria   19f
        Isaac   1m
726-699
    CREMEANS
        Winchester   42m VA labor
        Elizabeth   30f
        Michael   14m
        Isaac   12m
        Paulina   10m
        Burton   6m
        Catherine   4f
727-700
    ROY
        Isaac   49m VA farmer
        Elizabeth   55f
        Beverly   21m   farmer
        Letha   16f
        Amanda   12f
    COHEN
        Rodolph   3m
728-701
    PAINE
        Stephen   38m Va farmer
        Lucy   37f
        Valeria   12f

728-701 PAINE (con't)
        Mary   10f
        Aquillla   4f
        Martha   2f
729-702
    CREMEANS
        Sanders   44m OH farmer
        Sarah   44f VA
        Richard   20m   farmer
        Edith   16f
        Joycey   15f
        Joseph   13m
        Thomas   12m
        Julia   8f
        James   3m
730-703
    McCOMAS
        Isaac   72m VA farmer
        Nancy   67f
        Jefferson   31m   farmer
        Jackson   29m   farmer
        Isaac   27m   farmer
        Isabella   5f
    CHAPSCOTT
        George   30m ENG labor
731-704
    FRANKLIN
        John   43m VA shoemkr
        Eleanor   42f
        Elizabeth   17f
        Evermont   12m
    McCOMAS
        Ballard   3m
732-705
    KETCHAM
        Alonzo   38m VA farmer
        Margaret   38f
        Eliza   15f
        Vanilla   10f
        Hugh   6m
        John W.   3m
        Mary F.   6/12f
    BEEVERS
        Mathias   17m   labor

72

733-706
    SCITZ
        Christopher 49m GER farmer
        Elizabeth   35f VA
        Henry   15m
        Mary   13f
        Hiram   11m
        Catherine   8f
        Sarah   6f
        Nancy   4f
734-
735-707
    McCOMAS
        Harrison   45m VA farmer
        Catherine   32f
        Benjamin   20m
        Nancy   18f
        Blackburn   16m
        Elisha   12m
        Alonzo   8m
        Rush   3m
        Jefferson   2m
        Martha   5/12f
736-708
    KINCAID
        Wm.   50m VA labor
        Sarah   40f
        Wesley   14m
        Cynthia   12f
        Malinda   10m
        Henry   4m
        Clarrissa   1f
737-
738-709
    ADKINS
        Joseph   40m VA labor
        Margaret   45f
        Nelsina   20f
        Sarah   16f
        Daniel   13m
739-710
    McCOMAS
        David   59m VA farmer
        Docia   47f TN

739-710 McCOMAS (con't)
        Dyke   19m VA
        Arminda   15f
    HOLT
        James   57m   stone msn
740-711
    McCOMAS
        Lewis   21m VA farmer
        Minerva   18f
        George   1m
741-712
    McCOMAS
        Henderson   25m Va farmer
        Cynthia   27f
        Hester   4f
        William   3m
        Chloe   1f
742-713
    ANDERSON
        James   45m OH farmer
        Francis   40f VA
        Naoma   19f
        Isabella   16f
        Julia   12f
    ANDERSON
        Catherine   21f
743-714
    RIDGEWAY
        John   26m VA farmer
        Sarah   23f
        James   8m
        Henrietta   5f
        John   4m
        Mary   2f
    TURNER
        Richard   53m   farmer
744-715
    FRANKLIN
        David   25m VA farmer
        Elizabeth   18f
745-716
    FRANKLIN
        Edward   70m VA farmer
        Christiana   64f

745-716 FRANKLIN (con't)

William	36m		
Malinda	32f		
Elisha	30m		
James	21m		

746-717

FRANKLIN

Olivar G.	27m	VA farmer	
Mary E.	21f		

747-718

LUSHER

Irving	49m	VA farmer	
Jane	49f		
R. M.	22m	sawyer	
John	20m	farmer	
Charles	18m	farmer	
Henry	14m		
Mary	12f		
Alice	9f		

ADKINS

Emanuel	18m	labor	

LUSHER

Lewis	24m	farmer	
Cynthia	3/12f		

748-719

ADKINS

Sherod	49m	farmer	
Abagail	45f		
Paris	18m		
Clayton	17m		
James	16m		
Henry	14m		
Julia	13f		
Mary	13f		
Sarah	11f		
Archabald	9m		
Sarilda	7f		
Bazel M.	4m		
Jerome S.	2m		
Mildred	1f		

749-720

LUCAS

Parker	48m	VA farmer	
Chloe	42f		

749-720 LUCAS (con't)

John M.	20m		
Sarah	18f		
Rebecca	16f		
Malvina	12f		
Calvin	19m		

ADKINS

Wm. P.	21m	labor	

750-721

VAUGHAN

Henry	36m	VA farmer	
Malinda	32f		
Martha	10f		
Mary	9f		
Sarah	7f		
Henrietta	5f		
Margaret	3f		

751-722

VAUGHAN

John	36m	VA farmer	
Lucy	34f		
Andrew	12m		
Maria	9f		
Virginia	7f		
Julia	4f		
James	2m		

VAUGHAN

Henrietta	54f		
Richard	25m		
Erastus	23m	labor	

752-723

COWAN

Thomas	45m	VA farmer	
Levina	46f		
Mary	20f		
James	18m	labor	
Willis	15m		
Henrietta	13f		
Hester	10f		
Alexander	7m		
Walter	2m		

74

753-724
 DICK
   Joseph   60m VA farmer
   Catherine 40f
   Frances   17f
   Rhoda   11f
   Benjamin   10m
   Ballard   8m
   Spurlock   6m
   Margaret   4f
   Henry J.   3m
   Catherine 1f
754-725
 McCOMAS
   Jesse   36m VA shoemkr
   Mary   36f
   Cynthia   10f
   Mary   9f
   Frances   5f
   H. A. W.   2m
755-726
 LIBBY
   A. H.   27m ME farmer
   Ellen   22f MA
   Charles   3m MA
756-
757-727
 SHELTON
   David   33m VA farmer
   Elizabeth 37f
   Virginia   9f
   Letha   4f
   Robert   1m
758-728
 WOLCOTT
   W. B.   26m OH mercht
   Martha   25f KY
   Mary   6f
   Henry   2m VA
759-729
 BOWDEN
   Sidney   39m VA mercht
   Mary   38f

759-729 BOWDEN (con't)
   Charles   15m
   Alonzo   14m
   Rolanders 12m
   Mary   9f
   David   6m
   William   4m
   Innius   2m
 KELLER
   Mary   18f
760-730
 SHELTON
   Jerome   39m VA farmer
   Malinda   32f
   Lourana   16f
   Eliza   14f
   Susan   11f
   Henry   7m
   Mary   5f
   William   10/12m
761-731
 BIAS
   James C.   26m VA farmer
   Mary   26f
   Amanda   3f
   Larkin   1m
 BIAS
   Obidiah   21m   labor
 BURNS
   Zilla   52f
762-732
 PEYTON
   Henry   42m VA farmer
   Margaret   36f
   Cynthia   11f
   Elizabeth 8f
   Wm.H.   6m
   Louis   4m
 PEYTON
   Margaret   60f
763-733
 BIAS
   Larkin   50m VA farmer
   Ruth   45f

763-733 BIAS (con't)

Thomas	17m	farmer
Cornelius	14m	

BIAS

Linsey	27m	farmer
Malinda	7f	
Sarah	5f	
Wm. W.	3m	

764-734

ADKINS

Randolph	50m VA	farmer
Elsey	45f	
Sylvester	16m	farmer
Ballard	15m	
Charity	12f	
Parker	6m	

765-735

WILLIAMS

Matilda	50f VA

CURTIS

Mary	25f
Eliza	6f
Matthew	2m

766-736

NOWELL

Winston	59m VA	farmer
Mary	44f	
Angelina	24f	
Emaline	23f	
Mary	20f	
Willis	18m	farmer
Matilda	16f	
Nancy	12f	
Maria	8f	

BEECH

John	13m

767-737

SIMPSON

Charles	50m ENG teacher
Catherine	40f GER

786-738

MITCHELL

Saml.	53m VA	farmer
Eliza	49f	

786-738 MITCHELL (con't)

Absalom	23m	farmer
John L.	18m	farmer
Susan	9f	
Charles W.	5m	

MITCHELL

Pleasant G.	29m	labor
Fanny	17f	

769-739

KECK

John W.	38m VA	blacksm
Sarina	35f	
Daniel B.	16m OH	farmer
Phillip	14m VA	
William	12m	
Lucinda	10f OH	
Jonathan	9m	
John W.	4m VA	
Esther	1f	

MITCHELL

Saml.	12m

770-740

MESSINGER

Nicholas	75m VA	millwrt
Mary	65f	
John	21m	farmer
George	16m	farmer

McCOMAS

Mary J.	28f
Mary	15f
Blackburn	3m

771-741

MILLER

Henry	33m VA	farmer
Rhoda	65f	

772-742

McMILLEN

J. W.	29m VA	millwrt
Catherine	29f	
Enoch	4m	
Frances	3f	
Letitia	1f	

JOHNSON

Eveline	15f

773-743
  PETRY
    Martin   38m VA labor
    Mary   29f
    Marion   17m   labor
    Robert   10m OH
    John   7m VA
    Martha   7f
    George   5m
    Maria   1f
774-744
  ADKINS
    Price   46m KY farmer
    Eliza   45f VA
    Sarilda   20f
    Lucinda   15f
    Catherine   13f
    Abagail   10f
    Allen   6m
    Paris   1m
775-
776-745
  TULEY (Tooley)
    Charles   61m VA farmer
    Elizabeth   56f
    John   16m   farmer
    Polly   14f
    Amanda   12f
777-746
  ADKINS
    John C.   39m VA farmer
    Nancy   36f
    Elizabeth   15f
    George W.   13m
    Julia   11f
    Nancy   8f
    Martha   6f
    John W.   4m
    Mary M.   2f
778-747
  TULEY (Tooley)
    Charles Jr.   21m VA farmer
    Martha   18f OH
    George W.   11/12m VA

779-748
  JOHNSON
    Maxwell   23m VA farmer
    Polly   24f
780-749
  PRITCHARD
    Lewis   26m KY labor
    Eveline   23f VA
    Clarissa   5f
    Nancy   3f
781-750
  ADKINS
    Elizabeth   31f VA
    Ephraim   14m
    Delphia   7f
782-751
  DIAL
    Lucinda   55f NC
    Mary A.   17f VA
    Panthea   15f
783-752
  JOHNSON
    John   50m VA farmer
    Elizabeth   46f
    Louisa   24f
    Susan   23f
    Margaret   22f
    William   20m   farmer
    Franklin   18m   farmer
    Melitta   17f
    Isham   14m
    Joseph   10m
    Elizabeth   7f
    Irwin   4m
    Lucinda   3f
    Jesse   4/12m
  JOHNSON
    Sarah   85f
784-
785-753
  TERRY
    Emily   41f KY
    Elizabeth   16f
    James   14m

785-753 TERRY (con't)
Emily	11f	
Parker	7m	VA
Polly	6f	
Sarilda	3f	

786-754

ADKINS
Green	32m	KY farmer
Anna	33f	VA
Martin	10m	
Candus	8f	
Sarah	7f	
Alice	5f	
Garrett	4m	
Almeda		

787-755

PARSONS
Susan	76f	VA
Nancy	19f	

788-756

EPLIN
Wm.	40m	VA labor
Susanna	40f	
Melissa	12f	

789-757

EPLIN
Elizabeth	34f	VA
Mahala	15f	
Sherrod	12m	
Sarilda	10f	
Mary	6f	
Frederick	2m	

EPLIN
Lydia	68f

790-758

PORTER
Saml.	30m	VA labor
Sarah	30f	
Letha	11f	
John	9m	
Alexander	5m	
Mildred	3f	
Malinda	2f	

791-759

JOHNSON
Merritt	40m	VA farmer
Rhoda	50f	
Zerilda	17f	
Marion	16m	

792-760

EPLIN
Randolph	40m	VA farmer
Polly	30f	
Amasetta	8f	
Elizabeth	6f	
Merritt	3m	

793-761

MIDKIFF
Abraham	25m	VA farmer
Isabella	23f	
John	3m	
Mary	2f	

McQUIE
Andrew	61m	KY teacher

794-762

MIDKIFF
Spencer	50m	VA farmer
Vituria	43f	
Sarah	18f	
Alexander	16m	
Walden	14m	
Emma	12f	
Albert	10m	
Ivy	8f	
Spencer	6m	
Mary	3f	

795-763

ESKIN
John	29m	VA labor
Henrietta	24f	
Dyke B.	8m	
Guy F.	7m	
John W.	3m	
Sarah	1f	

796-764
    McCOMAS
        James   50m VA farmer
        Elizabeth   26f
        Alexander   24m   farmer
        David   22m
        Cynthia   21f
797-765
    WOOD
        Saml.   36m VA farmer
        Sarah   44f
        Betsey   11f
        Amanda   9f
        Bestie (Bettie) 6f
        Alexander   2m
        Benjamin   8/12m
    MILES
        Elijah   9m
(oldest 2 his, Elijah hers
    youngest 3 theirs ??)
798-
799-766
    CRABTREE
        Rachel   22f VA
        Pricy   2m

End Falls Mills

Paw Paw Bottom Post Office
800-767   (Salt Rock E)
   BUKLEY
      Charles   46m VA farmer
      Elvira   40f
      Martha   24f
      Sarah   21f
      William   18m   farmer
      Christiana   14f
801-768
   KEENAN
      Patrick   76m VA farmer
      Rebecca   60f
      Cynthia   30f
802-769
   McKEAND
      John   48m VA farmer
      America   46f
      William   24m   farmer
      Alexander   23m   farmer
      Sarah   15f
      Eliza   13f
      Emily   10f
      Mary   8f
      Eleanor   6f
803-770
   PERRY
      Benjamin   52m VA farmer
      Julia   52f
      Peter   20m   farmer
      Benjamin   18m   farmer
      Thomas H.   14m
      John   13m
      Martha   10f
   SMITH
      Margaret   24f   dom
804-771
   SHELTON
      Elisha   43m VA farmer
      Elizabeth   42f
      John   20m
      Sarah   16f
      Alderson   10m
      Victor   6m

805-772
   McCOMAS
      James   58m VA farmer
      Emily   20f
      Wirt   18m   farmer
806-773
   ROFFE
      James H.   44m VA farmer
      Polly   44f
      Armilda   14f
      Beatrice M.   9f
      Wm. H.   2m
807-774
   McCOMAS
      David   25m Va farmer
      Sarah   23f
      Emily   1f
      Herbert   4/12m
808-775
   KEENAN
      David   31m VA farmer
      Rebecca   29f
      Albert M.   9m
      Eliza   6f
      James   5m
      Eleanor   4f
      America   1f
809-776
   BELL
      James C.   26m VA farmer
      Mary B.   21f
810-777
   HEATH
      Sarah   42f VA
      Joshua   21m   farmer
      Juda   19f
      John   17m   farmer
      Eliza   15f
      Wm. B.   13m
      Sarah   8f
   GILL
      Wm.   23m   labor

811-778			
BLEDSOE			
Rachel	46f	ENG	
John T.	22m	labor	
James	21m	labor	
Lewis	17m	labor	
Mildred	14f		
Alfred	12m		
812-779			
McCALLISTER			
James	26m	VA	labor
Ann	25f		
Polly	5f		
Thomas	3m		
Wm. G.	2m		
813-780			
PERRY			
Wm. B.	28m	VA	farmer
Mary	29f		
Mary	5f	AR	
William	4m	VA	
David	2m		
JORDAN			
Matilda	14f		
814-781			
BELL			
John R.	24m	VA	mercht
Louisa	18f		
815-782			
McLEARY			
Alexander	55m	VA	farmer
Lucretia	49f		
Alexander	20m		farmer
P Catherine	9f		
O Charles	8m		
O McCOGGLE			
R John	66m	PA	blksm/pau
SMITH			
H Mary	30f	VA	pauper
O HOLTEN			
U Minerva	28f		pauper
S HILL			
E Benjamin	22m		pauper

815-782 McLEARY (con't)			
SMITH			
Joseph	12m		pauper
Nathaniel	3m		pauper
816-783			
SMITH			
A. J.	30m	VA	carpntr
Mary J.	28f		
Sarah M.	10f		
Joseph M.	2m		
Lewis H.	3/12m		
817-784			
FORTH			
John	55m	VA	farmer
Nancy	55f		
REYNOLDS			
Lorenzo	6m		
Henry	4m		
John	2m		
JORDAN			
Abagail	35f		
George	8m		
818-785			
McCALLISTER			
Richard	69m	VA	farmer
Cynthia	37f		
Dason	11m		
William	8m		
Dicey	2f		
Wesley	10/12m		
819-786			
ROBERTS			
Harrison	44m	VA	farmer
Susan	47f		
John	23m		farmer
America	11f		
ASHWORTH			
Joel	21m		labor
820-787			
JOHNSON			
Harvey	43m	VA	farmer
Mary	34f		
William	15m		
Rebecca	13f		

820-787 JOHNSON (con't)

Joseph	5m	
Sarah	3f	
Isabella	2f	
Emma	5/12f	

821-788

JOHNSON

Perry	49m	VA farmer
Sarina	46f	
Cynthia	24f	
America	19f	
Louara	16f	

822-789

JOHNSON

Andrew	26m	VA farmer
Betsey	27f	
Ennis	3m	
Sarah	1f	

SHOWANS

Sally	55f	

823-790

JOHNSON

John	38m	VA farmer
Henrietta	30f	
Mary	13f	
Tennessee	9f	
Perry	5m	

824-791

JOHNSON

Wm.	46m	VA farmer
Sarah	42m	
Jefferson	19m	farmer
John	17m	farmer
Gordon	15m	

825-792

JOHNSON

Andrew	51m	VA farmer
Ailsey	48f	
Harvey	23m	farmer
Jefferson	21m	farmer
Rebecca	19f	
Emeline	17f	
William	15m	
Henry	12m	

825-792 JOHNSON (con't)

Willis	8m	
David	3m	

826-793

WILLIAMS

A. W.	40m	VA farmer
Mary	34f	
Thomas	13m	
Walter	11m	
James	8m	
Patrick	6m	
David	4m	
Sarah	2f	

827-794

JOHNSON

James	34m	VA farmer
Sarah	28f	

JOHNSON

Mary	72f	
Eliza	38f	
Wilson	15m	

MESSINGER

John	8m	

828-795

JOHNSON

Minerva	40f	NC
Columbus	14m	VA
Eliza	12f	
Emily	10f	
James	6m	

JOHNSON

Olive	50f	
Delilah	26f	
Eliza	2f	

829-796

JOHNSON

Andrew	36m	VA farmer
Lucinda	27f	OH
Mary	9f	VA
Burwell	6m	OH
John	4m	
James	2m	

830-797
JOHNSON

Burwell	69m	VA farmer
Sarah	37f	
Mary	14f	
Wm. A.	11m	
Louisa	9f	
Lucy	7f	
Christopher	4m	
Randolph	4/12m	

831-798
SCITZ

John	47m	WIR farmr
Susan	45f	VA
John	17m	farmer
Charles	13m	
Catherine	12m	
James	10m	
Mary	8f	
America	5f	

832-799
SCITZ

Christopher	74m	WIR farmer
Sarah	73f	VA

833-800
BIAS

James	43m	VA farmer
Polly	35f	
Crosby	21m	farmer
Dicey	18f	
Lourana	17f	
Rolin	16m	farmer
Clarrissa	14f	
Angelina	12f	
Millington	9m	
Blackburn	7m	
Marion	5m	
Letha	2f	

834-801
MIDKIFF

Gordon	29m	Va farmer
Elizabeth	28f	
Harvey	8m	
Solomon	6m	

834-801 MIDKIFF (con't)

Emily	3f	
Eliza	1f	

835-802
NICELY

Zach.	48m	VA farmer
Elizabeth	36f	
James	14m	
Lucinda	12f	
America	8f	
Amanda	8f	
Melvina	5f	
Wm. D.	3m	
Emily	6/12f	

836-803
McCOMAS

Thomas J.	44m	VA dep shrff
Catherine	44f	
Julia	18f	
Sarah	16f	
Blackburn	13m	
America	9f	
Billington S.	7m	
Adaline	5f	
Emily	3f	
John M.B.	1m	

McCOMAS

Thomas	24m	farmer
Elvira	18f	

837-

838-804
McCOMAS

Mary	79f	VA
Paulina	6f	

839-805
HATFIELD

Henry	53m	VA farmer
Catherine	45f	
David J.	26m	farmer
John L.	24m	farmer
Andrew	22m	farmer
Nancy	19f	
Elizabeth	17f	
Catherine	14f	

83

839-805 HATFIELD (con't)
    Henry   13m
    Emily   11f
    Eliza   9f
    Isaac   8/12m
840-806
  McCOMAS
    Thomas Sr.   57m VA farmer
    Elizabeth   31f
    John   11m
    Elisha   6m
841-807
  SWANN
    Hezekiah   63m VA farmer
    Catherine   50f
    Ballard   31m   farmer
    Nancy   26f
    Patrick   1m
  PAINE
    Nancy   18f   dom
842-808
  SWANN
    H.C.   30m VA farmer
    Mary   19f
    Nancy   1f
843-809
  BIAS
    Rolin   36m VA minstr
    Martha   35f
    Sarah   18f
    Rachel   16f
    Mary   12f
    Elisha   8m
    Sereptia   6f
    Lucy   4f
  SWANN
    Mary A.   2f
844-810
  HATFIELD
    George   59m VA farmer
    Eliza   42f
    Josephine   17f
    Adam   15m
    James   14m

844-810 HATFIELD (con't)
    Eliza   11f
    John M.   9m
    Margaret   4f
    Charles   2m
    Lucinda   10/12f
845-811
  RAY
    Catherine   33f VA
    Blackburn   10m
    Greenville   8m
    Wm. W.   7m
    Ulysses   1m
846-812
  ROUSEY
    James   49m VA farmer
    Mary   50f
    William   20m   farmer
    Henry   19m   farmer
    Martha   14f
    James   13m
    Mary   9f
    John   4m
847-813
  REYNOLDS
    Archibald   59m VA farmer
    Susan   56f
  ROUSEY
    Archibald   15m (see 846)
848-814
  MORRISON
    John E.   40m VA farmer
    Mary   39f
    Mary   11f
    James   9m
    Catherine   7f
    Wm.E.   4m
849-815
  MORRISON
    Wm. E.   23m VA farmer
    Margaret   22f

850-816
   BIAS
      Obidiah   36m VA farmer
      Martha   32f
      Louisa   4f
      Cynthia   3f
      Wm.M.   2/12m

851-817
   MITCHELL
      Joseph   24m VA carpntr
      Nancy   21f

852-818
   PERRY
      Elijah   23m VA farmer
      Cynthia   18f
      Bula   1f
   CANNON
      Albert   10m

853-819
   MORRIS
      Benjamin   30m VA farmer
      Betsey   24f
      Mahlon   4m
      Benjamin   2m
      Bula   4/12f

854-820
   GLEN
      Thomas   23m VA farmer
      Elizabeth   18f
   DEACON
      Henry C.   23m   labor

855-821
   MAIB
      Wolfred   55m VA labor
      Elizabeth   45f

856-822
   DEACON
      Andrew   27m VA millwrt
      Elizabeth   21f
      Laura   2f
      Mary J.   3/12f

857-823
   PERRY
      S. B.   26m VA farmer
      Martha   27f
      Cynthia   6f
      Charles   3m
      Sarah   1f
   HATFIELD
      Edith   25f   dom
   ADKINS
      Polly A.   9f

858-824
   SCITZ
      Cutlope   39m WIR farmer
      Catharine   39f VA
      Henrietta   13f
      Elias   11f
   MYERS
      Margaret   15f

859-825
   McCALLISTER
      Preston   33m VA farmer
      America   26f
      Mary   11f
      Isabella   7f
      James   6m
      Lafayette   3m

860-826
   JOHNSON
      Joseph W.   33m VA labor
      Lucy   28f
      John   7m
      Lucy   6f
      Emily   5f
      Joseph   2m
   BLEDSOE
      Peter   18m   labor

861-
862-827
   BLEDSOE
      Wm.   26m VA labor
      Melissa   25f
      Amos   4m

862-827 BLEDSOE (con't)

Wm.	3m	
Mary	1f	
BEECH		
Columbus	14m	
Sarah	9f	

863-828

McCALLISTER

Alexander	37m	VA farmer
Helen	37f	
Emma	14f	
Henry	12m	
Albert	10m	
Eveline	9f	
Louisa	5f	
Joseph	1m	

864-829

PEYTON

Harrison	39m	VA farmer
Elizabeth	34f	
Henrietta	11f	
Jennetta	8f	
Frank	7m	
Marietta	6f	
Amasetta	4f	
Emma	2f	

865-830

PEYTON

Wm.	36m	VA labor
Eliza	31f	
Nancy	9f	
Betsey	6f	
Amanda	2f	
Alvin	3/12m	

PEYTON

Charles	71m	labor
Catlett	13m	

866-831

McCALLISTER

John	43m	VA farmer
Maria	35f	
Martha	16f	
Preston	14m	
Malinda	12f	

886-831 McCALLISTER (con't)

Isaac H.	10m	
Susannah	8f	
Sarah	6f	
Harrison	3f	

867-832

IRVING

Robert	43m	VA farmer
Sarah	36f	
Wm.T.	15m	
Sarah	12f	
James	9m	
Martha	4f	AR
Amanda	2f	AR
Samatha	3/12f	VA

868-833

DAVIS

Alvin	26m	VA farmer
Adaline	21f	
Milton J.	3m	
Daniel	11/12m	

869-834

STANLEY

Robert	23m	VA farmer
Henrietta	22f	

870-835

STANLEY

John H.	61m	VA farmer
Elizabeth	67f	

PEYTON

Clara	35f	
Randolph	5m	
Charles	1m	

871-836

RAY

Wm.	57m	VA farmer
Julia	50f	
Morris	25m	farmer
Andrew	23m	farmer
John	18m	

SMITH

Susan	7f	

872-837
  PORTER
    James   39m VA farmer
  PORTER
    Sarah   85f
  JOHNSON
    Jefferson   3m
873-838
  SCITZ
    Godfrey   38m VA farmer(GER
    Mary   25f
    Cynthia   3f
    Mary   2f
    Frank M.   9/12m
  BEECH
    Hannah   18f   dom
874-839
  MIDKIFF
    Solomon   55m VA farmer
    America   29f
    Emily   16f
    Henry   4m
    Lewis   1m
875-840
  MORRISON
    Thompson   48m VA farmer
    Mary A.   45f
    Elizabeth   21f
    Albert   19m
    John   16m
    Calvin   14m
    Mary   11m
876-841
  MORRISON
    Thomas   23m VA farmer
    Elizabeth   23f
    Henry   3m
877-842
  PORTER
    Jernal   52m VA farmer
    Juda   41f
    Sarah   23f
    Adaline   21f
    Jacob   19m

877-842 PORTER (con't)
    James H.   16m
    Nelssina   14f
    Nancy   11f
    Louisa   8f
    Rolin   6m
    John J.   2m
878-843
  MORRISON
    John T.   42m VA farmer
    Nancy   38f
    Martha   17m
    Nancy   15f
    John S.   11m
    Margaret   8f
    Calvery   4m
    Napoleon   2m
  MORRISON
    John   75m
879-844
  SAVAGE
    George W.   52m KY labor
    Minerva   37f VA
    Juda   5f
    George   3m
880-845
  ADKINS
    Edward   26m VA farmer
    Susan   20f
    Jefferson   2m

End Paw Paw Bottom

Ten Mile Post Office   (LC)

881-846
  ADKINS
    Richard   57m VA farmer
    Lucinda   61f
    James   23m   farmer
    Roffe   18m   farmer
  HOLT
    Ida   19f   dom
882-847
  KENNISON
    Griffin   28m VA farmer
    Nancy   22f
    Victoria   5f
    Malinda   2f
883-848
  ADKINS
    Lykins   31m KY farmer
    Eliza   28f VA
    William   7m
    Lucinda   5f
    Martha   3f
    Paulina   1f
  ADKINS
    Mahala   23f
    James L.   8m
    Nancy   2f
884-849
  ADKINS
    Samuel   28m VA farmer
    Nancy   23f
  SAXTON
    Wm.   19m   labor
  BELCHER
    Peggy   17f
    Paulina   13m
885-850
  ADKINS
    Alfred   29m VA farmer
    Lucetta   23f
    Wirt   4m
    Letha   2f

886-851
  STEPHENSON
    George   57m KY farmer
    Nancy   57f VA
887-852
  STEPHENSON
    Armstrong   37m VA farmer
    Caroline   26f
    Christopher 14m
    Edney   7f
    Patterson   5m
    Martha   3f
    Nancy   2f
888-853
  STEVENSON
    Thomas   35m VA farmer
    Malinda   39f
    America   13f
    Adaline   11f
    Francis   9m
    Louisa   7f
    Arnold   5m
    Lucy   3f
889-854
  ELKINS
    St.Clair   30m VA farmer
    Elizabeth   35f
    Margaret   10f
    Susan   8f
    James   6m
    Lucinda   3f
    Nancy   1f
890-855
  NASH
    Thomas   40m OH farmer
    America   23f
    Emeline   3f
    Mary   1f
891-856
  DEFOE
    Wm.   49m VA labor
    Elizabeth   39f
    John   18m   labor
    Martha   15f

891-856 DEFOE (con't)

Sarah	13f		
Rachel	10f		
James	8m		
Albert	6m		
Wm.M.	4m		
Charles L.	1m		

892-857

BURDETT

Leonard	75m	VA	farmer
Ailsey	75f	NC	

893-858

McCOY

Robert	43m	VA	farmer
Malinda	37 f	NC	
Meredith	17m	VA	farmer
Dicy	14f		
Ailsey	10f		
James	7m		

894-859

WARRICK

Fielding	34m	VA	farmer
Rhoda	32f		
Robert	11m		
Thomas	8m		
Nancy	6f		
Wm.W.	5m		
Mary	3f		
James	1m		

895-860

WARRICK

Wesley	24m	VA	farmer
Elizabeth	24f		

896-861

BRUMFIELD

John S.	25m	VA	farmer
Cynthia	24f		
Frances	11/12m		

SMITH

James	46m		labor
Rebecca	14f		

897-862

LUCAS

John	76m	VA	farmer
Mary	72f		
William	36m		farmer
Emily	27f		
Leonard	10m		
Andrew	7m		
Minerva	4f		
Paris	2m		

898-863

ELKINS

Overton	26m	VA	farmer
Nancy	22f		
Floyd	5m		
Elizabeth	2f		
Mary W.	3/12f		

899-864

LUCAS

Price	39m	VA	farmer
Amanda	39f		
Letta	20f		
Ralph	18m		farmer
Nancy	12f		
William	9m		
Emily	6f		
Moses	2m		
Sarah	2f		

ELKINS

Henry	23m		labor

900-865

HATFIELD

Addison	34m	VA	teacher
Zerilda	60f		
Elisha	24m		
America	17f		
Samantha	15f		

901-866

SMITH

Isaac	30m	VA	farmer
Elizabeth	35f		
Harriett	10f		

SMITH

Matilda	33f		

89

901-866 SMITH (con't)
    Eleanor   30f
902-867
  SMITH
    Ballard   42m VA farmer
    Sina   30f
    David   12m
    Lourana   9f
    Crozby   8m
    Huldah   6f
    Sarah   4f
    Lewis   2m
    Frances   1m
903-868
  PARSONS
    Saml.   70m VA farmer
    Theresa   70f
    John   24m
    Cynthia   18f
    Margaret   7m
904-869
  COLLINS
    Issac   36m VA farmer
    Sarah   24f
905-
906-870
  BREWER
    Martin   25m TN farmer
    Margaret   25f VA
    Missouri   4f
    Sydney   1f KY
907-871
  FARLEY
    John   30m VA farmer
    Rebecca   32f
    Minerva   10f
    Matilda   8f
    Elizabeth   6f
    Wm.A.   4m
    Susannah   2f
908-872
  BRUMFIELD
    Wm.   28m VA farmer
    Mary   30f

908-872 BRUMFIELD (con't)
    Letta   8f
    Lafayette   6m
    Lucinda   5f
    Martha   4f
    Wm. B.   2m
    John   1m
    Eliza   3/12f
  BRUMFIELD
    Charles   14m
909-873
  ELKINS
    Joel   35m VA farmer
    Elizabeth   24f
    Panthea   8f
    Louis   2m
910-874
  BLANKENSHIP
    Wm. P.   31m VA farmer
    Mary   29f
    Irvin   10m
    Melvin   8m
    Maria   5f
    Eliza   3f
    Ralph   1m
911-875
  SARTIN
    John W.   32m VA
    Margaret   32f
    Sarah   9f
  SARTIN
    Anna   60f OH
912-876
  ADKINS
    Lewis   47m VA farmer
    Milsey   36f TN
    Evermont   21m VA labor
    Anderville   17m
    Albert   14m
    Hansford   13m
    Emily   10f
    Carpenter   6m
    John H.   4m

912-876 ADKINS (con't)
ADKINS
   Mary   21f VA
   Jerome N.   4/12m
HATFIELD
   Carperton   26m VA shoemkr
LUCAS
   Susan   21f   dom
913-877
CONLEY
   Bayley   41m VA farmer
   Adaline   28f
   Mary   8f
   Isadora   5f
   Laura   4f
   Ira   1m
SMITH
   Luke   24m   labor
914-878
HATFIELD
   F.F.   34m VA farmer
   Nancy A.   21f
   Julia   15f
   Elizabeth 12f
   Adriana S. 9f
   Wm. G.   7m
   Rufus   3m
   Marsina   1f
915-879
DRAKE
   Henderson 53m VA farmer
   Amasetta 39f
   Penelope 24f
   Guy F.   18m   farmer
   Blackburn 16m
   Osborn   14m
   Paulina   5f
916-880
McCOMAS
   James M. 25m
   Emily   21f
   Victoria   2f
   Mary   1f

916-880 McCOMAS (con't)
BAKER
   Louis   47m   farmer
   Arminta   47f
DRAKE
   Elizabeth
917-881
McCOMAS
   Aquilla   25f VA
   Thomas   9m
   James   5m
   Moses   4m
   Mary   1f
McCOMAS
   Milton   36m   farmer
WEIGER
   Joseph   40m BAV baker
   Frank   39m   baker
918-882
McCOMAS
   Elizabeth 56f VA
   Emberson 34m
   Wm. P.   21m   farmer
   Sarah   16f
   Valeria   8f
HARRISON
   Moses   28m   labor
   Ellen   17f
   Guy   16m   labor
919-883
ADKINS
   Elisha   35m VA farmer
   Louisa   40f
   Sarah   10f
   Elizabeth 8f
   William P. 6m
920-884
SPEARS
   Wm.   49m VA
   Sarah   44f
   Wiley   21f
PEYTON
   John   8m

920-884 SPEARS (con't)
  McCOMAS
    Elizabeth   5f
921-885
  SPEARS
    Peyton   40m VA farmer
    Telitha   35f
    Wesley   15m
    Lucinda   12f
    Harmon   10m
    Hamilton   8m
    Emily   6f
    Nancy   4f
    Henry   6/12m
922-886
  COOPER
    Polly   35f VA
    Pheobe   10f
    Nancy   8f
    Saml.   6m
    Frances   4f
    Sally   2f
923-887
  SMITH
    Juda   35f VA
    America   14f
    Mary   1f
924-888
  COOPER
    Catherine   46f VA
    Mildred   24f
    Sarah   18f
    Thomas   9m
    Floyd   5m
925-889
  BALLARD
    Wm.   30m VA farmer
    Elizabeth   26f
    Wilson   8m
    Washington 6m
    James   5m
    Margaret   3f

926-890
  LANDRUM
    James   26m VA farmer
    Sarah   26f
    John   3m
    Wm.   3/12m
    Mary   3/12f
  VEST
    Rhoda   46f
    John   16m   labor
    Norman   13m
927-891
  ADKINS
    Robert   34m VA labor
    Harriett   32f
    Sophia   7f
    Abby   3f
928-892
  WADDLETON
    Harvey   46m VA farmer
    Alabama   40f
    John R.   12m
    Jeremiah   7m
929-893
  VICKERS
    Simeon   43m VA farmer
    John   19m   farmer
    Wm.   19m   farmer
    Mary   18f
    Charles   16m   farmer
    James   14m
    Thomas   12m
    Edmund   10m
    Simeon   4m
    Alexander 2m
  JONES
    Wm. H.   21m   labor
    Rosanna   22f
930-894
  SMITH
    Jessee D. 25m VA farmer
    Mary   22f
    Nathan   3m
    Sinate   1m

92

931-895
  KINDER
    Saml.   35m VA farmer
    Nancy   35f
    Mary   11f
    Elizabeth   9f
    Frances   7f
    Julia   6f
    Jasper   5m
    Samantha   3f
932-896
  HUNTER
    Elizabeth   60f VA
    Charles   22m   farmer
    William   14m

End Ten Mile District

Hamlin District   LC

933-897
  BALLARD
    John W.   38m VA farmer
    Matilda   35f
    Cora   3f
    Mollie   1f
  KINDER
    Jackson   24m   labor
  CYRUS
    James   21m   labor
  LAVENDER
    Emily   19f   dom
  PEARSON
    Nancy   13f
934-898
  BIAS
    Anderson   47m VA farmer
    Nancy   34f
    William A.   22m   farmer
    Evermont   21m   farmer
    Lenville   16m
    Rohn   10m
    Calvery   5m
    Daniel   3m
    Mary   2f
    Julia A.   1f
935-899
  BIAS
    Ennis   24m VA farmer
    Louisa   20f
936-900
  WILKINSON
    John   40m VA dpty shf
    Permelia   41f
    Barbary   15f
    George   13m
    Ira   11m
    Mary T.   9m
    Wilbur   7m
    David   4m

937-901
  THOMPSON
    James   37m MA carpntr
    Elizabeth   27f VA
    Emily   4f
    Henry   3m
  WEBB
    Saml.   25m
    Jane   25f
938-902
  WEBB
    James   57m VA farmer
    Lowis   55f
    Sarah   15f
    Marinda   13f
    James   10m OH
    Eliza   8m
    Emogene   5f
  WEBB
    John B.   20m Va farmer
    Ann E.   21f
    Theodore   18m
    Isabella   15f
  WEBB
    Elizabeth   77f
  SHEPERD
    Lucinda   22f
    Maria   3f
    George W.   7/12m
939-903
  CARROLL
    James   70m VA farmer
    Cynthia   60f
    Cynthia   25f
  BURNS
    Delilah   20f
940-904
  YEAGER
    John T.   36m OH farmer
    Rebecca   32f VA
    James   13m OH
    George   11m
    Wm.   10m
    John   8m

940-904 YEAGER (con't)
    Amelia   7f VA
    Martha   3f
    Pheobe   1f
941-905
  BURNS
    David P.   45m VA farmer
    Ebba   46f
    Elizabeth   24f
    Robert   20m
    Thomas   19m
    Taylor   15m
    Mary   13f
    Peter   12m
    David   11m
    James   6m
942-906
  SNODGRASS
    James   50m VA farmer
    Mildred   34f
    Joseph   23m   farmer
    Rebecca   21m
    George   14m
    William   12m
    Adaline   10f
    Mildred   9f
    Sarah   7f
    Thomas   5f
    John   1f
943-907
  SNODGRASS
    James H.   24m VA farmer
    Rebecca   17f
944-908
  MAHONE
    Wm. C.   38m VA farmer
    Nancy   39f
    Mahala   16m
    Virgil   14m
    Bennett   11m
    Alphous   7m
    Almeda   5f
  PINE
    Washington   23m   labor

94

945-909
SHORT

Robert	44m VA farmer		
Saml.	13m		
Ellen	11f		
Emily	3f		

SHORT

Jeremiah	76m	
Catherine	50f	
Sophia	34f	

946-
947-910
ADKINS

Hamilton	26m VA farmer	
Malinda	24f	
Wm.	8m	
Simon	6/12m	

PEARSON

Simon	70m
Sarah	17f

948-911
JOHNSON

Frank	59m VA farmer	
Ida	43f	
Charles	23m	farmer
Benjamin	21m	farmer
James A.	18m	farmer
Sarah	16f	
Martha	14f	
Mathilda	7f	
Elisha	4m	
Enoch	1m	

JOHNSON

Squire	24m	carpntr
Rhoda	23f	
Greenville	7/12m	

CAMERON

John D.	30m	teacher

949-912
HOLTEN

Allen	45m VA farmer	
Jane	45f	
Ruth	25f	
Harrison	23m	labor

949-912 HOLTEN (con't)

Sally	22f	
Julila	20f	
Calvin	18m	labor
Nancy	16f	
Wm.	14m	
Emily	12f	
Calvery	4m	

950-913
COOPER

Silas	70m VA farmer	
Lucinda	74f	
Henderson	25m	

951-914
LAWRENCE

Charles	53m VA farmer	
Elizabeth	46f	
Joseph	22m	
Preston	19m	
Elizabeth	15f	
Charles	12m	
Rachel	11f	
George M.	9m	
Saml.	7m	

BLACK

Mary	23f
James	2m

952-
953-915
HOLLY

Andrew	65m VA farmer	
Frank	35m	

HOLT

Sally	52f
Rebecca	15f

954-916
BLANKENSHIP

E. D.	38m VA farmer	
Louisa	34f	
Charlotte	12f	
Lenora	10f	
Elizabeth	8f	
Girard	7m	

954-916 BLANKENSHIP (con't)

Mary	4f		
Sarah	2f		

955-917

LAWRENCE

Wm. H.	26m	VA	farmer
Permelia	24f		
Emily	2f		
Theodore T.	2/12m		

SMITH

Lewis	30m	labor

PEARSON

Lewis	23m	labor

956-918

BALLARD

James R.	45m	VA	farmer
Amanda	38f		
Elizabeth	14f		
Preston	12m		
William	10m		
Martha	8f		
Sarah J.	6f		
Mary J.	5f		

BALLARD

Wilson	70m	farmer

957-919

COLLINS

Elias	45m	VA	farmer
Celicia	31f		
Merritt	10m		
Wm.R.	9m		
Timothy	6m		
Elijah	4m		
Andrew	2m		
Vincent	4/12m		

ADKINS

Lawrence	8m

958-920

CLENDENIN

Ballard	27m	VA	blacksm

959-921

CARROLL

William A.	22m	VA	farmer
Nancy	20f		

959-921 CARROLL (con't)

Eugenia	7/12f

960-922

CARROLL

James.T.	33m	VA	farmer
Susan	31f		
Adam	12m		
Samanthia	10f		
Martha A.C.	5f		
Mary M.B.	3f		
Nancy A.F.	2f		

961-923

HOLLEY

James A.	40m	VA	farmer
Margaret	38f		
David	14m		
Warren	12m		
Julia	11f		
Elisha	9m		
Margaret	7f		
James A.	6m		
Wm.H.	3m		
Joel	2/12m		

HOLLEY

Edward	20m	labor

HOLTEN

Mary A.	18f	MO	dom

962-924

CURRY

Wm.	58m	VA	doctor
Margaret	58f		
Washington	18m		farmer
Wm.H.	15m		

ADKINS

Levica	22f
Parker	4m

963-925

BLACK

James C.	54m	VA	farmer
Lucy	49f		
Adam	22m		farmer
Sarah	18f		
Eliza	16f		
John	13m		

96

963-925 BLACK (con't)

William	11m	
Caroline	10f	

964-926

SEXTON

Joseph	30m	VA farmer
Lucinda	27f	
Melissa	10f	
William	8m	
Ira	1m	

965-927

MORRIS

Wm.	32m	VA labor
Gensia	22f	
John	5m	
James	4m	
Rebecca	3f	

966-928

ADKINS

Timothy	31m	VA farmer
Mary	30f	
Nathaniel	13f	
Charles	11m	
Matilda	9m	
Napoleon B.	7m	
Millard F.	5m	
George A.	3m	
Sarah	2f	

967-929

WILKINSON

Stephen	44m	VA blacksm
Wm. W.	19m	farmer
John H.	14m	

PULLEN

Rebecca	50f	

CHITAM

Thomas	19m	labor

968-930

LYKINS

John	61m	VA farmer
Rebecca	50f	
James	34m	farmer
Peter	25m	farmer
Andrew	24m	farmer

968-930 LYKINS (con't)

Littleberry	19m	farmer
Erasmus	16m	farmer
Wm.	14m	
Herod	11m	
Mary	8f	

LYKINS

Frances M.	21m	
Nancy	18f	

969-

970-931

HOLTEN

George A.	36m	Va farmer
Nancy	35f	
John H.	14m	
Priscilla	12f	
Arisba	10f	
Thornton	8m	
Louisa	6m	
George A.	3m	

HOLTEN

Charles	68m	farmer

971-932

PULLEN

William	35m	VA farmer
Martha	37f	
James	11m	
John B.	9m	
Melissa	8f	
Susan	7f	
Danville	6m	
Charles	4m	
Andrew	2m	

PULLEN

Elizabeth	72f	

972-

973-933

POWELL

Andrew	22m	VA farmer
Nancy	23f	OH
Rebecca	2f	
Mary A.	1f	

974-934
BRAGG
Saml. 32m VA farmer
Ann 38f
Sophia 13f
Cynthia 11f
Mary 9f
Permelia 7f
Eliza 2f
Emily 1f
975-935
EKSS
Lewis 42m VA farmer
Elizabeth 14f
John 11m
William 9m
James 6m
BRUCE
Sarah E. 19f
976-936
POWELL
Phillip 52m Va farmer
Mary 56f
Henry 17m farmer
977-937
SMITH
Saml. 50m Va labor
Mahala 50f
Nancy 17f
John 15m
Alexander 13m
Harvey 11m
Lafayette 8m
Lucy 6f
SMITH
Almina 21f
Emily 2f
978-938
SPURLOCK
Thomas 60m Va farmer
Rebecca 42f
Nancy 16f
ROBERTS
John 14m

979-939
HOLTEN
A. J. 28m VA farmer
Mary 31f
John 3m
Frances 2f
Mary 6/12f
980-940
EGGLESTON
Thomas 76m IRE farmer
Agnes 65f VA
Elizabeth 22f
Almira 20f
Susan 18f
Frances 15f
David 12m
Cornelius 10m
981-941
LAVENDER
Joseph 29m VA farmer
Nancy 33f
John W. 9m
982-942
HOLLY
William 34m VA labor
Margaret 36f
Andrew 15m
Lucy 12f
James 9m
Cynthia 7f
Saml. 4m
Rebecca 8/12f
ADKINS
Lucinda 34f
Christiana 5f
983-943
COTTON
Charles 47m VA
Julia 30f
William 14m
James 10m
Richard 8m
Holland 6m
Susan 4f

984-944
    ADKINS
        Thomas T.   41m VA farmer
        Malinda   36f
        Trausina   18f
        Sarah   17f
        Iva   13f
        John W.   11f
        Wm. A.   10m
        Callowhill   8m
        Emeline   5f
        Louisa   2f
985-945
    ADKINS
        Jesse   25m VA labor
        Letha   22f
        Wm.C.M.   2m
    ADKINS
        Isabella   18f
986-946
    ADKINS
        Jonas   24m VA labor
        Sarah   23f
        Asina   5f
        Sinclair   3m
        Frank G.   2/12m
987-947
    SMITH
        James   45m VA farmer
        Pheobe   38f
        Nancy   16f
        Betsey   15f
        Martha   14f
        Joseph   12m
        Sarah   10f
        Andrew   9m
        Cynthia   7f
        William   6m
        Thomas   3m
        Samanthia   1f
    HOLTEN
        Cynthia   36f
        Rebecca   6f

988-948
    HOLTEN
        Joseph Jr.   25m VA farmer
        Lucinda   20f
        Eliza   2f
        Albert G.Jenkins 4/12m
989-949
    HOLTEN
        Wm.   24m Va farmer
        Lucinda   25f
        Mary E.   11/12f
990-950
    HOLTEN
        Joseph   63m VA farmer
        Sarah   71f PA
        Nancy   34f VA
        Frances   31f
        Toliver   2m
        Nelson   6/12m
    ADKINS
        Wm.A.   29m   gentleman
991-951
    WITCHER
        Jeremiah   63m VA farmer
        Polly   60f
        Emily   23f
        John   21m   farmer
        America   14f
        Valeria   10f
    ANDERSON
        Marion   23m   labor
992-952
    WALLS
        Anderson   25m VA
        Erastus   47m
        Nancy   47f
        Polly   15f
        Moses   13m
        Preston   11m
        Rebecca   9f
        Ermida   7f

(son before parents ??)

993-953
    MILLER
        Moses   75m VA farmer
        Ruth   65f
    OLSTEAD
        Lucinda   30f
        Letha   10f
        Benjamin   5m
        Zedic   1m
994-954
    BARRETT
        Harvey   38m VA farmer
        Lucy   33f
        Andrew   13m
        Thomas   10m
        Elisha   7m
        Julia   3/12f
    ADKINS
        Ballard S.   20m   labor
995-955
    ROBERTS
        A. B.   23m VA farmer
        Rachel   24f
        Eli   1m
    SHORT
        Skelton   22m   labor
    JONES
        Saml.   26m   labor
996-956
    GRASS
        Peter   40m VA farmer
        Maliinda   23f
        Emily   6f
        Thomas J.   4m
        John   2m
        Lucy   3/12f
997-957
    ROBERTS
        Thomas   32m VA farmer
        Emily   23f
        Vicotria   4f
        Sylvannis   3f
    HOLTEN
        Anna   20f

997-957 ROBERTS (con't)
    BURNS
        George   18m
998-958
    ROBERTS
        Henry   24m VA farmer
        Catherine   23f
        Charles   6m
        Frank   5m
        Erasmus   4m
        Saml.   2m
        Hugh   6/12m
999-959
    ROBERTS
        Frank   25m VA farmer
        Mary   21f
        Emily   6/12f
    VICKERS
        Robert   3m
1000-960
    MILLER
        Wm.   29m VA farmer
        Dollie   25f
        Charles   7m
        Susan   6f
        Thomas   4m
        Mary   2f
        Catherine   1f
1001-961
    ROBERTS
        Mason   28m VA farmer
        Phoebe   28f
1002-962
    ROBERTS
        A. B. SR.   59m VA
        Susan   53f
        Matilda   16f
        Dorothea   14f
        A.B.   12m (Alex.Bird)
        Jeremiah   10m
    SMITH
        Lewis   4m

100

1003-963
  ROBERTS
    Joseph   26m VA farmer
    Nancy   27f
    Everett   7m
    John   5m
    Rebecca   4f
    Emily   2f
1004-964
  HAGER
    George   45m VA farmer
    Wesley   14m
    Amy   12f
    Hester Ann 8f
    Washington 3m
1005-965
  LAWSON
    David   67m VA farmer
    Kesine   67m
1006-966
  HARMON
    Thomas   71m VA farmer
    Jane   71f
1007-967
  SANFORD
    Marine   41m VA merchnt
    Jane   38f
    Vanlinden   17m   farmer
    Wm.   15m
    Milton   14m
    Martha   12f
    Viola   8f
    Louginnis   1m
  ASHWORTH
    Wm.B.   22m   farmer
1008-968
  HARMON
    John M.   43m VA
    Thomas   17m
    Emily   16f
    Eliza   13f
    John   10m
    William   8m
    Harriett   6f

1008-968 HARMON (con't)
    Miranda   4f
    Lewis   1m
1009-969
  CARPENTER
    Lewis   35m VA
    Tabitha   37f
    Elsey   9f
    Valeria   4f
    Luvina   1f
1010-970
  HARBOUR
    Jesse   55m VA farmer
    Jane   60f
    Joseph   20m
    Elizabeth   19f
    James   1m
1011-971
  ROBERTS
    James   59m VA farmer
    Lucy   53f
    Marion   20m   farmer
    Daniel   16m
    Mary J.   12f
  KING
    Mary   80f
    Sarah   35f
1012-972
  WEBB
    Wm. W.   56m VA farmer
    Jane   53f
    John   20m   farmer
    Hannah   18f
    Helen   14f
    Theresa   8f
1013-973
  KING
    Jesse   47m VA wheelwrt
    Juda   40f
  HOLTEN
    Martha   14f

1014-974
   ROBERTS
      Henry   25m VA farmer
      Nancy   24f
      Richard   1m
1015-975
   HARMON
      Thomas Jr. 35m VA farmer
      Annie   25f KY
      Adam   5m VA
      Columbus   4m
      Leonidus   2m
   MARTIN
      Aaron   23m   labor
1016-976
   RAMSEY
      Allen   35m VA farmer
      Ellen   34f
      Nancy   14f
      Edward   12m
      William   7m
      Nicholas   5m
      Bula   2f
1017-977
   NELSON
      Jonathan   36m VA farmer
      Eliza   34f
      Jonathan   16m
      William   13m
      Chloe   10f
      Napoleon   8m
      Robert   6m
      Emma   3f
      Joanna   6/12f
   SPONOGLE
      Emily   24f
1018-978
   HAWKINS
      Thomas   66m VA farmer
      Polly   61f
1019-979
   ADKINS
      Elizabeth   50f
      Mary   18f

1020-980
   VICKERS
      Thomas   45m VA farmer
      Margaret   35f
      Frances   16f
      George   14m
      California   11m
      Nancy   8f
      John   6m
      Thomas   3m
1021-981
   WYSONG
      Catherine   64f
      Susan   37f
1022-982
   WYSONG
      Creed   43m VA farmer
      Emeline   39f
      John   22m
      Calvin   16m
      Wm.   15m
      Mary J.   12f
      Granville   9m
      Charles   7m
      George   4m
1023-983
   WYSONG
      Eding   20m VA farmer
      Louisa   19f
1024-984
   ASHLEY
      Henry   61m VA farmer
      Jane   50f
      Mary   20f
      Saml.   15m
      Sarah   7f
1025-985
   REYNOLDS
      Simon   54m VA farmer
      Jane   49f
      Mary   21f
      James F.   18m   labor
      Joseph H.   12m
      John   8m

1026-986
  KAYSER
    G.J.   31m VA farmer
    Rebecca   29f
    Eli   10m
    Mary   7f
    Caroline   5f
    John D.   3m
    Wm.W.   1m
1027-987
  JOHNSON
    Wesley   39m VA farmer
    Sina   36f
    Ritta Ann   14f
    Angelina   11f
    America   9f
    Sarah   8f
    James   6m
    Rina   1f
1028-988
  ASHWORTH
    Henry   44m VA farmer
    Susan   41f
    Lewis   18f   farmer
    Lelia   16f
    Adaline   11f
    Linsey   8m
    George   7m
    Caroline   4f
    Amanda   1f
1029-989
  WOOD
    Joel   28m VA farmer
    Martha   26f
    John H.   7m
    Rosabella   4f
1030-990
  WILKINSON
    Benjamin   49m VA farmer
    Anna   48f
    Augustan   23m   labor
    Martha   20f
    Wm.G.   18m   farmer
    Eli   10m

1031-991
  JOHNSON
    Squire   52m VA farmer
    Dempsey   48f
    Elizabeth   22f
    Susanna   19f
    Polly   16f
    Sarah   15f
    Sampson   13m
    Lucinda   10f
    Catherine   7f
  THOMAS
    Joseph   2m OH
1032-992
  PORTER
    David   58m VA farmer
    Mary   50f
    John W.   28m   farmer
    James H.   22m   farmer
    Martha J.   20f
    Mary   14f
    Joseph   10m
  McCOMAS
    Sally   60f
1033-993
  ADKINS
    Wm.M.   35m VA labor
    Edith   30f
    Nancy   4f
    Sarah   2f
    Thomas   5/12m
10 34-994
  CURRY
    Hiram   46m VA farmer
    Barbary   41f
    Benjamin   21m
    Granville   18m
    Martha   16f
    Pemelia   14f
    George   12m
    Blackburn   9m
    Emily   7f
    Elmira   4f
    Alfred H.   2m

1035-995
  ACHERS
    Nathaniel   28m VA farmer
    Louisa   26f
    Henry   7m
    Julina   5f
    Rebecca   3f
    John   1m
1036-996
  REYNOLDS
    Ezekiel   52m VA farmer
    Amy   53f
    Thomas   18m   labor
    Isaiah   17m   labor
    Jackson   14m
    Alfred   8m
    Sarah   5f
1037-997
  NEWLEY
    Abagail   43f
    Mary J.   35f
  PINE
    Victoria   14f
    John   12m
  McCOMAS
    Charles   3m
1038-998
  ROBERTS
    John L.   34m VA farmer
    Frances E.   26f
    David A.M.   3m
    John L.N.   2m
    Charles H.L. 2/12m
1039-
1040-999
  ASHWORTH
    John   31m VA farmer
    Leah   27f
    Jonathan   7m
    Alfred   4m
    Jeremiah   3m
    Greenville   1m
    Nancy   7/12f

1041-1000
  ASHWORTH
    Hillary   24m VA farmer
    Rocksalina 21f
1042-1001
  JORDAN
    Morris   32m VA farmer
    Rebecca   25f
    Mary   10f
    Caroline   9f
    John   7m
    Louisa   5f
    Thomas   3m
    Rebecca   1f
1043-1002
  BROWN
    Thomas   21m VA labor
    Cynthia   20f
    Greenville 4/12m
  McCOMAS
    Edney   9f
1044-1003
  BURNS
    Isaiah   38m VA farmer
    Lucy   34m
    Mary   10f
    Artemisia   10f
  GRASS
    Jacob   82m   farmer
    Jemimah   84f
    Jacob   17m   farmer
  REYNOLDS
    Jasper   24m   labor
1045-1004
  PATTON
    Robinson   45m VA farmer
    Harriett   30f
  KEYTON
    John   26m
1046-1005
  ROSE
    Fleming   30m
    Peggy   25f

104

1046-1005 ROSE (con't)
    Robert   4m
    Harriet   1f
1047-1006
  HINCKLEY
    Livingston 55m NY farmer
    Permelia   50f VA
    Jacob   24m   labor
    Malvina   22f
    Hiram   18m   labor
    Ruth   15f
  ROSE
    Saml.   32m   labor
1048-1007
  BURNS
    James   20m VA farmer
    Cindrilla 20f
1049-1008
  BODEN
    John   26m VA labor
    Cynthia   26f
    Mary   5f
    Sarah   2f
    Alice   2/12f
  WEBB
    Cynthia   24f
    Mary   2f
    Nancy   3/12f
1050-1009
  THOMPSON
    Robert   27m VA farmer
    Elsey   21f
    Mary   4f
    Andrew   1m
  ASHWORTH
    VanBuren 30m   labor
1051-1010
  THOMPSON
    Hasting   24m VA farmer
    Virginia   20f
    Ellender   3f
    Angelina 1f

1052-1011
  THOMPSON
    Robert   59m OH farmer
    Ellender 59f
  THOMPSON
    Fountain 76m or 16m
1053-1012
  BOBBITT
    James F. 24m Va labor
    Malinda   25f
    Joseph   1m
1054-1013
  ASHWORTH
    John   60m VA farmer
    Nancy   50f
    Elizabeth 25f
    Ona   18f
    John   14m
    Aaron   9m
1055-1014
  BECKETT
    Wm.   58m VA farmer
    Martha   35f
    Eliza   12f
1056-1015
  GARRETT
    Stephen   23m VA farmer
    Catherine 22f
    Hezekiah 9/12m
1057-1016
  ROUSEY
    Seaton B. 39m VA farmer
    Drucilla   35f
    Susan   14f
    John   12m
    Henry M. 11m
1058-1017
  BECKETT
    Ahaz H.   22m VA farmer
    Margaret   22f
    Mary   3f
    Andrew   1m

1059-1018		
BURNS		
Job. Sr.	54m	VA farmer
Elizabeth	15f	
Allen	12m	
James	7m	

1060-1019		
THOMPSON		
John	24m	Va labor
Julia	19f	
James	3m	
John W.	2m	
Mary M.	4/12f	

1061-1020		
BURTON		
Wm.	40m	VA farmer
Mary	39f	
Joseph	14m	
John K.	12m	
Ann	10f	
Moses	8m	
Andrew	5m	
Queen Victoria	3f	
America	1f	

1062-1021		
LAWRENCE		
Charles	42m	VA farmer
Sarah	32f	
Arabella	10f	
Parthenia	9f	

1063-1022		
ASHWORTH		
Asa	37m	VA farmer
Mildred	26f	
Wm. H.	16m	
Andrew	11m	
John	10m	
Emily	7m	
Mary	6f	
Albert	3m	
Mildred	6/12f	

1064-1023		
LAWSON		
Joseph	36m	VA farmer
Lucy	30f	
David	12m	
Mary	8f	
Henry E.	6m	
James	4m	
Zach.	3m	
Scott	2m	

1065-1024		
LAWSON		
Wm.	30m	Va farmer
Julia	30f	
Lucinda	9f	
John	7m	
Mary A.	4f	
Sarilda	5/12f	

1066-1025		
PRIDEMORE		
Joseph	33m	VA farmer
Nancy	21f	
Rhoda	4f	
Jeremiah	3m	

1067-1026		
LAWSON		
John	28m	VA farmer
Lucretia	19f	
Mason	1m	
COOPER		
Rebecca	9f	

1068-1027		
MILLER		
Jacob	46m	VA farmer
Mary	36f	
Alice	15f	
Burwell	13m	
Martha	11f	
Atha	9f	
Edney	6f	
Valeria	3f	
Henry A. W.	1m	
WINGFIELD		
John	24m	teacher

1069-1028
  ALFORD
    Robert   46m VA farmer
    George   23m   farmer
    Joseph   21m   farmer
    Adam   19m   farmer
    Alzina   18f
    Lorenzo   16m   farmer
    Cynthia   12f
    Lafayette   10m
    Mary   6f
    James   5m
    Bellidona   4f
    Elizabeth   6/12f
1070-1029
  ALFORD
    James   35m VA farmer
    Mary   26f
    Emily   2m
    Olivia   1f
1071-1030
  EDWARDS
    James M.   35m VA farmer
    Elizabeth   27f
    Samuel   10m
    James   7m
    John   5m
    Mary   3f
1072-1031
  HAGER
    James   71m VA farmer
    Sarah   50f
    Sarilda   25f
    Benjamin   24m   farmer
    Lorenzo   23m   farmer
    Mary   21f
    Rachel   19f
    Clement   17m   farmer
    Nancy   14f
    Solomon   11m
1073-1032
  STANLEY
    Martin   40m VA farmer
    Sarah   30f

1073-1032 STANLEY (con't)
    John   4m
    George W.   2m
    Lucinda   4/12f
1074-1033
  HAGER
    Andrew   26m VA farmer
    Margaret   21f
    Elizabeth   3f
    Ann   9/12f
  FRAZIER
    Mary   18f
1075-1034
  SPURLOCK
    Burwell   36m VA farmer
    Nancy   33f
    Thomas   11m
    Rebecca   9f
    Elizabeth   8f
    Lucy   7f
    Fanny   6f
    Julia   4f
    Rosalie   9/12f

End Hamlin

Griffithville   LC
1076-1035
  MAY

Jacob	45m	VA	farmer
Ann	40f		
Jacob	19m		farmer
Cynthia	15f		
Octavia	13f		
Elvira	12f		
James	10m		
Charles	9m		
John	7m		
Sarilda	5f		
Eveline	4f		
Wm.	3m		
Ann	1f		
Emma	4/12f		

1077-1036
  HALDRON

Charles	33m	Va	farmer
Sarah	28f		
Eliza	2f		
Martha	3/12f		

1078-1037
  KING

John A.	31m	VA	farmer
Frances	22f		
Emma	2f		

1079-1038
  GOODE

Thomas	30m	OH
Louisa	16f	

1080-1039
  BOSTICK

Joseph	38m	VA
Betsey	38f	
Henderson	17m	
Nancy	13f	
Mary	5f	
Anderson	2m	

1081-1040
  BOSTICK

Joshua	44m
Mary	41f

1081-1040 BOSTICK (con't)

Elizabeth	22f

  FISHER

Andrew	25m	labor

1082-1041
  BAYS

Riley	37m	NC	farmer
Elizabeth	35f	VA	
Richard	11m		
Eliza	7f		
Mary	5f		
Susan	2f		
Lucinda	4/12f		

1083-1042
  BAYS

John	31m	NC	farmer
Sarah	37f	VA	
Jane	10f		
Wm.H.	8m		
James	6m		
Sarah E.	3f		
Isaac	1m		

1084-1043
  ELKINS

Patterson	22m	VA	farmer
Mary A.	20f	NC	
Martha	2m	VA	

1085-1044
  OXLEY

Alfred	39m	Va	farmer
Sarah	33f		
Saml.	13m		
Nancy	10f		
Thomas	9m		
Arnold	6m		
Martha	4f		
Lewis	6/12m		

1086-1045
  FLOWERS

Betsey	40f	VA
Emasetta	8m	
Matilda	6f	
Jacob	5m	

108

1086-1045 FLOWERS (con't)
    William   3m
    Amanda   1f
1087-1046
  EGNOR
    Archibald   49m VA farmer
    Susan   36f
    Josiah   20m OH farmer
    Archibald   18m
    Mary S.   16f
    Martha   14f
    James   12m
    Saml.   5m
1088-1047
  LAWRENCE
    John   46m VA farmer
    Sarah   29f
    Julia   7f
    Elizabeth   5f
    Michael   2m
1089-1048
  BREWER
    Floyd   23m VA labor
    Sarah   24f
    John W.   7/12m
1090-1049
  TONEY
    David   45m VA farmer
    Cynthia   39f
    Mary   9f
    Elizabeth   7f
    Wm. H.   3m
    James   6/12m
1091-1050
  CARROLL
    Thomas   70m VA farmer
    Sarah   56f
1092-1051
  HOLTEN
    George   45m Va farmer
    Elizabeth   63f
    Elizabeth   19f
    Rebecca   5f

1093-1052
  GRIFFITH
    Lorenzo D.   26m Va farmer
    Lucy   27f
  FLINT
    Oliver   8m
1094-1053
  DRAPER
    Wm.   36m Va farmer
    Mary   36f
    Sarah   13f
    Nancy   11f
    John   9m
    Solomon   6m
    Thomas   4m
1095-1054
  HOLSTEIN
    Wm. A.   39m Va farmer
    Cynthia   40f
    James R.   16m   farmer
    Mary   16f
    Addison   13m
    John   10m
    Elizabeth   8f
    Calbert   5m
    Arabella   3f
    Emma M.   2/12f
1096-1055
  WILLIAMS
    Matthew   35m VA blacksm
    Lucy   35f
    John   13m
    Felix   11m
    Saml.   9m
    Austin   6m
    Sarah   1f
1097-1056
  EGNOR
    John W.   30m VA farmer
    Lucinda   22f
    Mary   6f
    Greenville   5m
    Martin P.   3m

1098-1057			
GUNNOE			
Ralph	48m	VA	farmer
Jane	40f		
Julia	19f	KY	
Sarah	17f	VA	
Mary	14f		
John	12m		
Matilda	8f		
Rosa	5f		
Lucy	9/12f		

1099-1058			
EGNOR			
Wm. G.	25m	VA	farmer
Elizabeth	28f		

1100-1059			
GRIFFITH			
Ephraim	66m	VA	farmer
Mary	61f		
Addison	17m		farmer
Preston	15m		

1101-1060			
McCLURE			
William	25m	VA	farmer
Nancy A.	24f		
John	4m		
Asberry	1m		

1102-1061			
GRIFFITH			
Valeria	29f	VA	
Tunsell	8m		
John	4m		
Hester	2f		

1103-1062			
GRIFFITHS			
Ephraim Jr.	27m	VA	farmer
Nancy	24f		
Mary	8f		
Columbus	6m		
Washington	3m		

1104-1063			
MOORE			
Wm.	40m	VA	farmer
Sarah	35f		

1104-1063 MOORE (con't)			
Nancy	12f		
Alice	10f		
Anderson	8m		
Sarah	6f		
Susan	5f		
Elizabeth	3f		

1105-1064			
HAGLEY			
Preston	30m	VA	farmer
Letha	21f		
WHEELER			
Vernila	15f		
Matilda	13f		

1106-1065			
McCLURE			
Allen	25m	VA	farmer
Julia	20f		
James	3m		
Rhoda	6/12f		

1107-1066			
OTT			
William	59m	VA	farmer
Simeon	45m		farmer
OTT			
Catherine	82f		
Julia	60f		
WIKOSS			
Lucinda			

1108-1067			
ROBERTS			
Wm. H.	37m	VA	farmer
Susan	36f		
Elvira	12f		
Andrew	11m		
James	6m		
Jewett	1m		

1109-1068			
JOHNSON			
Lott	43m	VA	farmer
Juda	40f		
Martha	19f		
Joseph	18m		farmer
Caledoria	16f		

1109-1068 JOHNSON (con't)

Thomas	15m	
Henry	13m	

1110-1069

SPURLOCK

Mary	33f	Va
John H.	13m	
Thomas	12m	
Andrew	11m	
Edney	9f	
Malinda	8f	
Mary	6f	
Leander	4m	
Joseph	3m	
James	1m	

1111-1070

HAGER

Joseph	43m Va farmer
Rachel	42f
James	19m farmer
Hezikiah	18m farmer
Arrisba	15f
Vernalla	13f
Minerva	11f
Lucy	9f
Andrew	7m
Permelia	3f

BYERS

James	22m gentleman

1112-1071

SPURLOCK

Harrison	32m VA farmer
Delilah	30f
Matthew	7m
Amanda	6f
Martha	4f
Harriett	2f

1113-1072

HARMON

Eli	45m Va farmer
Lucinda	34f
John	6m

REYNOLDS

Nancy	20f

1114-1073

GRIFFITH

H.B.	23m Va farmer
Louisa	22f
Levanna	2m
James A.	1m

1115-1074

GRIFFITH

Sarah	57f Va
Lewis	21m farmer
Joseph	16m farmer

HOLTEN

Sarah	16f

1116-

1117-1075

ROBERTS

William	46m Va farmer
Elizabeth	33f
Laura	12f
Juda	11f
Henry	8m
Rocksalina	6f
Green	4m
Sarah	3f
Elijah	8/12m

1118-1076

SMITH

Ralph	38m VA farmer
Mahala	30f
Louisa	8f
Telitha	5f
Allen	1m

1119-1077

KIRK

John E.	36m Va farmer
Mary	35f
Jessee	15m
William J.	13m
Preston	10m
Andrew	7m
Leander	4m
Nancy	2f

1120-1078
 KIRK
  Jordan   26m VA farmer
  Julia   26f
  Manderville 4m
  Martin   2m
  POLLY
  Wm.   25m   labor
  Amos E.   1m
1121-1079
 McCALLISTER
  Richard   27m Va farmer
  Nancy   20f
  Sarah   1f
1122-1080
 McCALLISTER
  Perry   27m VA farmer
  Parthenia   20f
  Sarah   1f
  McCALLISTER
  Sarah   60f
  Senith   20f
  Catherine   14f
  NICHOLAS
  John   84m NC farmer
1123-1081
 CHANDLER
  H. M.   29m VA farmer
  Martha   19f
  HILL
  Sarah W.   13f
1124-1082
 BURNS
  Job   22m Va farmer
  Lucinda   16f
1125-1083
 CUMMINGS
  Charles   45m VA farmer
  Sydney   44f
  Minerva   17f
  Mary   14f
  Ellender   12f
  John   6m

1125-1083 CUMMINGS (con't)
  Adaline   5f
  Angeline   3f
1126-1084
 SMITH
  Peter   55m VA farmer
  Asinth   53f
  Nancy   24f
  Alfred   23m
  Sarah   20f
  Julia   19f
  Columbus   14m
  Wm.H.   10m
  Anderson   6m
  CHANDLER
  Peter   4m
1127-1085
 HARVEY
  John   61m VA farmer
  Jane   62f
  John   23m
  James   17m
  POLLY
  Mary A.   14f
1128-1086
 EGGLESTON
  J. T.   36m VA farmer
  Barbary   25f
  Mary   6f
  Isabella   4f
  Josephine   1f
1129-1087
 HALL
  John C.   43m VA farmer
  Elizabeth   39f
  James R.M. 14m
  Mary M.   13f
  Wm. H.   11f
  Seaton B.R. 9m
  Drucilla P.J. 6f
  Joshua V.T. 3m

End Griffithsville   LC

Greenbottom Post Office

1130-1088
  EMERSON
    Lyman   38m OH labor
    Elizabeth   32f VA
    Sylvester   11m
    Leander   9m
    Millard   6m
    Sarah   1f

1131-1089
  JENKINS
    Wm. A.   31m VA farmer
    Julia M.   28f MO
    Jennetta   5f OH
    Wm. G.   3m VA

1132-1090
  JENKINS
    A. G.   28m VA farmer
    Jennie S. 20f MO
    James Bowlin 6/12m VA

1133-1091
  WALLACE
    Toliver   56m VA farmer
    Malinda   36f OH
    Emily   3f VA
  McCOMAS
    John   14m OH
    Wm.   13m
    Julia   11f
    Elisha   8m

1134-1092
  RARDON
    Lyman   23m OH labor
    Araminta 22f VA

1135-1093
  BOWEN
    Sylvester 25m VA labor
    Susan   22f
    Henry M. 5/12m

1136-1094
  EMERSON
    Mary   40f OH
    Benjamin 23m OH labor
    Levina   21f OH

1137-1095
  JENKINS
    T. J.   33m VA farmer
    Susan   23f
    Julia   3f
    Laura   10/12f

1138-1096
  BLOM
    Wm.   40m OH labor
    Jane   41f KY
    Rachel   16f Oh
    Mary   12f
    John   10m
    Sarah   8f
    George   6m
    Elizabeth 3f
    Frances   1f

1139-1097
  SOUTHERS
    Wm.   24m VA labor
    Hester   17f OH

1140-1098
  BOWEN
    Wm.   40m VA farmer
    Adalaide 35f
    Jane   14f
    Sarah   12f
    Ezekiel   10m
    Margaret 8f
    Abner   6m
    Lewellyn 4f
    Frances   2f
    Albert G.J. 5/12m

1141-1099
  RICHARDSON
    Richard   30m VA overseer
J Mary   32f
E LINKFIELD
N Frances   12m
K Riley   10m
I Ida   8f
N Alice   6f
S GATEWOOD
    Charles   30m   labor

1141-1099 RICHARDSON (con't)				
F	CANTERBERRY			
A	Joseph	25m	OH	labor
R	TURNER			
M	William	24m	VA	labor
	CLOSE			
	Allen	24m	OH	labor
	HAWTHORN			
	Wm.	22m	VA	labor
	BICKEL			
	John	21m	VA	labor
	TURNER			
	Thomas	20m	VA	labor
	John	16m	VA	labor

1142-1100
CHRISTY

Thomas	25m	OH	labor
Jeremiah	30f	VA	
Jerome	7f		
William	1m		
HUGHES			
DeKalb	14m		

1143-1101
STEVENS

Hooper	39m	MD	carpntr
Emily	38f		
Hooper	14m		
Caroline	6f	KY	
Edwin	4m	VA	
Emma	3/12f		

1144-1102
LACY

David R.	62m	VA	brickms
Eustacia	50f		

1145-1103
CHRISTY

Abraham	26m	VA	labor
Catherine	19f		
Susan	2f		

1146-1104
CHRISLIP

A. R.	34m	Va	ministr
Martha	32f		
Mary	13f		

1146-1104 CHRISLIP(con't)

Solome	11f		
Eugenia	1f		

1147-1105
CALDWELL

Wm. H.	25m	OH	farmer
Elizabeth	27f	VA	
Nangasett	1f		

1148-1106
THOMPSON

Wm.	28m	VA	farmer
THOMPSON			
Winnie	70f		
Mary	23f		

1149-1107
WILLIAMSON

John	27m	VA	ministr
S. O.	24f		
Emma	3f		
BLOM			
Nancy A.	18f	OH	dom

1150-1108
MICHAEL

Wm.	40m	VA	farmer
Polly	38f		
John	18m	OH	
David	16m		
Daniel	15m		
Sarah	13f		
Elizabeth	11f		
Melissa	8f		
Andrews	7m		

1151-1109
BLAKE

Morris	44m	VA	farmer
Telitha	37f		
Wm. H.	19m		farmer
Julia	17f		teacher
Mary	15f		
Sarah	10f		
Clarissa	8f		
John M.	6m		
Lucetta	4f		

1151-1109 BLAKE (con't)
    Daniel   2m
    Nancy   2/12f
1152-1110
  HARMON
    Edmund   40m VA labor
    Jane   30f
    Virginia   2f
    Henry J.   8/12m OH
    George W. 8/12m OH
1153-1111
  SPURLOCK
    Jesse   45m VA farmer
    Margaret   39f
    Simeon   17m   farmer
    Thomas B. 11m
    John M.   9m
1154-1112
  SPURLOCK
    Harvey   47m VA farmer
    Elizabeth 45f
    James H.   17m   farmer
    Levi   15m
    David   13m
    Charles   10m
    Jesse   6m
1155-1113
  SPURLOCK
    Thomas   49m VA farmer
    Catherine 25f PA
    Wm.   8m VA
    Leonora   5f
    Sarah   3f
    Ira   4/12m
  SPURLOCK
    Eliza   16f
    Daniel A.   5m
1156-1114
  KNIGHT
    Susan   29f VA
    Eliza   6f
    Abagail   4f

1157-1115
  HOUCHINS
    Frances   31m VA farmer
    Rebecca   27f
    James H.   5m
    Wm.F.   3m
    Mary A.   1f
1158-1116
  BOWEN
    Sarah   53f VA
    Jefferson 22m
    Isaiah   18m   farmer
1159-1117
  BOWEN
    Ezekiel   37m VA farmer
    Ann   33f
    Wm. H.   8m
    Missouri   7f
    Charles   5m
    Albert   3m
    Thomas J. 8/12m
1160-1118
  SPURLOCK
    Daniel   74m VA farmer
    Stephen   33m   farmer
    Jane   34f
    Elizabeth 13f
    William   11m
    Sarah   9f
    Abner   6m
    Nancy   9/12f
1161-1119
  PERRY
    John   55m NC carpntr
    Lucy   54f
    Wm.W.   29m   farmer
    Eliza   23f VA
    John H.   7m
    Susan   5f
    Lucy   3f
    Albert   10/12m

1162-1120
  PERRY
    Wm.   65m NC farmer
    Nancy   39f VA
1163-1121
  BRYANT
    Lawrence   40m VA farmer
    Mary   33f
    Wm.P.   14m
    Mary A.   12f
    Theresa   10f
    John H.   7m
    Parthenia   6f
    Adaline   5f
    Nimrod   3m
  PINCHIN
    Elizabeth   17f ENG dom
1164-1122
  WHITE
    James H.   30m VA farmer
    Eustacia   40f
    Sarah   10f
    Catherine   7f
    John   3m
    Nimrod   1m
1165-1123
  BRYANT
    Nimrod   38m VA farmer
    Nancy   34f
    Matilda   12f
    Catherine   10f
    Gabriel   8m
    Jefferson   6m
    Mary   4f
    Julia   10/12f
1166-1124
  SMITH
    Jacob   25m VA labor
    Matilda   25f KY
    Mary   5f VA
    Lawrence   3m
    John   1m

1166-1124 SMITH (con't)
  FOX
    James   13m KY
    Wm. J.   8m
1167-1125
  AMOS
    Joshua   37m OH farmer
    Mary   32f VA
    Wm. P.   11m
    Sarah C.   4f
    Mary F.   10/12f
  CREMEANS
    Sarah   78f
1168-1126
  HOLLY
    Moses   22m Va farmer
    Eveline   27f
  DORAN
    Mary   5f
1169-1127
  RIGGS
    Cecelia   58f VA
    Elizabeth   21f
    Esom   16m
    Albert   13m
    Jefferson   10m
    Francis   8f
1170-1128
  JENNINGS
    Saml. R.   58m VA doctor
    Mary   62f ENG
  SIDEBOTTOM
    John C.   19m VA farmer
1171-1129
  QUINTIN
    James M.   34m VA
    Calpernia   27f
    Mahala   7f
    Ahaz   6m
    Mary   4f
    Elizabeth   1f
    Frances   62f
    Caroline   32f
1172-------------------End Greenbottom

Mud Bridge Post Office (Milton)
1173-1130
    GARRETT
        James   62m VA farmer
        Margaret   40f
        John H.   23m
        Robert   21m
        Albert   19m
        Alexander   17m
        Virginia   15f
        Jeremiah   14m
        Andrew   6m
    WILLIAMS
        Saml.   35m VA doctor
    STONE
        Rebecca   70f
1174-1131
    ROBERTS
        Jones   48m VA farmer
        Nancy   34f
        Columbus   13m
        Sampson   10m
        James   8m
        Mary   6f
        Sarah   4f
        Minerva   2f
    DAVIS
        Elizabeth   13f
    ASHWORTH
        Michael   34m VA labor
1175-1132
    ASHWORTH
        Thomas   30m Va farmer
        Julia   27f
        Mary   3f
        James   1m
1176-1133
    BURNS
        Andrew   36m VA farmer
        Mary   28f
        Janthe   7f
        Elizabeth   5f
        Henry   2m
        Mary   5/12f

1176-1133 BURNS (con't)
    BURNS
        Nancy   69f
1177-1134
    BURNS
        Peter   41m VA farmer
        Ruth   36f
        Robinson   11m
        John   9m
        Lafayette   7m
        Virginia   5f
        Wm.S.   3/12m
    BURNS
        Fredrick   14m
        Venila   12f
1178-1135
    JORDAN
        A.H.   28m VA shoemkr
        Celicia   23f
        Celicia Jr. 6f
        Lucy   3f
1179-1136
    BROWN
        Thomas   53m VA farmer
        Mary   53f SC
        John   24m   farmer
        George   22m   farmer
        Mary   17f
    BROWN
        James   79m PA farmer
        Mary   82f PA
1180-1137
    WHEELER
        William   68m VA farmer
        Peggy   26f
1181-1138
    NICHOLAS
        John S.   58m VA farmer
        Lucinda   47f
        James   19m
        Calahill   16m
        Preston   14m
        Ahaz   11m
        Francis   8m

1181-1138 NICHOLAS (con't)
  NICHOLAS
    John A.   22m   labor
1182-1139
  PORTER
    William   55m VA farmer
    Sarah   31f   (2nd w?)
    Sarah   27f
    Emily   14f
    Matilda   12f
    Martha   10f
    William   8m
    Allbert   8m
    Nancy   6f
    Jessee   3m
    Edney   6/12f
1183-1140
  REYNOLDS
    Peter   24m VA farmer
    Ruth   22f
    John   1m
1184-1141
  WHEELER
    Zach.   23m VA labor
    Hansley   29f
1185-1142
  CHAPMAN
    Eli   30m VA farmer
    Armilda   30f
    Jennetta   7f
    Charles   5m
    Henry   3m
1186-1143
  BROWN
    James H.   29m VA farmer
    Louisa   24f
    Joseph   2m
    Lucinda   1f
  McCOMAS
    Elizabeth   15f
1187-1144
  WHEELER
    Reason   40m VA farmer
    Mary   31f

1187-1144 WHEELER (con't)
    Lucinda   9f
    John   8m
    Louisa   3f
1188-1145
  JEFFERSON
    Wm.   28m VA farmer
    Rhoda   26f
    Louisa   6f
    German   2m
    William   2/12m
  CHAPMAN
    William   28m   farmer
1189-1146
  WILLIAMS
    Mourning   68f VA
    Nancy   45f
  HOLTEN
    Nancy   13f
1190-1147
  BLEDSOE
    Moses   22m VA farmer
    Louisa   19f
    Susan   3f
    Mary   11/12f
  HOLTEN
    Rachel   7f
1191-1148
  MORRISON
    Washington   44m VA farmer
    Margaret   43f (33?)
    James L.   19m   farmer
    Patrick   18m   farmer
    John   14m
    Eliza A.   13f
    Emily   9f
    Benjamin   7m
    Catherine   5f
    Wilson   1m
  MORRISON
    Wm.W.   21m   labor
    Sarah   19f
    Thomas   8/12m
(number change)

118

1191-1149
  BALL
    Henry   60m Va farmer
    Telitha   50f
    John D.   8m
    Henry   6m
    Edney   4f
    Charles   3m
    Randolph   3/12m

1192-1150
  CONNER
    Wm.   93m NC farmer
    Susan   85f

1193-1151
  BLACK
    Andrew   34m VA farmer
    Lucinda   24f
    Araminta   8f
    John   4m

1194-1152
  KEYTON
    William   31m Va farmer
    Mary   40f
    Wm.H.   8m
    John W.   7m
    Lucinda   1f

1195--1153
  CHAPMAN
    German   23m VA farmer
    Ellender   20f
    Charles   9/12m

1196-1154
  JORDAN
    Saml. J.   23m VA farmer
    Jane   24f
    Madison   3m
    Charles   2m

1197-1155
  KEYTON
    Riland   58m VA farmer
    Lucinda   54f
    Preston   18m   farmer
    Henry   17m   farmer
    John L.   15m

1197-1155 KEYTON (con't)
    Adaline   12f
    Amanda   10f
    Armilda   6f

1198-1156
  CHAPMAN
    John   65m VA farmer
    Lucy   62f
    Araminta   44f
    Martha   21f
    Albert   16m
    Lucy   7f
  COOK
    Peter   39m VA labor

1199-1157
  JOHNSON
    H. M.   34m VA farmer
    Ann   26f
    Josiah   10m
    Theodore   8m
    May   6m
    Leonidas   3m
    Grace   6/12f
  HANDLEY
    Jackson   13m
    Bonaparte 13m

1200-1158
  BECKET
    Moses   60m VA farmer
    Mary   39f
    Julia   10f
    Josiah   7m
    Susan   5f
    Wm.C.   3m
  BECKET
    Charles   26m VA labor

1201-1159
  WOODWARD
    Wm.   60m VA farmer
    Henrietta 51f
    Mary   15f
    William   11m
    Matthew   9m

1201-1159 WOODWARD (con't)		
Martha	7f	
John	6m	
1202-1160		
CHAPMAN		
Harrison	39m	VA farmer
Julia	32f	
Nelsina	14f	
Ellen	12f	
William	10m	
Malinda	8f	
Henrietta	5f	
Charles	10/12m	
1203-1161		
JOHNSON		
Madison	48m	VA farmer
Martha	43f	
Eugenia	22f	
Almedia	19f	
Elizabeth	17f	
Warren	15m	
James M.	13m	
Wm. M.	7m	
1204-1162		
BARKER		
Wm.R.	24m	VA farmer
Martha	27f	
CHAPMAN		
Phoebe	40f	
Tazewell	22m	
1205-1163		
TEMPLETON		
James	96m	VA farmer
Anna	65f	
1206-1164		
CURRY		
Franklin	49m	VA farmer
Sophia	47f	
Sarah A.	15f	
John C.	14m	
Laura	8f	
Joseph	7m	

1207-1165		
CONNER		
Michael	59m	VA labor
Amy	22f	
1208-1166		
MORRIS		
John	66m	farmer
Mary	69f	
Armstead	63m	farmer
Charles	8m	
PEDRO		
S.M.	26m	VA carpntr
1209-1167		
HEREFORD		
B. G.	31m	VA labor
Mary	25f	
Virginia	8f	
Ellen	5f	
Robert	2m	
1210-1168		
ARTHUR		
F. T.	55m	VA blacksm
Jane	41f	
Sarah	15f	
Missouri	10f	
Nathaniel	9m	
Jessee	7m	
Hugh	5m	
John W.	1m	
STNY (Stiry-Stivy)		
Mary	16f	OH
1211-1169		
TEMPELTON		
Harvey	41m	VA labor
Mary	41f	
John	18m	labor
Ransom	16m	labor
Isaac	14m	
Esom	12m	
William	10m	
Mary E.	9f	
Lucinda	7f	
Addison	5m	
Charles	2m	

120

1212-1170
  McCALLISTER
    Joseph   41m VA farmer
    Eliza   32f
    Jackson   14m
    Hamilton   9m
    John   6m
    Patrick   4m
    Nancy   1f
1213-1171
  MARTIN
    Wm.   21m VA farmer
    Susan   28f
1214-1172
  MARTIN
    James   28m VA farmer
    Martha   29f
    Calvin   1m
1215-1173
  NIMO
    Wm.   50m VA carpntr
    Susan   41f
    Mary   15f
    Wm. H.   7m
    Sarah   4f
    Charles   1m
  SPENCER
    James   64m VA blacksm
1216-1174
  MORRIS
    Joseph W.   35m VA
    Sarah   37f
    John   15m
    Mary   12f
    Helen   10f
    Edney   3f
  RYAN
    Thomas   46m IRE labor
1217-1175
  McCALLISTER
    Malcom   46m VA farmer
    Sarah   38f
    Henry   19m   farmer
    Edney   16f

1217-1175 McCALLISTER (con't)
    Margery   14f
    Elizabeth   12f
    Edgar   10m
1218-1176
  McCALLISTER
    Olivia   50f VA
    Allen   30m
1219-1177
  McCALLISTER
    Isaac   19m VA farmer
    Mary   19f
1220-1178
  SMALLRIDGE
    John W.   33m VA labor
    Elizabeth   24f
    John   4m
    James   3m
  SMALLRIDGE
    Sampson   33m   labor
1221-1179
  GIBSON
    Burwell   70m VA labor
    Elizabeth   50f
    William   20m   labor
    Martha   17f
    Sarah   15f OH
    Elizabeth   9f
1222-1180
  ROBERTS
    Henry   61m VA farmer
    Elilzabeth 54f
    Bartholomew 51m   farmer
1223-1181
  BILLUPS
    James   21m VA laobr
    Ann   20f
    Mary J.   7/12f
1224-1182
  REYNOLDS
    James   57m Va farmer
    Jane   57f
    James   18m   farmer

1224-1182 REYNOLDS (con't)
  HACKWORTH
    George   25m KY clerk
1225-1183
  SPENCER
    Ann E.   38f VA
    Mary J.   7f
    James   5m
1226-1184
  BRANNON
    Peter   35m IRE labor
    Catherine 29f
    Michael   8m IN
    Mary   7f VA
    John   3m
    Peter   1m
    Catherine 3/12f
1227-1185
  BROWN
    George   44m VA blacksm
    Alleghany 49f
    James   18m   farmer
    John   17m   farmer
    Wm.   15m
    Lucretia 14f
    Robert   8m
    Sarah   5f
  McCOMAS
    Eliza   18f
1228-1186
  HARSHBARGER
    Jacob   46m VA farmer
    Elizabeth 41f
    Peter   18m   farmer
    Henry   14m
    Eliza   12f
    Joseph W. 10m
    Charles   5m
    William   3m
1229-1187
  ROSE
    George   29m VA labor
    Cynthia   25f
    Malinda   5f

1229-1187 ROSE (con't)
    Mary   3f
    Sarah   2f
  CHAPMAN
    Polly   40f
1230-1188
  RECE
    John M.   47m VA mercht
    Miram   34f
    Joseph L. 16m   clerk
    Mary   3f
1231-1189
  CURRY
    Harrison 22m VA labor
    Martha   21f
1232-1190
  RECE
    Abia   76m VA farmer
    Elizabeth 74f
    Warren P. 38m   farmer
    Madira   10f
  JARRETT
    Martha   65f
  MORRISON
    David   60m   labor
1233-1191
  SMITH
    Traverse 36m VA farmer
    Harriett 18f
    James   1m
  LAKEMAN
    Jane   35f
1234-1192
  RECE
    Thomas H. 49m VA farmer
    Martha   40f
    Calvin   20m   farmer
    James   18m   farmer
    Georgia   4f
1235-1193
  RECE
    Addison   31m VA blacksm
    Amellia   24f
    Leonard   2m

1236-1194
  RECE
      Edmund   49m VA carpntr
      Sophia   47f
      Alice   15f
      Theodore   13m
1237-1195
  BLACKWOOD
      Joseph   29m Va farmer
      Adaline   21f
      Charles   3m
      James   1m
  WADE
      Jesse   18m   labor
1238-1196
  PARSLEY
      Richard   39m VA labor
      Bridget   39f IRE
      Daniel   10m VA
      John   9m
      Franklin   7m
      Mary   6f
      Sarah   3f
      Nathaniel   G. 5/12m
1239-1197
  SNAPP
      William   27m VA labor
      Lucy   26f
      Melissa   6f
      Celicia   2f
      Mary   2/12f
1240-1198
  TEMPLETON
      Jessee   34m VA farmer
      Sarah   27f
      Wm. H.   10m
      Julia   8f
      John   7m
      Martin   5m
      Charles   3m
      Frances   2f
      Thomas   3/12m

1241-1199
  LEGG
      Willis   40m VA farmer
      Rebecca   30f
      John H.   12m
      Eli   9m
      Addison   4m KY
      Thomas   3m VA
      Charles   4/12m
1242-1200
  ANGEL
      Washington 37m VA farmer
      Louisa   37f
      Charles   5m
      Fanny   3f
1243-1201
  LEGG
      Thomas   25m VA farmer
      Elizabeth   24f
      Allen   4m
  LEGG
      Vileta   60f
1244-1202
  CREMANS
      John   26m VA farmer
      Julia   18f
1245-1203
  CREMANS
      Nathan   46m VA farmer
      Elizabeth   48f
      Nathan   22m   farmer
      Mary   15f
      Martha S.   13f
      John W.   9m
      Sarah C.   7f   OH
1246-1204
  CARROLL
      Saml.   43m VA farmer
      Lucinda   38f
      Isabella   20f
      Charles T. 18m   farmer
      Nancy   16f
      Mary   13f
      Betsey   10f

1246-1204 CARROLL (con't)
    Naoma   6f
    Henry B.   4m
1247-105
  CHAPMAN
    Sampson   27m VA farmer
    Malinda   25f
    Joseph   2m
    James   1m
1248-1206
  ESTES
    James   38m VA farmer
    Elizabeth 30f
    Virginia   11f
    John M.   3m
    Edney   3/12f
1249-1207
  LUNCEFORD
    Joshua   44mf
    Sarah   40f
    Susan   20f
    Wm. T.   19f   farmer
    Mary E.   15f
    George W. 11m
    John   9m
    Peter   6m
    Hugh M.   9/12m
1250-1208
  WALLACE
    Benjamin 76m VA farmer
    Letta   64f
    Jessee   30m   farmer
  FORTH
    Elizabeth 39f
    William   16m
    Mahala   12f
    Hugh   7m AR
    Frances   5f AR
    Martha   3f AR
    Mary   1f AR
1251-1209
  WALLACE
    Thenia   45f VA
    Peggy   18f

1251-1209 WALLACE (con't)
    Betha   16f
1252-1210
  WALLACE
    Edmund   36m Va farmer
    Mary   31f
    Susan   13f
    Charles   10m
    America   8f
    Abagail   7f
    Mary   6f
    Missouri   3f
    Sarah   2f
1253-1211
  CHAPMAN
    James   21m VA farmer
    Mary   21f
    Elizabeth 7/12f
  SMITH
    Rebecca   18f
1254-1212
  WALLACE
    Henry M.   24m VA farmer
    Naoma   23f
    Georgia   1f
1255-1213
  CONNER
    James   54m VA labor
    Levina   48f
    Abagail   17f
    Samanthia 16f
    John M.   14m
    James   8m
1256-1214
  SMITH
    John W.   49m VA farmer
    Margaret   30f
    Wm.H.   11m
    Victoria   9f
    Mary   4f
1257-1215
  CONNER
    Addison   25m VA farmer
    Emaretta 23f

124

1258-1216
 DEAL
   Henry H.   45m Va farmer
   Lucy   50f
   John   23m   farmer
   Ebenzer   20m   farmer
   Cadmus   18m   farmer
   Martha   13f
1259-1217
 SMITH
   Thomas   76m Va farmer
   Polly   76f
 BLACK
   Elizabeth   12f
1260-1218
 PARISH
   James   43m Va farmer
   Julia   43f
   Mary C.   17f
   Frances M.   15m
   Elizabeth   8f
   Julia   4f
   Millard F.   3m
 SMITH
   Barbary   41f   milliner
   Virginia   8f
   Isadore   5f
1261-1219
 BILLUPS
   Mary   44f VA
   Charles   14m
   Louisa   3f
1262-1220
 GIBSON
   Thomas   39m VA farmer
   Sarah   42f
   Nancy A.   14f
   Andrew   8m
1263-1221
 CURRY
   Timothy   23m VA farmer
   Mary   24f
   John   3m
   Sophia   1f

1263-1221 CURRY (con't)
 CURRY
   Harrison   20m   labor
   Martha   23f
1264-1222
 CHAPMAN
   Milton   23m VA farmer
   Mary   16f
   William   3/12m
1265-1223
 SUMMERS
   George W.   48m Va farmer
   Sarah   46f
   Sylvester   22m   farmer
   Constantine   18m   farmer
   Edgar   16m   farmer
   Thomas B.   13m
   Tyre C.   11m
   Matthew   8m
 CURRY
   Mayberry   21m   labor
1266-1224
 PAINE
   Charles W.   29m VA teacher
   Margaret   23f OH
   William   3m VA
   Ellen   1f
1267-1225
 JORDAN
   Wm.   45m VA farmer
   Esther   45f
   Andrew J.   20m   labor
   Mary   18f
   Linda   16f
   John   14m
   Henry   13m
   Sarah   8f
   Morris   6m
   Abraham   3m
1268-1226
 FORTH
   Wm.J.   24m VA farmer
   Louisa   26f
   Andrew   4m

1268-1226 FORTH (con't)			
Charles	3m		
1269-1227			
BRYANT			
W. P.	26m	VA	farmer
Eveline	20f		
Anna	11/12f		
1270-1228			
KINNARD			
Howard	54m	Va	famer
Nancy	49f		
Ephraim	23m		labor
Wm.H.	22m		labor
George R.	20m		labor
Joseph	16m		labor
Harriett	13f		
Jane	11f		
Ann	6f		
Margaret	6f		
1271-1229			
BALL			
Isaac M.	57m	Va	farmer
Susan	26f		
Francis M.	21m		farmer
Calvin	6m		
Conwesley	5m		
George W.	1m		
1272-1230			
CHAPMAN			
William	60m	Va	farmer
Elizabeth	49f		
Nehemiah	17m		farmer
Martha	15f		
Minerva	13f		
America	11f		
James	9m		
Sarah	7f		
Joseph	5m		
1273-1231			
Davis			
John	30m	VA	
Sarah	35f		
George	1m		
Sarah	8/12f		

1274-1232			
BECKETT			
Emsley	28m	Va	shoemkr
Mary S.	21f		
John H.	4m		
Louisa	3f		
James	2m		
Rebecca	2/12f		
CHAPMAN			
Albert	17m		labor
1275-1233			
JORDAN			
Andrew	75m	VA	farmer
Mary	75f		
Mary	35f		
1276-1234			
SMITH			
Daniel P.	54m	Va	farmer
Eliza A.	24f		
Joshua	19m		labor
Charles	18m		labor
Catherine	16f		
Sarah	12f		
Elijah	11m		
Paulina	9f		
John C.	3m		
1277-1235			
KILLGORE			
Wm.	26m	Va	farmer
Rachel	24f		
George	4m		
Nancy	3f		
James	1m		
1278-1236			
ROBERTS			
Anderson	54m	Va	farmer
Jane	45f		
Dicey	22f		
Maurice	20m		
Nancy	17f		
John H.	15m		
Allen	14m		
Bradford	12m		
William M.	9m		

1278-1236 ROBERTS (con't)
    JORDAN
      Abagail   40f
      George A.   9m
1279-1237
    RECE
      James H.   48m VA farmer
      Rebecca   40f
      James   16m   farmer
      Martha   14f
      Thomas H. 13m
      Rebecca   11f
      Mary   5f
1280-1238
    REYNOLDS
      Griffin B.   60m VA labor
      Elizabeth   64f
1281-1239
    REYNOLDS
      Harden E.   25m VA labor
      Quintina   22f
    HUDSON
      Mary   5f
1282-1240
    GWINN
      Henry   29m VA faremr
      Ann E.   21f
      Edward   3m
      Joseph   1m
    NEWMAN
      Sarah   18f
      Henry   16m   labor
      James   15m
1283-1241
    KILLGORE
      Thomas   38m Va farmer
      Mary   32f
      Joseph   13m
      John   11m
      Charles   6m
      Marshall   4m
    KILGORE
      Nancy   63f

1282-1241 KILLOGRE (con't)
    POOR
      Francis   16f   dom

End Mud Bridge

Thorndyke Post Office
1284-1242
   GWINN

Andrew	63m	Va faremr	
Rachel	55f		
Wm.	22m		
Louisa	18f		
Emily	15f		
Jefferson	13m		

1285-1243
   GWINN

John	33m	VA farmer	
Hetty	30f		
Emma	7f		
Albert	5m		
Randolph	3/12m		

   SPENCER

Thomas	32m	labor	

1286-1244
   SANDERS

Isham	62m B VA labor	
Sarah	60f B	
Diana	15f B	

1287-1245
   POOR

Elisha	49m	VA farmer	
Tasey	49f		
Alfred	20m		farmer
Stephen	18m		farmer
Elias	9m		
Allen	8m		

1288-1246
   BRYANT

Jacob	55m	KY farmer	
Lucy	46f	VA	
John	17m		farmer
Sarah	16f		
Francis M.	13m		
Chapman M.	11m		
Marcellus	4m		

1289-1247
   McCOMAS

John	37m	Va farmer
Lucinda	34f	

1289-1247 McCOMAS (con't)

Benjamin	13m	
Mary	11f	
Wm.H.	7m	
Job	5m	
Julia	2f	

1290-1248
   MILLER

John M.	50m	VA farmer
Martha	40f	
Emily	16f	
James	14m	
Eliza	12f	
John M.	7m	
Jane	6f	

1291-1249
   CARTER

John W.	44m	VA farmer	
Nancy	43f		
William	18m		farmer
John D.	15m		
Salem	11m OH		
Albert	9m		
Matilda	7f		
Leonidas	2/12m VA		

   DEFOE

Rachel	16f	VA dom

1292-1250
   SHEFF

Andrew	59m	VA farmer
America	22f	
Caroline	33f	

   WILKES

Mary	17f	

1293-1251
   HODGE

Preston	45m	VA farmer
Ellis	35f	
Amanda	13f	
Theodore	12m	
Sarilda	11f	
Emily	9f	
Cynthia	7f	
Ellen	5f	

1293-1251 HODGE (con't)

    Leah   3f

    POTEET

    James   25m   labor

    PRICE

    Evin   38m   labor

1294-1252

    PEYTON

    Archibald 39m VA farmer

    Susan   28f

    Sarah   10f

    Mary   4f

    Emma   2f

    PEYTON

    Frances   20f

    TONEY

    John   8m

1295-1253

    LOVE

    William   78m VA farmer

    THOMAS

    Susan   16f

1296-1254

    BLACK

    Wm.   41m VA farmer

    Virginia   38f

    Isabella   16f

    Rufus   13m

    Ezra   10m

    John   6m

    Cynthia   3f

    Ann   1f

    BARKER

    John   20m   labor

1297-1255

    MILLER

    James   72m VA farmer

    Mary   70f

1298-1256

    STEPHENSON

    Abraham 50m Va farmer

    Mary   49f

    James   20m   farmer

    Wm. H.   10m

1298-1256 STEPHENSON (con't)

    POOR

    Mary J.   16f   dom

1299-1257

    POOR

    David   42m Va labor

    Eliza   26f

    Joseph L.   9m

    George W. 4m

    Sarah   2f

    Frances M. 11m

1300-1258

    THOMAS

    Susan   49f VA

    Mary   29f

    Nancy   15f

    David   9m

1301-1259

    SHEFF

    John H.   26m VA merchnt

    Mary   22f IL

    Joseph   2m VA

    Wm. A.   9/12m

1302-1260

    BLACK

    Wm.   36m VA farmer

    Elizabeth 28f

    George   12m MO

    Samantha 9f VA

    Amastis   7f

    Lowell   3m

    Theodore 1m

    BLACK

    Elizabeth 76f

1304-1261

    BALL

    Lafayette 27m VA farmer

    Mary   21f

    Josephus 2m

    William   8/12m

    BALL

    Jeremiah 23m   farmer

    Martha   19f

1305-1263
  MALCOMB
    John   50m VA farmer
    Ann   47f
    William   17m   farmer
    Bruce   15m
    Charles   13m
    Mary   12f
    Ellen   10f
    John   8m
    Martha   7f
1306-1264
  MALCOMB
    Margaret   45f
  NEWMAN
    James   8m
1307-1265
  DUFFY
    Patrick   32m IRE labor
    Martha   23f VA
    Mary   6f
    John B.   2m
1308-1266
  GWINN
    Washington 31m VA farmer
    Emasetta   25f
    Elizabeth   8f
    Sampson   5m
    Conwesley 3m
    Charles   2m
    Thomas   2/12m
  BALL
    Hetty   21f
  CONNER
    Lewis   25m   labor
1309-1267
  MALCOMB
    Edward   36m VA farmer
    Virginia   35f
    Joseph   7m
    Edward   5m
    Frances   3f
  NEWMAN
    Marcey   9f

1310-1268
  ROACH
    William H. 27m VA farmer
    Lovie   22f
    John   3m
    Mary   1f
1311-1269
  DOUGLAS
    Wm. H.   38m Va farmer
    Rachel   37f
    Mary   3f
  HOLTEN
    Elizabeth 9f
1312-1270
  FULLERTON
    Lewis   65m B VA farmer
1313-1271
  SHEFF
    George   30m VA farmer
    Margaret 26f
    Mary   6f
    Elisha   4m
    America   2f
1314-1272
  WOODWARD
    Hezekiah 31m VA farmer
    Sarah   35f
    Sarah Jr. 7f
    Angeline 5f
    John W.   3m
1315-1273
  TAYLOR
    Allen   46m VA farmer
    Esther   36f
    Margaret 14f
    Susan   5f
  YOUNG
    Susan   65f
1316-1274
  BECKETT
    Andrew L. 36m VA farmer
    Emily S. 30f
    Lewis L. 9m

1317-1275
  BECKETT
    Charles   33m VA farmer
    Susan   31f
    James   9m
    Samuel   6m AR
    Julia   5f AR
    John   3m VA
    Mary   1f
1318-1276
  BECKETT
    James   86m VA farmer
    Hannah   72f
  McCALLISTER
    Lucinda   38f
    Adaline   12f
1319-1277
  YATES
    William B.   38m VA farmer
    Rebecca   32f
    Lucretia   11f
    Ezra   10m
    Julia   4f
    Mary E.R. 3/12f
1320-1278
  BIAS
    Reuben   47m VA farmer
    Malinda   36f
    Lucy   17f
    Eliza   8f
1321-1279
  BARKER
    John   64m VA farmer
    Dicey   50f
1322-1280
  CHAPMAN
    Greenberry   37m VA farmer
    Lucy   37f
    William   18m   labor
    Sophia   16f
    Nancy   14f
    John   9m
    James   7m
    Washington   6m

1322-1280 CHAPMAN(con't)
    Charles   2m
1323-1281
  BEECH
    James   47m VA farmer
    Jane   30f
    Mary   16f
    Caroline   13f
    William   12m
    John H.   11m
    Eliza   9f
    Elizabeth   8f
    Sarah   6f
    James   4m
  SPENCER
    William   29m VA labor
1324-1282
  DENNISON
    John   45m ENG farmer
    Mahala   36f VA
    John   14m ENG
    Mary   8f   VA
    George   6m
    Margaret   5f
    Jane   4f
    Jennetta   2f
1325-1283
  HANDLEY
    Wm. A.   23m VA blacksm
    Adaline   18f
  CREMANS
    Julia   16f
1326-1284
  MAUPIN
    Chapman   49m VA farmer
    Matilda   35f KY
    Frances   14f VA
    Thomas   12m
    Lucy   10f
    Albert B.   8m
    Mary   6f
    Shelby   3m
  MAUPIN
    Margaret   80f

1326-1284 MAUPIN (con't)
BUCKNER
  J.A.   24m VA teacher
1327-1285
McDONIE
  James   26m PA farmer
  Mary   24f VA
  Wm.C.   3m
  Charles B. 4/12m
1328-1286
MAUPIN
  Beverly   52m VA farmer
  Juliet   34f
  William   23m
  Henry   18m
  Adaline   16f
1329-1287
LOVE
  Daniel   62m VA farmer
  Cynthia   59f KY
  Leonidas 16m VA
  Theodosius 13m
1330-1288
THORNBURG
  Moses   60m VA farmer
  Caroline 32f
  Sarah   7f
  Elizabeth 4f
  Sampson H. 8/12m
1331-1289
DOOLITTLE
  Luther   49m NY farmer
  Amanda   35f VA
  Ambrose 11f
  Alice   8f OH
  Virginia 4f VA
  Cedora   7/12f
HARSHBARGER
  William   14m
1332-1290
WHITE
  Peter   35m HOL sawyer
  Mary   30f VA
  Emma   5f

1332-1290 WHITE (con't)
BLACKWOOD
  Sarah   19f
1333-1291
HOWELL
  A.B.   50m VA miller
  Frances 55f
SMITH
  Martha   18f
DEIHL
  Catherine 16f
WOODWARD
  James   16m labor
1334-1292
SHEFF
  James   30m VA farmer
  Caroline 27f ENG
  Elizabeth 3/12f VA
1335-1293
ARTHUR
  Thomas   25m VA farmer
  Mary   15f
  Ann   1f
1336-1294
ADAMS
  William   45m VA farmer
  Elizabeth 50f
  Francis M. 11m
1337-1295
ARTHUR
  Washington 25m VA labor
  Julia   25f
  Mary A.   1f
1338-1296
DAVIS
  Saml. H. 32m VA farmer
  America 32f
  Thomas   13m
  Joseph   11m
  Nancy   9f
  Allen   6m
  Licia   3f

1339-1297
  WHITE
    Zach.   50m VA farmer
    Lucy   59f
    Jane   19f
    Mary   19f
    Theresa   16f
    Moses   14m
1340-1298
  CONNER
    Andrew   53m VA farmer
    Mildred   53f
    Premelia   18f
    Conwelsey   17m   farmer
    Joseph   14m
1341-1299
  DAVIS
    Sterling   46m VA farmer
    Elizabeth   44f
    Addison   20m   farmer
    Martha   18f
    Charles   14m
    Jessee   12m
    Sarah   9f
    Mary   5f
1342-1300
  TAYLOR
    George   23m
    Eveline   22f
  ARTHUR
    Cynthia   20f
    Theresa   13f

End Thorndyke

1860 Slave Schedule

(no names given)

owner-age-sex-color

HOLDERBY, Susan

60m B	8m B
35f B	9f B
33m B	12f B
30f B	7m B
27f B	6m B
19m B	5f B
21f B	5f B
16f B	4m B
13f B	3f B
12f B	6/12f B
10f B	
total 21	

WILLIAMS, Wm.

33f B	10m M
26f B	8m B
25m B	7f B
16f B	6m B
16f B	3m B
14m M	1m M
13f M	1m B
12m B	
total 15	

THORNBURG, Thomas

30m B
17f M
2m M
2/12m M
total 4

MORRRIS, John

67m B	19f B
35m B	12m M
23m B	8f B
23m B	6f M
21f B	6f M
19m B	4f B
total 12	

GARRETT, James

50m B	6m B
37f B	4f B
20f B	4m B
14m B	1m B
8m M	
total 9	

GWINN, Andrew

45f B	16f B
30m B	9m M
23f B	8m B
20m B	3f B
18m B	
total 9	

BUFFINGTON, P.C.

45f B	9f M
45f B	7f M
25f B	4f M
15m B	3f M
10m B	
total 9	

JOHNSON, Merritt

6f B

MILLER, John G.

27m B	9m B
23f M	5m B
14f M	2m M
9m M	2/12m M
total 8	

EVERETT, T.W.

60m B	5m B
42m B	3m B
30f B	1m B
8f B	
total 7	

EVERETT, John

58m B	32f B
52m M	3m B
35m M	1f M
total 6	

B=black   M=mulatto

HITE,John W.
    14f M   8m M
    12f M   6m M
    10f M   4m M
       total 6

FRAMPTON,David
    50m M
    50f M
    9f M
    6m M
    3f M

WATSON,Virginia
    50f B   16m M
    30f B   12f M
    20f M   10m M

SHELTON,James
    9f B

RICKETTS,Elijah
    57m M
    20f M
    18m B
    16f M
    11f M

BUFFINGTON,John
    40f B
    15f B
    12m B
    3f B

MORRIS,Charles
    45f B
    20m M
    15m M
    13f B

RECE,Abia
    25m B
    23f B
    20m B
    18f B
    13m B

BUFFINGTON,Nancy
    25f B   30m B
    24m B   30f B
    60m B   15m B
    60f B

STEWART,Robert
    23f B
    21m B
    19f B
    19f B
    5m B

WILSON,James
    26f B
    23m B
    18m B

WRIGHT,Edward
    30f M
    8m M
    3m M

THORNBURG,John W.
    60f B
    27m B
    8f M

McCOMAS,Wm.
    16m B
    14m B
    12f B

MORRIS,James B.
    30f B
    4f B
    2f B

SAMUELS,Henry J.
    65f M
    30m B
    7f M

CHAPMAN,A. P.
    45f M
    6m M
    1f M

McCORKLE, A.M.
    21m M
    17m B

MILLER,Henry H.
    21f M
    12f M
    1f M

1860 Cabell County Slaves
Owners name only - Slaves listed by age, sex, color

#Census Household/ owner

#15-15 - Henry J. Samuels
   65f M
   30m B
   7f M
#33-33 - John Samuels
   30f B
   2f B
#36-36 - W. B. Moore
   35m M
#37-37 - Mary Moore
   50f B
   16m M
#45-45 - William Merritt
   50f B
#53-52 - Arnold Westhoff
   40f B
   19m M
#54-53 - Albert Beckner
   45m B
57-56 - Henry B. Maupin
   47f B
   10m B
#58-57 - John G. Miller
   27m B
   23f M
   14f M
   9m M
   9m B
   5m B
   2m M
   2/12m M
#59-58 - William C. Miller
   26m M
   3f M
#61-59 -Thomas Thornburg
   30m B
   17f M
   2m M
   2/12m M
#66-63 - William McComas
   16m B
   14m B
   12f B
#67-64 - James B. Morris
   30f B
   4f B
   2f B
#75-72 - Sarah Blake
   16m B
   6f B

#98-95 - R.S. Bias
   19m B
#106-103 - James Shelton
   9f B
#151-148 - Virginia Watson
   50f B
   30f B
   20f M
   16m M
   12f M
   10m M
#227-219 - Henry W. Shelton
   50m M
   25f B
#230-222 John W. Thornburg
   60f B
   27m B
   8f M
#230-222 - James Everett
   29f M
   9f M
#231-223 - Elizabeth Griffin
   27f B
#308-297 - A. M. McCorkle
   21m M
   17m B
#331-320 - Charles Morris
   45f B
   20m M
   15m M
   13f B
#374-363 - C.L. Roffe
   40f B
   40f B
   14f B
   13m B
   8f B
   7m B
   4m B
#374-363 - Susan Shelton
   42m B
   40f B
   37m B
   30f B
   26m B
   19m B
   10m B
   7m B
#378-367 - Augustus Wolcott
   60f B

#381-370 - J.T. Dusenberry
   20f B
   6m B
#386-375 - A. P. Chapman
   45f M
   6m M
   1f M
#398-386 - John W. Hite
   14f M
   12f M
   10f M
   8m M
   6m M
   4m M
#401-389 - Elijah Ricketts
   57m M
   20f M
   18m M
   16f M
   11f M
#402-390 - William Hite
   38f B
   13m M
#422-410 - P.S. Smith
   45f B
   20f B
   19m B
#423-411 - Grace Stone
   40f B
#424-412 -William C. Rodgers
   13f B
#425-413 - E.H. Walton
   21f M
   5f M
   4f M
#444-431 - S.M. Clark
   50f B
#451-438 - A.B. McGinnis
   33m M
   27m M
#453-440 - John Everett
   58m B
   52m M
   35m M
   32f B
   3m B
   1f M
#473-459-Jas. H. Buffington
   17f M
   11f M
   9m B

34

#Census Household/ owner

#474-460 - P.C. Buffington
45f B
45f B
25f B
15m B
10m B
9f M
7f M
4f M
3f M
*   13m M (in trust
*   11m M for heirs)
#475-461 - Nancy Buffington
25f B
24m B
60m B
60f B
30m B
30f B
15m B
#476-462 - William H. Hagan
18f B
5f M
#477-463 - John Buffington
40f B
15f B
12m B
3f B
#493-479 - Robert Stewart
23f B
21m B
19f B
19f B
5m B
#497-483 - John Harden
16f M
#499-485 - John C. Rece
19f B
18m B
#501-487 - T.W. Everett
60m B
42m B
30f B
9f B
5m B
3m B
1m B
#503-489 - B.B.Burks
18f B
#504-490 - James H. Poage
13f B
#541-525 - James Thornburg
23m M
6f B

#548-532 - David Frampton
50m M
50f M
9f M
6m M
3f M
#550-534 - William Williams
33f B
26f B
25m B
16f B
16f B
14m M
13f M
12m B
10m M
8m B
7f B
6m B
3m B
1m M
1m B
#658-636 - Charles Everett
33f M
8f B
4f B
1f B
#621-601 - Henry H. Miller
21f M
12f M
1f M
(in trust for Sarah Holderby)
26m M
10m M
6f M
#641-619 - James Wilson
26f B
23m B
18m B
#646-624 - Edward Wright
30f M
8m M
3m M
#661-639 - Susan Holderby
60m B
35f B
33m B
30f B
27f B
19m B
21f B
16f B
13f B
12f B
10f B
8m B

#661-639 (con't)
9f B
12f B
7m B
6m B
5f B
5f B
4m B
3f B
6/12f B
#662-640 - John Everett
46m B
#791-759 - Merritt Johnson
6f B
#847-813- Archibald Reynolds
45f B
25m B
22f B
21f B
7f B
#848-814 - John E. Morrison
18f B
#872-837 - Sarah Porter
46f B
24f M
#976-936 - Phillip Powell
50m B
42f B
4m B
#1144-1102 - David Lacy
32f B
16f M
13f M
6m B
2f B
#1160-1118 - Daniel Spurlock
46m B
#1173-1130 - James Garrett
50m B
37f B
20f B
14m B
8m M
6m B
4f B
4m B
1m B
#1208-1166 - John Morris
67m B
35m B
23m B
23m B
21f B
19m B
19f B
12m M

#Census Household/ owner

#1208-1166 (con't)
    8f B
    6f M
    6f M
    4f B
#1217-1175 -
    Malcolm McCallister
    32f B
    31f B
    16m B
    8f B
    3f B
1228-1186
    David Harshbarger
    50m B
#1230-1188 - John M. Rece
    18m B
    15f B
#1232-1190 - Abia Rece
    25m B
    23f B
    20m B
    18f B
    13m B
#1236-1194 - Edmund Rece
    12f B
#1265-1223- George Summers
    26m B
    22f B
#1283-1241-Thos. W. Killgore
    35f B
    25m B
    11f B
    9f B
    6f B
    5f B
    1m B
#1283-1241 - Nancy Killgore
    40f B
    20m B
    13m B
#1284-1242 - Andrew Gwinn
    45f B
    30m B
    23f B
    20m B
    18m B
    16f B
    9m M
    8m B
    3f B
#1285-1243 - John Gwinn
    15f B

#1290-1848 - John M. Miller
    22m B
#1295-1253 - William Love
    46f M
    18m B
    15f B
    7f M
    5f B
#1296-1254 - William Black
    (employer)
    Thomas Summers(owner)
    22m B
#1302-1260 - Elizabeth Black
    50f B
    35f B
#1308-1266 -
    Washington Gwinn
    10f B
1326-1284- Chapman Maupin
    44f B
1329-1287 - Daniel Love
    44m B
    18f B

NOT EMUNERATED
George Gallaher
Cornwelsie Simmons
A.G. Jenkins (60 + slaves)

WHITE HOUSEHOLDS 1860

87 slave holders
       77 male owners
       10 female owners/widows

Owners by families
Buffington	26
Everett	20
Gwinn	11
Hite	8
Holderby	23
Kilgore	10
Love	7
Miller	14
Morris(2)	19
Rece	10
Shelton	11
Thornburg	9
Williams	15
Jenkins/Lacy	
Missing	60+

BLACK HOUSEHOLDS 1860

302 slaves
       136 male
       166 female

Age break out
male 6 and under	24
female 6 and under	32
males 7-15	40
females 7-15	45
males over 15	72
females over 15	89

Of the 87 households
       24 had a single slave
            15 male - 9 female
       10 had no adults
       18 more had no male adults

INDEX OF 1860 SLAVE HOLDERS
w/ =widow

SMITH, P.S.
45f B
20f B
19m B

WALTON,E.H.
21f M
5f M
4f M

BUFFINGTON,James H.
17f M
11f M
9m B

MILLER,H.H.(in trust for
Sarah Holderby)
26m M
10m M
6f M

BUFFINGTON,P.C.(in trust for
3 minor heirs)
13m M
11m B

HAGAN,Wm.H.
18f B
5f M

THORNBURG,James
23m M
6f B

SHELTON,Henry W.
50m M
25f B

EVERETT,James
29f M
9f M

SAMUELS,John
30f B
2f B

MOORE, W.B.
35m M

MOORE,Mary
50f B
16m M

WESTHOFF,Arnold
40f B
19m M

MERRITT, William
50f B

MAUPIN,Henry B.
47f B
10m B

BECKER,Albert
45m B

BLAKE,Sarah
16m B
6f B

MILLER,Wm.C.
26m M
3f M

BIAS,R.S.
19m B

DUSENBERRY,J.T.
20f B
6m B

WOLCOTT,Augustus
60f B

HITE,William
38f B
13m M

STONE,Grace
40f B

RODGERS,Wm.C.
13f B

CLARK, S.M.
50f B

McGINNIS,A.B.
33m M
27m M

RECE,John C.
19f B
18m B

HARDEN,John
    16f M

BURKS,B.B.
    18f B

POAGE,James H.
    13f B

McCALLISTER,Malcom
    32f B
    31f B
    16m B
    8f B
    3f B

EVERETT,Charles
    33f M
    8f B
    4f B
    1f B

LACY,David
    32f B
    16f M
    13f M
    6m B
    2f B

SPURLOCK,Daniel
    46m B

SUMMERS,George W.
    26m B
    22f B

KILLGORE,Thomas W.
    35f B
    25m B
    11f B
    9f B
    6f B
    5f B
    1m B

KILLGORE,Nancy
    40f B
    20m B
    13m B

LOVE,William
    46f M
    18m B
    15f B
    7f M
    5f B

MILLER,John M.
    22m B

POWELL,Phillip
    50m B
    42f B
    4m B

GWINN,John
    15f B

REYNOLDS,Archibald
    45f B
    25m B
    22f B
    21f B
    7f B

MORRISON,John E.
    18f B

LOVE,Daniel
    44m B
    18f B

MAUPIN,Chapman
    44f B

PORTER,Sarah
    46f B
    24f M

RECE,Edmund
    12f B

RECE,John M.
    18m B
    15f B

HARSHBARGER,Jacob
    50m B

BLACK,Elizabeth
    50f B
    35f B

GWINN,Washington
    10f B

EVERETT,John
    46m B

MIDKIFF,Spencer
    45m B

ROFFE,C.S.
    40f B
    40f B
    14f B
    13m B
     8f B
     7m B
     4m B

SHELTON,Susan
    42m B
    40f B
    37m B
    30f B
    26m B
    19m B
    10m B
     7m B

GRIFFIN,Elizabeth
    27f B

SUMMERS,Thomas(owner)
 BLACK,Wm.(employer)
    22m B

Slave Schedule

males over 35 22
females over 35.......28

males 16-34 50
females 16-34 61

males under 16 64
females under 16......77

total male 136
total female 166

                   _____
            total 302

Females outnumbered males in
each age group and only 14
households indicate families.

87 households with blacks
   (24 were single people)

     15 were single males
      9 were single females

of the remaining 63
10 had no adults
18 no male adults
 8 probable mother/s

Household Occupations

The 1860 Census lists households giving the occupation of
the head of the household and every male sixteen and older.
Most of women listed as head of household are either homemaker or
have no listed occupation. This is the first census with women
having occupations outside the home with a laundress,3 teachers
and 48 domestics. Please note that these are mostly teenage
girls.

The main occupation is farmer (792/1300 households), and
there are more laborers than 1850 as older sons look for work
(160 households). In addition 268 younger sons are listed as
farmers and 227 are listed as labors.

A small increase in the size of towns is noted with a
corresponding increase in "city" jobs. Almost all of the
professional and business people are located in either
Barboursville(the county seat) or Guyandotte
(a river port). Only 63 of 347 "city" are outside these two
communities (18%).

Several households have no listed occupation,perhaps an
oversite of the census taker.

1860 CABELL COUNTY OCCUPATIONS

139

baker
  C-Weiger,Frank (TM)
  C-Weiger,Joseph(TM)

barber
  Gy-Mays,Elisha

blacksmith
  C-Arthur,F.T.(MB)
  Gy-Baker,J.C.
  C-Brown,George(MB)
  Gy-Carter,Henry
  Mc-Clendinin,B.(Ha)
  Gy-Deitz,John K.
  Gy-Evicks,William
  Gy-Flowers,Nathaniel
  U-Handley,Wm.A./T-HM
  B-Harrison,Green
  Mc-Hunter,Samuel-FM
  B-Justice, P.V.
  Mc-Keck,John W.(FM)
  Gy-Larkin,Thomas
  B-Lattin,David
  Gy-Matthews,Sam(CC)
  Mc-McCoggle,John(PP)
  B-Metzer,Frank (7M)
  Gy-Noddle,Abraham
  Gy-Ohi,John (CC)
  B-Pine,William
  Gy-Scott,Sanford
  Gy-Scott,Sanford W.
  Gy-Shomburg,John B.
  C-Spenver,James(MB)
  B-Swann,Benjamin
  Mc-Wilkinson,S.(Ha)
  C-Williams,Matt(Gf)

brickmason
  B-Buckingham,Elisha
  U-Lacy,David R.(Gr)
  B-Leonard,Rufus(UR)
  Gy-Stewart,Isaac F.

Bridge Keeper
  Gy-McMahon,Wayne

Broker
  Gy-Hite,John B.

butcher
  B-Freutel,Julius
  Gy-Ong,John
  Gy-White,John

cabinet mkr
  B-Telginer,Emile

carpenter
  Gy,Arthur,James
  Gy-Deitz,Hugo
  Gy,Deitz,Rodoluphus
  Gy-Dotson,Thomas
  Gy-Emmons,Cyrus
  Gy-Ferguson,William
  B-Frelwiler,Geo. W.
  Gy-Gregg,James H.
  Gy-Hill,Frank
  B-Holyryde,Peter
  Mc-Johnson,Sq.(Ha)
  Gy-Johnson,Wm.R.(CC)
  B-Mather,Joel Ohio R
  B-McCune,Benjamin
  Gy-McGinnis,Achilles
  Gy-McLary,David (CC)
  Gy-Melcher,William
  Mc-Mitchell,Joe(PP)
  G-Nimo,William(MB)
  Gy-Paine,Henry
  C-Pedro,S.M.(MB)
  U-Perry,John(Gr)
  C-Rece,Edmund(MB)
  B-Shelton,Thomas
  Mc-Smith,A.J.(PP)
  Gy-Smith,William
  U-Stevens,Hooper(Gr)
  Mc-Thompson,JamesHa
  B-Underwood,E.M.(BS)
  B-Wade,Samuel
  Gy-Wellington,Eras.
  Gy-Wellington,E.Jr.
  Gy-Wellington,Jas W.
  Gy-Wellington,Nodiah
  B-Wingo,A.W.
  Gy-Wood,Thomas H.

clerk
  B-Apple,A.N.
  Gy-Davidson,Alex
  C-Hackworth,Geo(MB)
  B-Handley,Lycingus
  Gy-Hayslip,Samuel

B-Miller,Charles H.
Gy-Ong,John
Gy-Nesmith,Charles
B-Samuels,Alex
Gy-Smith,Dudley
Gy-Smith,Percival S.

clk/court
  B-Thornburg,Moses
  B-Wood,H.H.

clothier
  B-Proctor,George

coach maker
  Gy-McKinley,M.M.

collier
  B-Pulley,David

constable
  B-Feazel,Wm.E.
  Gy-Barbour,Robert

cooper
  Gy-Blake,Miles
  Gy-Blake,Miles L.
  B-Carson,Wm.A.
  Gy-Dudding,B.A.(CC)
  Gy-Hughes,R.B.(CC)
  B-Kinght,John OH
  B-Lesage,Francis OH
  B-Miller,John
  Gy-Petit,Hugh B.
  B-Rose,Enoch
  Gy-Smith,William
  Gy-Stephenson,G(4P)

currier
  B-Morey,Frank

dentist
  B-Boggess,George W.
  B-Dusenberry,W.F.FM
  Gy-Molesworth,W.W.

deputy sheriff
  Mc-McComas,T J.(PP)
  Mc-Wilkinson,J.(ha)

doctor
 Mc-Curry,Wm.(Ha)
 U-Jennings,S.R.(Gr)
 B-Maupin,H.B.
 B-McCorkle,A.M.
 Gy-McCullough,P.H.
 Gy-McGinnis,A.B.
 B-Moss,V.R. (Martha)
 B-Peyton,John W.
 Gy-Paine,Wm(4P)
 Gy-Rouse,James H.
 G-Williams,Sam (MB)

domestic
 B-Adkins,Clara
 Gy-Arthur,Agnes
 Gy-Arthur,Letitia
 Gy-Arthur,Mary
 Mc-Beech,Hannah(PP)
 C-Blom,Nancy A.(Gr)
 Gy-Boyd,Nancy
 B-Conner,Amanda
 B-Cook,Eliza
 B-Crumby,Elizabeth
 Gy-Davis,Mary
 C-Defoe,Rachel(T-HM)
 Gy-Evans,Laura
 B-Ferguson,Cynthia
 Gy-Freeman,Agnes
 Mc-Hatfield,Edithpp
 B-Hensley,Virginia
 C-Holt,Ida (TM)
 Mc-Holt,Minerva(PP)
 Mc-Holten,Mary A.Ha
 B-Houchins,Rebecca
 Gy-Hughes,Jane
 B-Johnson,Nancy
 B-Keyton,Harriett
 Gy-Jones,Elizabeth
 Gy-Kise,Harriet
 Gy-Knight,Ellen
 Mc-Lavender,EmilyHa
 C-Lucas,Susan(TM)
 Gy-Mathus,Sarah
 Mc-McQuie,Andrew(PP)
 Gy-Neffin,Melissa
 B-Paine,Julia
 Mc-Paine,Nancy(PP)
 B-Perry,Margaret
 B-Peyton,Francis
 U-Pinchen,Eliza.(Gr)
 C-Poor,Mary J.(T-HM)

 B-Poor,Susan
 Gy-Ray,Levina
 B-Roberts,Eveline
 B-Roberts,Mary S.
 Gy-Roberts,Sarah
 B-Sasson,Catherine
 Mc-Smith,Margrt(PP)
 B-Stanley,Sarah
 B-Stowater,Caroline
 Mc-Terry,Elizb(FM)

druggist
 Gy-Clark,Silas

engineer   '50-4
 Gy-Ayers,William A.
 Gy-Flowers,E.H.
 Gy-Flowers,Thaddeus
 B-Gill,Joseph

farmer   792/1300
 B-   190h (x41)
 Gy-   118 (x48)
 Mc (FM) 78   x38
 Mc(PP) 64   x25
 Mc(TM) 39   x10
 Mc(Ha) 113   x49
        (297) (122)
 C-(Gf) 44   x10
 C(MB)   77   x34
        (121) (44)
 U-(Gr) 20   7
 U(Tr)   46   x13
        (66) (20)
               268

ferryman
 B-Derton,John
 B-Dolen,George

gentleman
 Mc-Adkins,Wm A.(Ha)
 Gy-Baumgardner,Jacob
 C-Byus,James(Gf)
 B-Church,Octavius
 Gy-Hite,William
 B-Kraus,Walter
 B-Lusher,Johnson
 Gy-Moore,Orren
 Gy-Smith,Ralph F.
 Gy-Thompson,Charles

grocier
 Gy-Warren,George W.

gunsmith
 B-Jefferson,Henry7M
 B-Kyle,Thomas (7Mi)

hotel
 Gy-Carroll,Thomas
 B-Harshbarger,David
 Gy-Harshbarger,H.W.
 Gy-Harshbarger,J.M.
 B-Hatfield,J.T.
 B-McKendree,Ariana

jailor
 B-Shelton,Anthony
jeweler
 B-
Dusenberry,Chas(FM)

labor
 B-   56 x75
 Gy-   41 x60
 (FM) 16 x 17
 (PP) 5 x 9
 (TM) 2   9
 (Ha) 10   26
 Mc   35 x61
  (Gf) 1   2
  (MB) 15   21
 C   16 23
  (Tr) 3   4
  (Gr) 9   4
 U   12   8
      total 160 227

laundress
 B-Anderson,Nancy

lawyer
 B-Laidley,Albert
 Gy-Laidley,John
 Gy-Mann,George W.
 Gy-Parker,Greenville
 B-Samuels,H.J.
 B-Samuels,John
 Gy-Warren,G.D.

livery Stable
 Gy-Rodgers,William

merchant
  Gy-Beekman,Lewis
  Mc-Bell,John R. (PP)
  Mc-Bowden,Sidney(FM)
  B-Cann,Charles
  Gy-Chapman,A.P.
  B-Cox,James A. OH
  Gy-Dusenberry,J.T.
  Gy-Douthit,William
  Gy-Emsheimer,Joseph
  Gy-Everett,H.C.
  Gy-Ferguson,D.P.
  Gy-Holderby,G.W.
  B-Miller,George F.
  Gy-Miller,H.H.
  B-Miller,John G.
  B-Miller,Sigmund
  B-Miller,William C.
  B-Poteet,H.C. (4P)
  C-Rece,John M. (MB)
  Gy-Russell,St.M.E.
  B-Salmon,Joel K.
  Mc-Shelton,Jerome
  U-Sheff,John H.
  Gy-Smith,D.D.
  Gy-Smith,E.A.
  Gy-Smith,Percival
  Gy-Smith,Whitcomb
  Gy-Spurlock,M.J.
  B-Thompson,Matthew
  B-Thornburg,Thomas
  Gy-Walton,E.H.
  Gy-Wolcott,L.M.

miller
  U-Howell,A.B.(T-HM)
  B-Lloyd,R.J.
  Gy-Nesmith,John
  Gy-Nesmith,Wm M.
  Gy-Price,Joseph
  B-Sheff,Wm.P. HM
  B-Weiger,Lewis

milliner
  C-Barbary Smith(MB)

millwright
  Mc-Deacon,Andrew(PP)
  Gy-Flowers,Alfred
  Mc-McMillen,J.W./FM
  Mc-Messinger,Nich.FM

miner
  Mc-Jack,John (FM)

minister
  Mc-Bias,Rolin (PP)
  Gy-Brown,John R.
  C-Chrislip,A.R.(Gr)
  Gy-Hoffman,P.H.
  Gy-Monroe,Thomas H.
  Gy-Preble,Ulysus
  Gy-Rece,John C.
  Gy-Russell,S.M.
  U-Williamson,J.(Gr)

ostler
  Gy-Reynolds,L.M.

overseer
  U-Richardson,Richard

painter
  Gy-Bramer,Clark .
  Gy-Hayslip,Carey
  Gy-Peters,Lewis
  Gy-Scott,Harvey

pilot River
  Gy-Dotson,Jesse
  Gy-Russell,A.G.
  Gy-Shoemaker,Jas H.
  Gy-Thompson.John
  Gy-White,Albert

plaster
  B-Latimore,Robert
  B-Latimore,James M.
  Gy-Sedinger,James
  Gy-Wood,J.E.
  B-Tasson,John Fudge

raftman
  B-Dillon,John L.

saddler
  Gy-Chapdu,Peter
  Gy-Blanped,Elisha
  B-Fetter,H.A.
  Gy-Keenan,A.J.

sawyer
  B-Ansel,Abraham OH
  Mc-Lusher,R. (FM)

B-Seitzer,Jonathan
B-Smith,Harvey (4P)
U-White,Peter(T-HM)

seamtress
  B-Hatfield,Frances
  Gy-Jewell,Catherine
  Gy-Jewell,Helen

sheriff
  B-Moore,W.B.

sheperd
  B-Korn,David (Un R.)

shoemaker
  C-Becket,Emsley (MB)
  B-Beech,Walden
  B-Bryant,Dennis O.
  Gy-Dupine,Francis
  Gy-Eaves,Thos.Hodges
  B-Eggers,William
  Mc-Franklin,J. (FM)
  C-Hatfield,Caperton
  B-Hatfield,Thomas
  Gy-Hillman,William
  U-Jordan,A.J.(MD)
  Gy-Keller,Adam
  B-Lloyd,John
  Mc-McComas,Jesse(FM)
  Gy-Sedinger,Lewis
  B-Smith,David F.

silversmith
  Gy-Hatfield,Alex
  Gy-Louchime,Sol
  Gy-Moore,F.M.

stage drvr
  Gy-Hayslip,James

state agnt
  Gy-Vandivar,J.H.

stonemason
  Gy-Clark,Lyman
  Mc-Holt,James(FM)
  Gy-Huxom,Henry
  B-McKannon,Matthew
  B-Merritt,William
  Gy-Reed,Judson (C C)
  Gy-Stephenson,J.M.4P

142

Gy-Stewart,Burgess   B-Hollenback,F.P.4P
Gy-Stewart,James   B-Hollenback,Lorenzo

student   tinner
  B-Roffe,Thomas J.   Gy-Hiltbruner,Jacob
                             Gy-Hiltbruner,Steph
surveyor
  B-Felix,James   tobaccoist
  B-Lattin,Charles   Gy-McMahan,John
  B-Seamonds,Alfred   Gy-Summerson,Charles

tailor   vine dresser
  Gy-Campbell,James   Gy-Best,William
  B-Farrell,Francis M.   Gy-Stark,John
  B-Jones,Willim E.
  B-Mather,O.W.   wagon maker
  Gy-Ong,Isaac   Gy-Bierly,Joseph
                             Gy-Cunningham,I(4P)
tanner
  B-Becker,Albert   wharf master
  Gy-Hite,John B.   Gy-Wolcott,A.S.
  Gy-Suiter,Jacob(C C)
  B-Westhoff,Arnold   wheelwright
                             B-Hibbins,John T.
teacher   C-Jesse King(H)
  B-Algeo,William D.   U-Nelson Thomas(T-H
  Gy-Bent,J.M.
  U-Blake,Julia(Gr)
  B-Bryant,W.G. (HM)
  U-Buckner,J.A.(T-HM)
  C-Cameron,John(Ha)
  Gy-Cook,Mathew
  C-Hatfield,Addi(TM)
  Gy-Hayslip,T.J.
  B-Keene,Eliza (f)
  B-McGinnis,John B.
  Gy-Ong,Albina(f)
  U-Paine,Chas W.(MB)
  Mc-Simpson,Chas FM
  Gy-Stone,Elizabeth
  B-Thacketon,B.H.
  B-Vertigans,Edward
  C-Wingfield,John(H)

teamster
  Gy-Smith,Austin
  Gy-Turner,Leonard
  Gy-Walker,William

timberman
  B-Allen,R.B.
  B-Dillon,Rece W.

Please Note:
    Name Changes
(Present name first)

Falls Mill =
        Martha
        Bloomingdale
        Dusenberry Mill
        Saunders Mill
        Estes Mill

Districts:

Barboursville = B
Guyandotte   = GY   Paw Paw=
McComas   = Mc   Salt Rock
Union   = U
Carroll/Grant = C   Thorndyke=
                              Howells Mill
    Communities   Howell
                              Doolittle Mill
The census was taken   Lillard Mill
by district and post
office. It is
possible to place
several families in
their modern
location.

                          DIVIDED COMMUNITIES

Barboursville
 Thorndyke (T-HM)
   (Howell's Mill)   Barbourville District
 Howell(Howells Mill)   and McComas District
 Blue Sulphur (BS)   divide a community.
 Union Ridge (UR)
 7 Mile   (7M)   Falls Mill (Martha) a
 Ohio River   (OH)   river crossing and
Guyandotte   mill site, the com-
 4 Pole   (4P)   munity is on both
 Central City (CC)   sides of the
Falls Mill   (FM)   Guyandotte River in
Paw Paw   (PP)   Barboursville and
Ten Mile   (TM)   McComas Districts.
Hamlin   (Ha)
Griffithville (Gf)   Thorndyke (Howells
Greenbottom   (Gr)   Mill)is also a river
Mud Bridge   (MB)   crossing and mill
                        site on Mud River and
                        is in Barboursville
                        and Union Districts.

CENSUS DISTRICTS

1860

363 -- BARBOURSVILLE --- BARBOURSVILLE PO
163 -- CARROLL   --- MUD BRIDGE PO
                      --- GRIFFITHVILLE PO
                      --- HAMLIN PO
279 -- GUYANDOTTE   --- GUYANDOTTE PO
386 -- McCOMAS   --- FALLS MILLS PO
                      --- PAW PAW BOTTOM PO
                      --- TEN MILE PO
 99 -- UNION   --- GREENBOTTOM PO
                      --- THORNDYKE PO

Griffithville,Ten Mile and Hamlin were in present Lincoln County.

                1860 CENSUS
            by household number

    Cabell Court House (Barboursville) 1/374-363

    Guyandotte   375-365/666-644

    Falls Mills   667-645/799-766

    Paw Paw Bottom   800-767/880-845

    Ten Mile   (LC)   881-846/932-896

    Hamlin   (LC)   933-897/1075-1034

    Griffithville   (LC)   1076-1035/1129-1087

    Greenbottom   1130-1088/1171-1129

    Mud Bridge (Milton)   1172-1130/1283-1241

    Thorndyke (Howells Mill) 1284-1242/1342-1300

The Civil War affected Cabell County much like the rest of the nation. Although part of the new state of West Virginia, Cabell County had several ties to the South. The most important factor was Cabell County's location on the Ohio River. For many years prior to the War, this area of Virginia was known as a point on the Underground Railway. There were also several large farms along the Ohio whose owners dominated the county. The onset of the War broke Cabell County into factions and because of the "plantation" owners old power, this section of West Virginia was pro-southern for some time.

This strife sent many families out of the area. The population dropped by 1228 persons representing 200 households. (Please remember that Lincoln County was formed from Cabell County in 1867.) This figure should be further decreased because between 100 and 200 of the 1870 population was labor for the new railroad . This population moved on when it was completed.

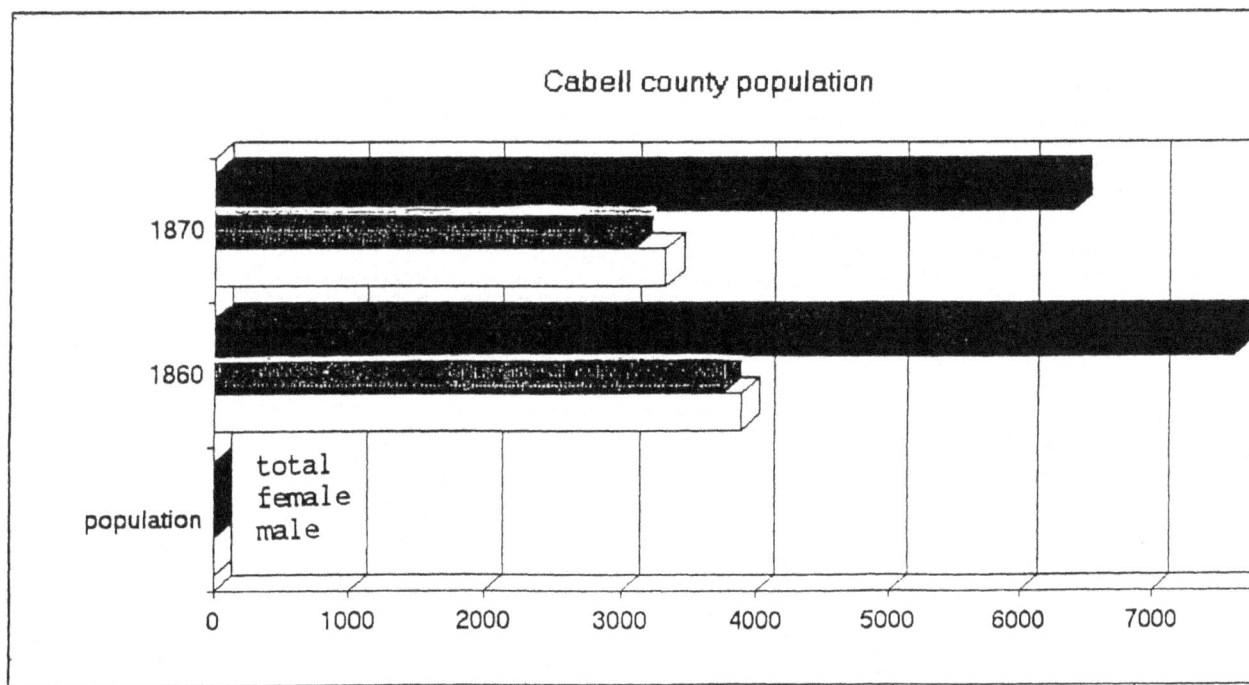

Cabell county population

population	1860	1870		
male	3884	3316	decrease	568
female	3740	3080	decrease	660
total	7624	6396	decrease	1228

The population decrease from 1860 to 1870 is at least partially due to the Civil War. Many families also moved west to escape the war torn East. One figure that is unexpected is the number of widows and widowers for the period.

	1860	1870
population	7624	6396
widows	185	145
	2.42%	2.26% of population

There were considerably more female than male in both periods.

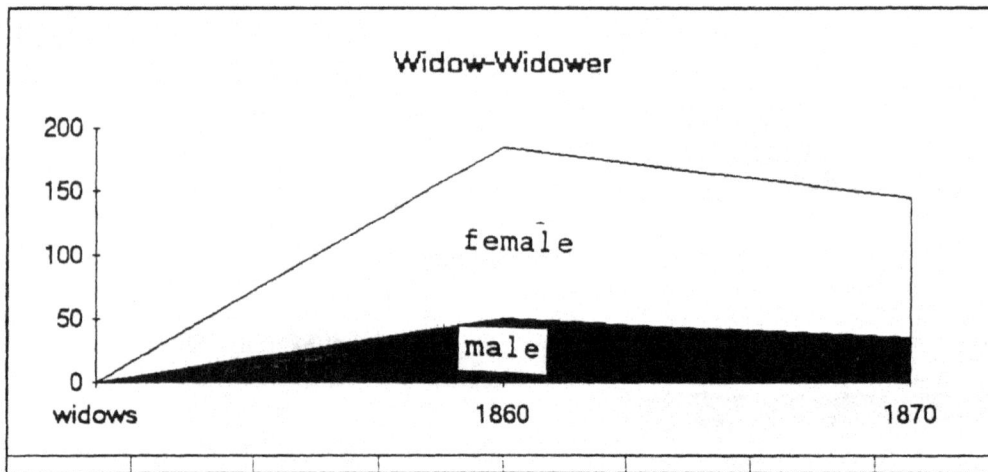

1860 female- 135	1860 male- 50
1870 female- 110	1870 male- 35

This figure is even more pronounced if you combine the widows with second spouses. (A figure that is difficult to accurately count without full knowledge of each family structure.)
        Counted if female was 10 years younger than spouse.
                Male was 5 years younger than spouse.

1860 198 persons	2.597%	combined 5.02%
1870 168 persons	2.626%	wid/spou 4.89%

Many widowers married as soon as possible after wife's death.

(If the cut off age had been 9 years at least 25 more females)

Working with the census can sometimes produce hidden information. Double families are those created when two widows with children marry. To find these families look for ages of both spouse and children that do not "fit".

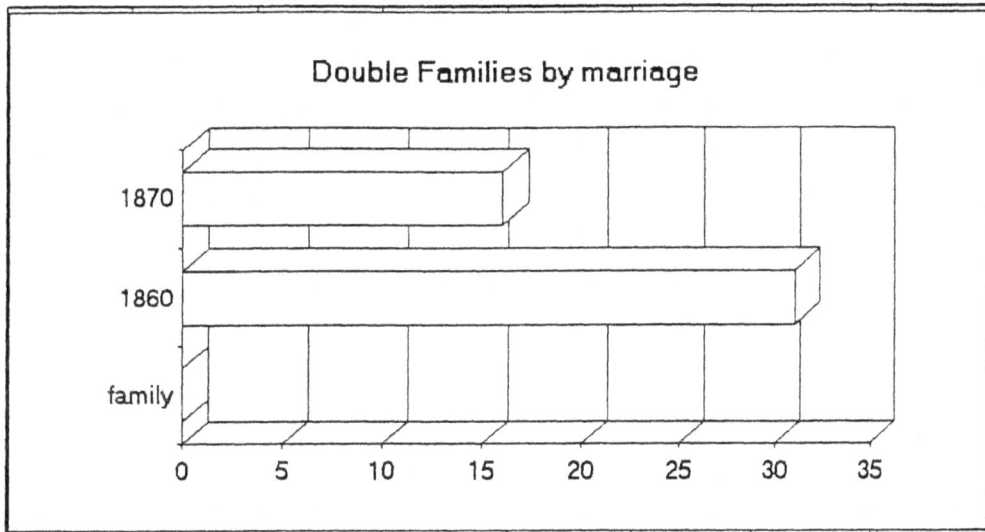

Double Families by marriage

(bar chart showing years 1870, 1860, and "family" on vertical axis; horizontal axis scaled 0, 5, 10, 15, 20, 25, 30, 35)

The extended family is very common in the census. It is a family with inlaws, brothers or sisters or grandchildren. Some times the family extension is difficult to spot. Remember, married sons and theirs wives and children follow the first family. (Some times a widow names her son as head of household and her name follows his before his wife.)

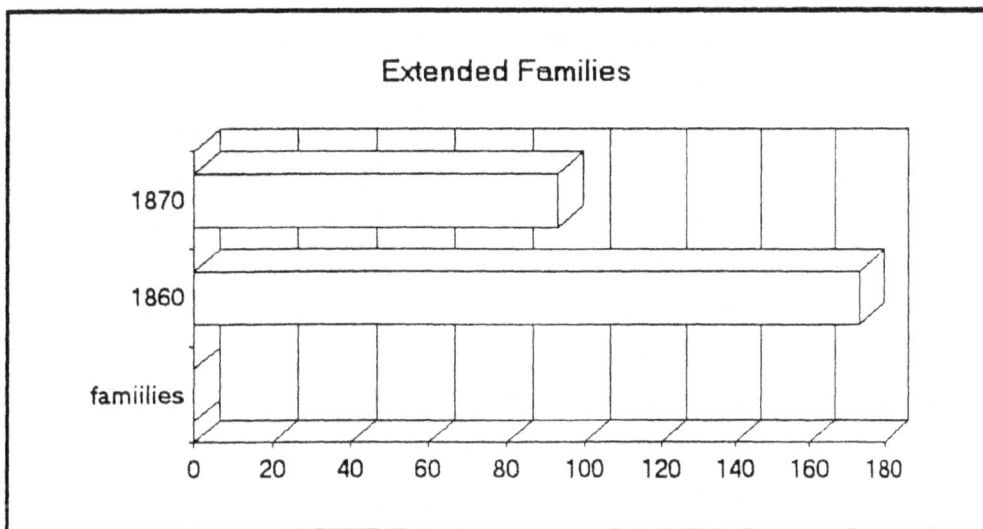

Extended Families

(bar chart showing years 1870, 1860, and "famiilies" on vertical axis; horizontal axis scaled 0, 20, 40, 60, 80, 100, 120, 140, 160, 180)

CENSUS OF POPULATION

	1850	1860	1870
Arkansas		7	2
Connecticutt	12	5	11
DC	1	-	-
Georgia	1	-	-
Illinois	6	5	7
Indiana	24	18	21
Iowa	-	2	5
Kentucky	74	100	131
Louisana	2	2	2
Maine	11	10	-
Maryland	36	15	17
Massachusetts	14	15	1
Mississippi	1	1	1
Missouri	3	11	10
Nebraska	-	1	-
New Hampshire	8	1	1
New Jersey	3	3	6
New York	41	26	53
North Carolina	18	34	29
Ohio	197	240	343
Pennslyvania	66	29	57
Rhode Island	-	1	-
South Carolina	2	2	2
Tennessee	24	9	17
Texas	-	1	-
Vermont	6	4	1
Wisconsin	-	1	7
Virginia	-	-	747

28 states and DC are represented in this thirty year period

	1850	1860	1870
AUSTRIA	-	2	6
CANADA	1	1	4
EAST INDIES	1	-	-
ENGLAND	35	27	25
FRANCE	5	15	10
GERMANY*	51	68	52
HOLLAND	-	1	2
IRELAND	8	19	58
POLAND	12	-	-
SANTO DOMINGO	1	-	-
SCOTLAND	10	9	1
SWEDEN	-	-	7
SWITZERLAND	13	8	-
WALES	4	1	-

14 foreign countries had citizens who moved to Cabell County.

*Combined German States

Households per District

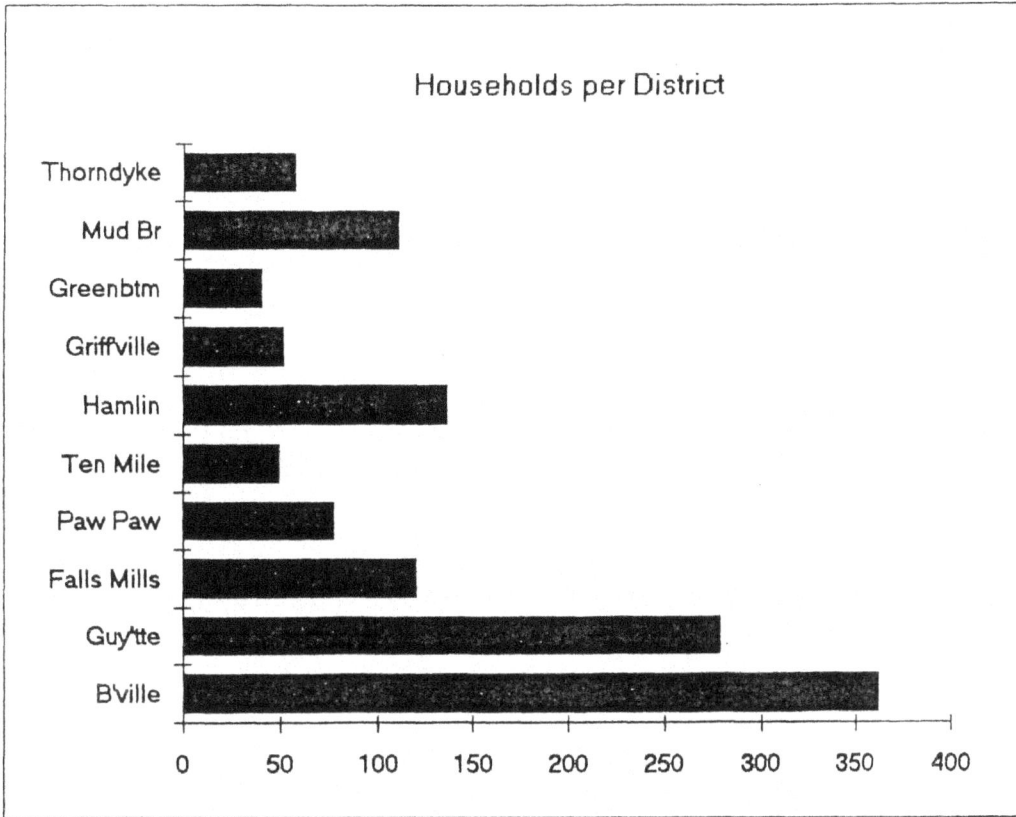

CARROLL-Mud Bridge   McCOMAS-Falls Mills   UNION-Greenbottom
    -Griffithville   -Paw Paw Bottom   -Thorndyke
    -Hamlin   -Ten Mile

DISTRICT vs POST OFFICE

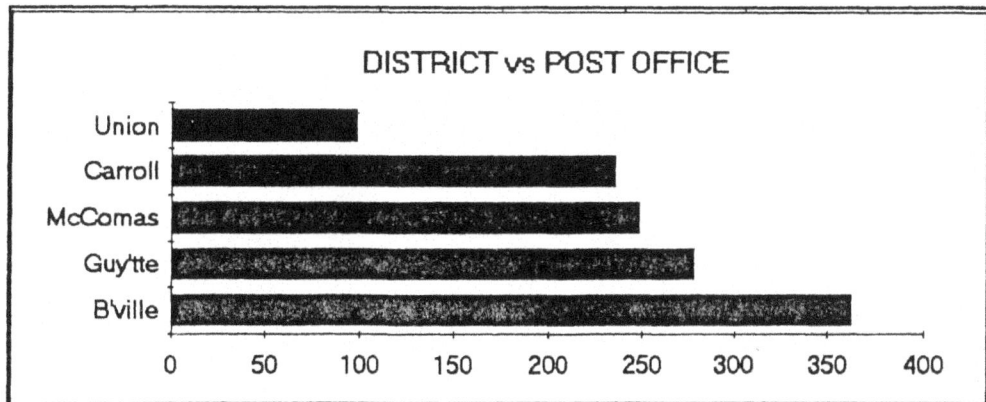

Who lived in Cabell County

Cabell County had excellent farm land along the Ohio River,
Mud River and Guyandotte River. Most of the farmers were small
land owners although Greenbottom (owned by the Jenkins family)
contained 4444 acres. In 1860 792 households out of 1300 listed
farmer as occupation. Census figures give value of property which
does not necessarily indicate size of farm, but information is
also given for occupation for every male over 16. Most large
property holders' sons are also listed as farmer while the sons
of small farms are listed as laborers.

The other 508 households have occupations ranging from none,
to "gentleman", craftsman and professional persons. There are 69
occupations other than farmer listed. Since every male over 16
was asked for his occupation, each household may have more than
one occupation. In some cases all the members of a business lived
in the same household, in others married children lived at home.

The most prominent occupations:

carpenter- 27	labor - 387	tailor - 5
cooper - 11	lawyer - 7	tanner - 4
doctor - 11	minister - 9	teacher - 18
domestic - 48	shoemaker- 16	timberman- 4
engineer - 4	stonemason 9	tobaccoist 2
gentleman- 10	surveyors- 3	vine dresser2

Cabell County Farmers 1860

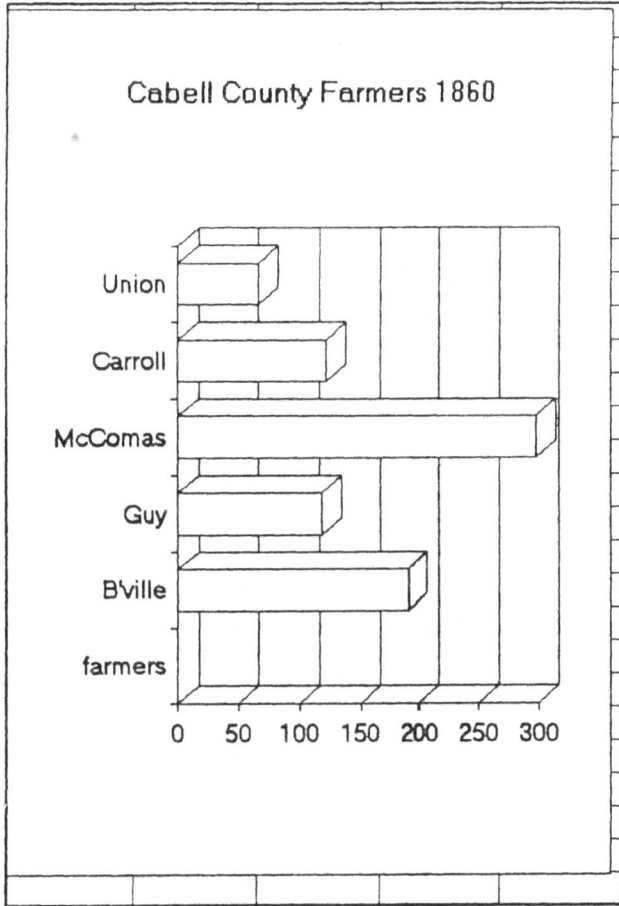

There are 1300 households in 1860 Cabell County. 792 list the head of household as a farmer(61%). The richest farms were in the Teays Valley on Mud River(Carroll District), along the Ohio River in Barboursville and Guyandotte Districts and along the Guyandotte River in McComas District. There were also 41 youngers sons or other non-heads who give the occupation farmer.

Occupation Non-Farmers

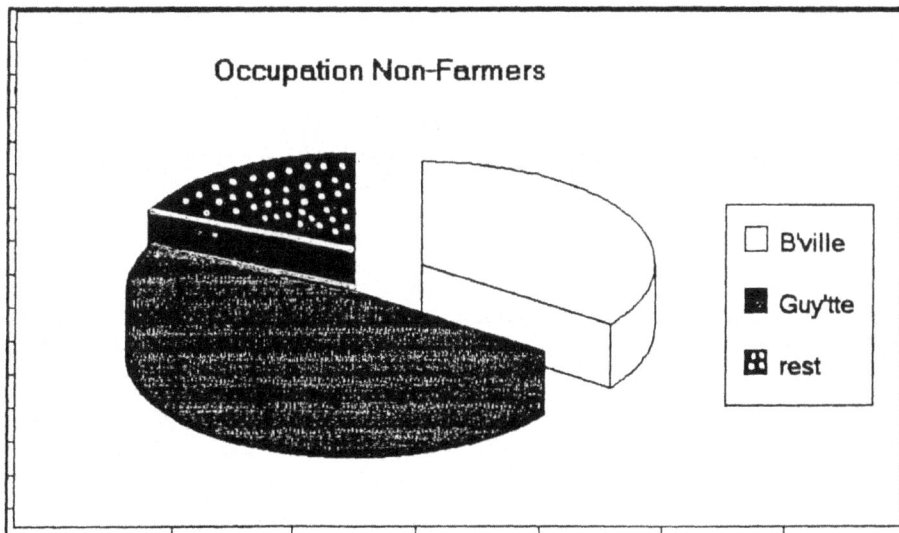

B'ville
Guy'tte
rest

There were two large communities in Cabell County, Baboursville and Guyandotte. These two communities contained 72% of the people who listed an occupation other than farming.

CABELL COUNTY SETTLERS

Cabell County was still a "western frontier" in 1860. Although many people moving west had reached Missouri, Oregon and California, some were still filling in the empty spaces in the East. Because of its location between two major Indian trails and its rugged terrain and lack of roads, Cabell County had few settlers before 1810 and settlement was slow. The western migration took people past the area, but some turned arround and settled Cabell County from the west. There is also a pattern of parents born in the area, moving west, birthing children and then returning to West Virginia.

Cabell County had a fair number of citizen of foreign birth. They came to the area for its good soils and oppertunity for success. Guyandotte was an important river port and gave frontier oppertunists a chance to make a good living. A group of people arriving from the German states made their way to Cabell County and settled Union Ridge while another family settled near Salt Rock. Frenchmen leaving Gallipolis choose to settle in Cabell County. Englishmen were deemed necessary teachers and located in many frontier towns. Why many of the foreign settlers came may never be known, but most came for a better way of life than the one they left.

Most of Cabell Counties's settlers were born in Virginia, but 553 persons were born in some other state and 154 were born outside the United States. The 553 born in the United States represent 25 states altough 240 were born in Ohio and 100 were born in Kentucky. Of the foreign born 68 were born in the German states, 27 in England, 19 in Ireland and 15 in France while the remaining 25 came from 9 different countries.

1860
ORIGIN
POPULATION
outside Virginia

AR	Arkansas	7	NC	North Carolina	34	
CT	Connecticutt	5	NH	New Hampshire	1	
IA	Iowa	2	NJ	New Jersey	3	
IL	Illinois	5	NY	New York	26	
IN	Indiana	18	OH	Ohio	240	
KY	Kentucky	100	PA	Penslyvania	29	
LA	Louisana	2	RI	Rhode Island	1	
MA	Massachusetts	15	SC	South Carolina	2	
MD	Maryland	15	TN	Tennessee	9	
ME	Maine	10	TX	Texas	1	
MI	Mississippi	1	VT	Vermont	4	
MO	Missouri	11	WI	Wisconsin	1	
NB	Nebraska	1			total	553

1860
ORIGIN OF
FOREIGN BORN POPULATION

AUS	Austria	2			
CAN	Canada	1	*GERMAN STATES		
ENG	England	27	Bavaria	5	
FRA	France	15	Bohemia	10	
GER	German*	68	Germany	9	
HOL	Holland	1	Hanover	4	
IRE	Ireland	19	Hesse Darmstaad	9	
SDo	Santo Domingo	1	Prussia	15(+1 (Russia)	
SCT	Scotland	9	Saxony	15	
SAm	South America	1	Shcamberg Lippi	1	
SWI	Switzerland	8	Wirtenburg	5	
WAL	Wales	1			

total 154
(at least one clerk was German)

DISTRICTS IN CABELL COUNTY

The present district system was created in West Virginia by a Township Commission in 1852 and revised in 1863. The Original Districts were: District 1 - Lower Guyan
                 District 2 - Barboursville
                 District 3 - Mud River and Ohio
                 District 4 - Valley and Upper Mud District
                 District 5 - Upper Guyan

In 1863, the new state of West Virginia renamed these districts, but kept the same division lines because "We are unabel at this time to have the line of the said townships surveyed for the reason that a large portion of the county is in the possession of the Rebels".(Cabell Commissioners)

District 1: Guyandotte - begining on the Ohio River at the mouth of 4 Pole at the Wayne County line hence up the river to the mouth of Files Branch(Pyles) hence across the ridge to the Guyandotte River to Widow Shelton's and toward the Wayne county line along the dividing ridge between 4 Pole and Davis Creek. (After Huntington was incorporated this district was sudivided adding Gideon and Kyle)

District 2: Barboursville - Begining on the Ohio River at the mouth of Files Branch with Guyandotte line hence up the river to James Knight's ferry across ridge to 9 Mile at Lemuel Cornell house hence along road to Richard Perry house, hence along road to James Cushing house then in a straight line to the Mud River Ford above Harshbarger's Mill hence to the Turnpike the south along the dividing ridge around the head waters of Fudge Creek and Little Cabell Creek and down the next ridge to the mouth of Little Cabell hence in a straight line to the Wayne County line at the old Carson place hence along county line to Guyandotte.

District 3: Union - Begining at the Ohio River with the Barbousville line hence to the line to the Turnpike the to Putnam County line hence north to Mason County line and to river.

District 4: Carroll (Grant) - Beginging at the Turnpike at junction of Union and Barboursville lines hence along Turnpike to Putnam County line south to the Boone County line the west to the Logan County line hence to the top of the dividing ridge between Mud River and Guyandotte River hence North along ridge to Barboursville line and then the begining. (Carroll included part of Lincoln County when that section was removed the District took the name Grant.)

District 5: McComas - Begining at the southwest corner of the Barboursville line at the Wayne County line hence to the Logan County line hence to Carroll District hence along said line to the Barboursville line and the begining. (Also contained part of Lincoln County)

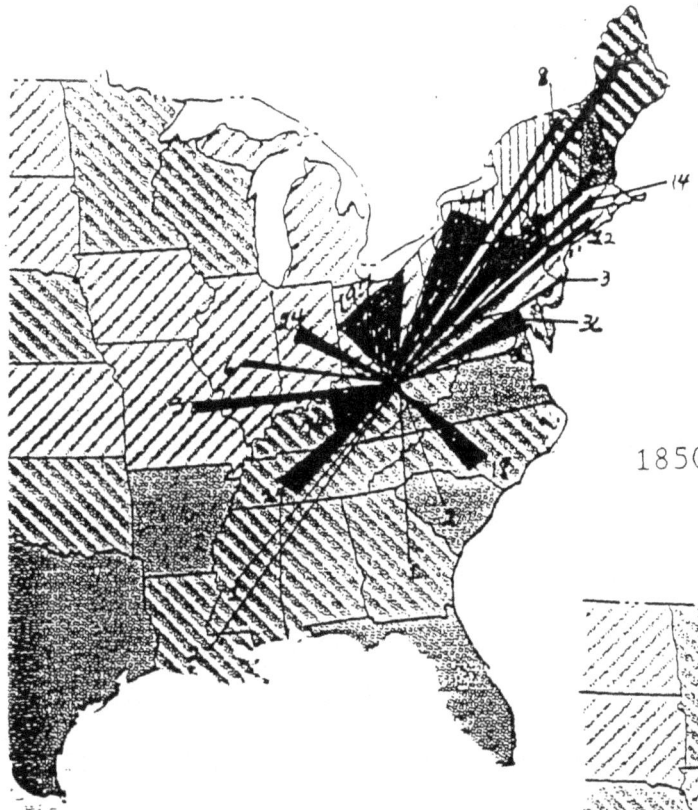

BIRTH LOCATION OF
PERSONS LIVING IN
CABELL COUNTY

1850

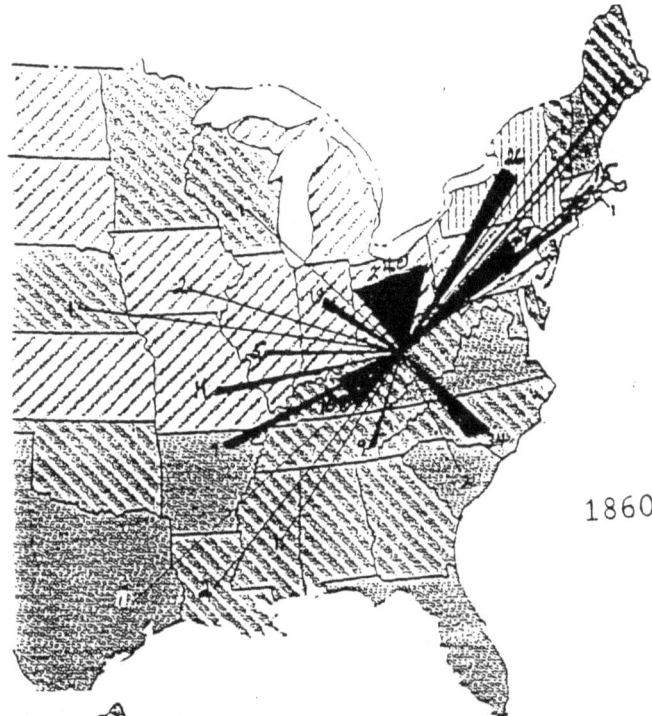

1860

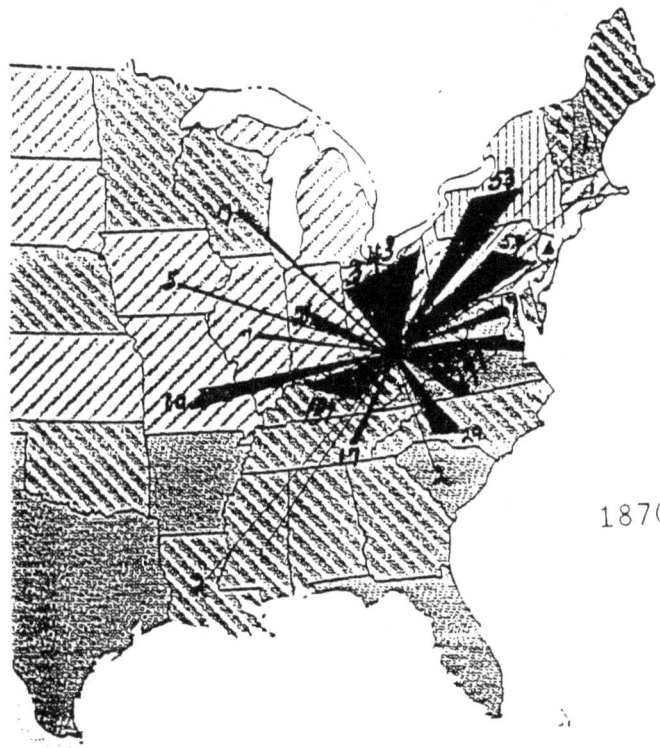

1870

#1 OHIO
#2 KENTUCKY
#3 PENNSLYVANIA
#4 NEW YORK
#5 NORTH CAROLINA

Each Census has been guilty of missing people.
Some wanted to be missed, others simply were
isolated, while others were skipped by the enumerator.

There are severals ways to double check for the missing. One is
to identify the elderly and follow them backwards because few
people willing moved so late in life.

    Cabell County had 112 elderly over 70 in 1860 and
97 elderly of 70 in 1870. Of these 30 and 26 were over 80.

	1870			1860	
house					
12	Edward Shy	84	467	Edward Shy	74
65	William Collins	86	167	William Collins	74
105	Sofia Peyton	80	148	S.M.Peyton	67
139	Samuel Morris	85			
166	Annie Witcher	90	358	Annie Witcher	70
206	Elizabeth Derton	86	35	Elizabeth Derton	74
214	William Yates	83	97	William P.Yates	74
247	Abia Rece	86	1190	Abia Rece	76
268	Letta Wallace	80	1208	Letta Wallace	64
395	Nancy Bates	80	594	Nancy Bates	65
450	Elizabeth Booten	80	507	Elizabeth Booten	65
506	Sarah Cook	81			
573	John Everett	82	440	John Everett	72
673	Sarah Hite	87	386	Sarah Hite	76
683	Rody McConnell	81			
916	Nancy Diel	83	140	Nancy Dial	70
951	Jeremiah Blake	80	166	Jeremiah Blake	66
953	Henry Jefferson	91	185	Henry Jefferson	79
953	Bettie Jefferson	84	185	Elizab.Jefferson	76
962	Richard Perry	86	189	Richard Perry	70
976	Samuel Rouse	80			
1045	John Lapool	84			
1072	Anderson Jenkins	94	642	Anderson Jenkins	85
1084	Sarah Cremeans	94	1125	Sarah Cremeans	78

Note the differences in ages.
Missing persons may have: 1. moved into area
                          2. been missed in 1860 count
                          3. different name spelling

Abbott
  *James, 29
  Margaret, 29
  Martha, 29
  Polly, 29
Achers
  Henry, 103
  John, 103
  Julina, 103
  Louisa, 103
  *Nathaniel, 103
  Rebecca, 103
Adams
  Elizabeth, 131
  Elizabeth x, 27
  Francis M., 131
  *John Q., 51
  Jordan, 51
  Julia x, 51
  Sarah A., 51
  Thomas x, 17
  *William, 131
Adkins
  Aaron, 57
  Abagail, 73, 76
  Abby, 91
  Albert, 89
  *Alfred, 87
  Alice, 77
  Allen, 76
  Almeda, 77
  America, 68
  Amos, 32
  *Anderson, 68
  Anderville, 89
  Anna, 69, 77
  Archabald, 73
  Arnold, 32
  Asina, 98
  Ballard, 75
  Ballard S. x, 99
  Bazel, 73
  *Benjamin, 32
  Blackburn, 68
  Cadman, 70
  Callowhill, 98
  Calvery x, 27
  Candus, 77
  Carpenter, 89
  Catherine, 76
  Cerilda x, 67
  Charity, 75
  Charles, 96
  Christiana x, 97
  Clara x, 7
  Clayton, 73
  Cynthia, 68, 69
  Daniel, 72
  Delphia, 76

  Edith, 102
  *Edward, 86
  *Elisha, 90
  Eliza, 70, 76, 87
  *Elizabeth, 57,
    68, 69, 70, 76,
    90, 101
  *Elliott, 68
  Elsey, 75
  Emanuel x, 73
  Emeline, 98
  Emily, 89
  Ephraim, 57, 76
  Evermont, 89
  Frank G., 98
  Garrett, 77
  George A., 96
  George W., 76
  Georgia, 57
  *Green, 77
  *Hamilton, 94
  Hansford, 89
  Harriett, 91
  Henry, 73
  Hiram, 69
  Ira, 98
  Isabella x, 98
  Jackson, 68
  Jacob, 69
  James, 73, 87
  James L.x, 87
  Jefferson, 86
  *Jeremiah, 57
  Jerome N., 90
  Jerome S, 73
  *Jesse, 98
  Jessee, 68
  John, 98
  *John C., 76
  John H., 89
  John L., 69
  *John T., 70
  John W., 76
  *Jonas, 98
  *Joseph, 70, 72
  Julia, 73, 76
  Lawrence x, 95
  Letha, 69, 87, 98
  Levica x, 95
  *Lewis, 89
  Louisa, 90, 98
  Lucetta, 87
  Lucinda, 69, 76,
    87
  Lucinda x, 97
  Lucy, 69
  *Lykins, 87
  Mahala x, 87
  Malinda, 94, 98
  Margaret, 72

  Maria, 69
  Martha, 76, 87
  Martin, 77
  Mary, 69, 73, 90,
    96, 101
  Mary M., 76
  *Mathew, 68
  Matilda, 96
  Merrett, 69
  Mildred, 73
  Millard, 96
  Milsey, 89
  Nancy, 32, 70,
    76, 87, 102
  Nancy x, 87
  Napoleon, 68, 96
  Nathaniel, 96
  Nelsina, 72
  Paralie, 32
  Paris, 73, 76
  *Parker, 69, 75
  Parker x, 95
  Paulina, 87
  *Perry G., 69
  Polly, 68, 70
  Polly A.x, 84
  *Price, 76
  Rachel, 70
  *Randolph, 68, 75
  Rebecca, 68
  *Richard, 70, 87
  *Robert, 91
  Ross, 87
  *Samuel, 87
  Sarah, 68, 69,
    72, 73, 77, 90,
    96, 98, 102
  Sarilda, 73, 76
  *Sherod, 73
  Simon, 94
  Sinclair, 98
  Sophia, 91
  Susan, 70, 86
  Sylvester, 69, 75
  Thomas, 57, 68,
    70
  Thomas L., 102
  *Thomas T., 98
  *Timothy, 96
  Trausina, 98
  *William, 68, 69,
    87, 94
  William A., 98
  William A. x, 98
  William C.M., 98
  *William D., 69
  *William M., 102
  William P., 90
  William P.x, 73
  Wirt, 87

Alford
  Adain, 106
  Alizina, 106
  Bellidovea, 106
  Cynthia, 106
  Elizabeth, 106
  Emily, 106
  George, 106
  *James, 106
  John x, 3
  Joseph, 106
  Lafayette, 106
  Lorenzo, 106
  Mary, 106
  Oliver, 106
  *Robert, 106
Algeo
  Amasetta, 6
  Beverly J., 6
  *William D., 6
Allen
  America, 2
  Cyrus, 55
  Elizabeth, 52
  Frances, 2
  Henry, 55
  Irving, 55
  *James, 52
  Jennie B., 2
  *John W., 55
  Mary J., 55
  Matilda, 55
  Missouri, 55
  Nancy, 55
  *R.B., 2
  Runnell, 55
  Samuel, 55
  Samuel V., 52
  Sarah, 55
  Virginia, 52
  *William, 55
  Willie B., 52
Amos
  *Joshua, 115
  Mary, 115
  Mary F., 115
  Sarah C., 115
  William P., 115
Anderson
  Catherine x, 72
  Edmund, 5
  Frances, 72
  Isabella, 72
  *James, 72
  Julia, 72
  Marion x, 98
  *Nancy, 5
  Naoma, 72
Angel
  Charles, 122

*head of household   X EXTRA PERSON

Baum
Barbary, 4
* George, 4
John x, 23

Baumgardner
Armana, 22
Arminta, 13
Charles A., 1
Cora V., 1
Elizabeth, 13
Emma, 22
Frank, 22
Frederick, 22
George F., 13
Henrietta, 13
Henry J., 13
Henry W., 46
* Jacob, 46
* James, 13
James M., 46
* John, 22
John A., 13
John B., 1
John P., 22
Lawrence K., 1
Louisa C., 1
Malinda, 22
Margaret, 22
Mary, 22, 46
Mildred, 46
Millard, 13
Rebecca, 46
Sarah E., 13
Welcome A., 13
William, 22
William J., 13
William L., 1

Bays
Eliza, 107
Elizabeth, 107
Isaac, 107
James, 107
Jane, 107
* John, 107
Lucinda, 107
Mary, 107
Richard, 107
* Riley, 107
Sarah, 107
Sarah E., 107
Susan, 107
William H., 107

Becker
* Albert, 6, 135
Frederick, 6
George, 6
Jo Anna, 6
Matilda, 6
Mildred, 6
Thomas, 6

Wilhelmine, 6
Beckett
* Ahaz H., 104
Andrew, 104
* Andrew L., 129
* Charles, 29, 130
Charles x, 118
Eliza, 104
Emily S., 129
* Emsley, 125
Francis M., 29
Hannah, 130
* James, 130
James A., 125
John, 130
John S., 125
Jonah, 118
Julia, 118, 130
* Lewis, 29
Lewis L., 120
Louisa, 125
Margaret, 104
Martha, 104
Mary, 104, 118, 130
Mary S., 125
* Moses, 118
Rebecca, 125
Samuel, 130
Susan, 29, 118, 130
* William, 104
William C., 118
William L,, 29

Beech
Caroline, 130
Columbus x, 85
Eliza, 130
Elizabeth, 130
Hannah x, 86
* James, 130
Jane, 130
John H., 130
John x, 75
Mary, 130
Saml. x, 8
Sarah, 130
Sarah x, 85
Walden x, 25
William, 130

Beekman
Betty A., 39
Ellen V., 39
* Lewis, 39
Pauline, 39
Samuel M., 39

Beevers
Mathias x, 71

Belcher
Paulina x, 87

Peggy x, 87
Bell
* James C., 79
* John R., 80
Louisa, 80
Mary B., 79

Bellamy
Armstead, 53
* E., 53
John M., 53
Melissa J., 53
Nelsina, 53
Samuel, 53

Belsoe (Bledsoe)
Alfred, 80
James, 80
John T., 80
Lewis, 80
Mildred, 80
* Rachel, 80

Berry
Corila, 35
John, 35
Letitia, 35
Mary, 35(2)
* Philo B., 35

Best
Carrie, 51
Elizabeth, 51
John, 51
Mary, 51
* William, 51

Beuhring
Emma, 50
* F.D., 50
Fanny, 50

Bexfield
James, 36
Joseph, 36
Mary, 36
* Richard, 36

Bias
Adalaide, 30
Adolphus, 27
Amanda, 74
America, 10
Anabella, 10
* Anderson, 92
Andrea, 18
Andrew, 10
Angelina, 82
Augusta, 10
* Berry, 10
Blackburn, 82
Calvery, 92
Catherine, 30
Charles L., 10
Clarrissa, 82
Cordelia, 27
Cornelus, 75

Crosby, 82
Cynthia, 84
* Daniel, 26, 92
Daniel B., 27
* David H., 27
Dicey, 82
Drucilla, 30
Elisha, 83
Eliza, 130
Elizabeth, 18, 27, 30, 55
Emerine, 10
Emilly, 57
Emily A., 92
Emily x, 10
* Ennis, 92
Evermont, 92
George W., 57
* James, 82
* James A., 55
* James C., 74
James R. x, 10
* James S., 57
Jennetta, 26
John, 10
Julia, 26
Julia A., 92
* Larkin, 18, 74
Lenville, 92
Letha, 82
Lily A., 55
* Linsey, 14
Linsey x, 75
Louisa, 84, 92
Lourana, 82
Lucinda, 18
Lucy, 83, 130
Malinda, 130
Margaret, 10
Mariam x, 10
Marion, 82
Martha, 14, 30, 83, 84
Mary, 74, 83, 92
Mary A., 10
Matilda, 14
Matilda x, 17
Millington, 82
Nalinda x, 75
Nancy, 92
Nancy M., 18
* Obidiah, 84
Obidiah x, 74
Polly, 82
* R.S., 10, 135
Rachel, 83
* Reuben, 130
Rohn, 92
* Rolin, 30, 82, 83
Ruth, 27, 74

154

Bias (continued)
Saml. A., 10
Sarah, 10, 27, 57, 83
Sarah x, 75
Sereptia, 83
Thomas, 26, 75
William, 30, 57
William A., 92
★William E., 18
William M., 84
William W.x, 75

Bickel
John x, 113

Bicker
★Henry, 36
Joanna, 36

Bierly
Eliza, 43
John D., 43
★Joseph, 43
Samuel, 43
Sarah M., 43
Tucker, 43

Billups
Adalaide, 14
Ann, 120
Chalres, 124
Charles A., 14
Elliott T., 14
Huldah, 14
★James, 120
James B., 14
John W., 14
Louisa, 124
★Mary, 124
Mary J., 120
★R.A., 14
Robert H., 14

Black
Adam, 95
Amastis, 128
★Andrew, 118
Ann, 128
Araminta, 118
Caroline, 96
Cynthia, 128
Eliza, 95
Elizabeth, 128, 136
Elizabeth x, 124, 128
Ezra, 128
George, 128
Isabella, 128
★James C., 95
James x, 94
John, 95, 118, 128
Lowell, 128

Lucinda, 118
Lucy, 95
Mary x, 94
Peter x, 124
Rufus, 128
Samantha, 128
Sarah, 95
Theodore, 128
Virginia, 128
★William, 96, 128, 137
William C., 128

Blackwood
Adaline, 122
Charles, 122
James, 122
★Joseph, 122
Robert x, 62

Blair (Blom)
Elizabeth, 112
Frances, 112
George, 112
Jane, 112
John, 112
Mary, 112
Rachel, 112
Sarah, 112
★William, 112

Blake
Albert, 21
Alice, 62
Amasetta, 62
Anna, 8
Anselon, 14
Charles, 62
Christian S., 21
Clarrissa, 113
Daniel, 114
Dolph, 21
Elizabeth, 21
Emma, 8
Frances, 62
Frederick, 14
★Isaac, 7, 21
James, 14
★Jeremiah, 17, 21
JoAnna, 21
John, 21
John M., 21, 113
Julia, 113
Louisana, 21
Lucetta, 113
Margaret, 14, 17
Margaret x, 17
Martha, 62
Mary, 14, 62, 113
Mary A, 7
★Miles, 62
★Morris, 113
Nancy, 14, 114

★Pinnell, 14
Preston, 14
★Sarah, 8, 21, 113, 135
Sarah C., 14
Telitha, 113
Thomas, 14
William H., 113

Blankenship
Ariana x, 32
Charlotte, 94
★E.D., 94
Eliza, 89
Elizabeth, 94
Frances, 58
George, 57
Girard, 58, 94
Henry, 59
Irvin, 89
Jessee, 59
John T., 57
Lalila, 57
Leonara, 94
Louisa, 94
Lucy, 58
Maria, 89
Marlin x, 23
Mary, 89, 95
Melvin, 89
Permelia, 59
Ralph, 89
Reece, 58
Salome x, 57
★Samuel, 57
Sarah, 95
William J., 58
William P., 89

Blanped
★Elisha, 43
Isabella, 43
Mary E., 43

Bledsoe
Alfred, 80
Amos, 84
James, 80
John T., 80
Lewis, 80
Louisa, 117
Mary, 85, 117
Melissa, 84
Mildred, 80
★Moses, 117
Peter x, 84
★Rachel, 80
Susan, 117
★William, 84, 85

Blom
Elizabeth, 112
Frances, 112
George, 112

Jane, 112
John, 112
Mary, 112
Nancy A.x, 113
Rachel, 112
Sarah, 112
★William, 112

Blume
Ada, 26
Albert, 26
★E.W., 26
Eveline, 26
George, 26

Bobbitt
★James F., 104
Joseph, 104
Malinda, 104

Boden
Alice, 104
Cynthia, 104
★John, 104
Mary, 104
Sarah, 104

Boggess
George W. x, 2

Booten
Elizabeth x, 52

Booth
Alexander, 67
Artemisia, 67
Ballard, 67
Charles, 67
Edith, 66
Elias, 66
James, 66, 67
★John, 66
Julia, 66
Martha, 67
Mildred, 66
★Nathan, 66
Rachel, 67
★Samuel, 67
William, 67
William E., 66

Bostick
Anderson, 107
Betsy, 107
Elizabeth, 107
Henderson, 107
★Joseph, 107
★Joshua, 107
Mary, 107
Nancy, 107

Bowden
Alonzo, 74
Charles, 74
David, 74
Innius, 74
Mary, 74

155

George x, 71
Chatterton
Amanda, 58
⁎George, 58
Henry, 58
Mary, 58
Richard, 58
Rocksalina, 58
Childers
⁎A.M., 7
Albert, 32
Alenda J, 7
Alexander, 7
Amanda, 28
⁎ Benjamin S, 8
Benton, 10
Catherine, 7, 28
Charles T., 7
Colonel, 32
Conwesley, 7
Elizabeth, 7, 10,
  32
Elizabeth A, 8
Ellenor, 10
Geneva, 8
George, 10
George W., 7
⁎ Green A., 8
Greenville, 32
Henry, 7
James, 7, 27
Jasper, 7
John, 28
John M., 7
Joseph B., 32
Louisa, 7
⁎M.M., 28
Malvina, 8
Mary, 8
Mary F., 32
Mary J, 7
Mary M, 8
Nancy, 32(2)
Nancy x, 28
Newton, 7
Philip, 7
⁎Royal, 32
⁎Samuel A., 7
Sarah, 32
Sarah E., 7
Spencer, 28
Thomas, 10
⁎Thomas A., 10
William, 10
William L., 32
William S., 7
Childs
Phoebe x, 55
Chitam
Thomas x, 96

Chrislip
⁎ A.R., 113
Eugenia, 113
Martha, 113
Mary, 113
Salome, 113
Christy
⁎Abraham, 113
Catherine, 113
Jeremiah, 113
Jerome, 113
Susan, 113
⁎ Thomas, 113
William, 113
Church
Francis, 1
Frederick, 1
George, 1
Henry L., 1
John W., 1
Margaret, 1
Octavius, 1
Clark
Alexander, 44
Angelin, 17
Catherine, 17
Charles R., 31
Clarence, 44
⁎Daniel, 64
David, 64
⁎ Elizabeth, 31, 39
⁎Ervin, 17
Eveline, 64
Frederick, 39
George, 39
Harvey, 64
Julia, 39
Lorenzo D., 39
⁎ Lyman, 39
Martha, 44
Rachel, 64
Robert, 44
Robert x, 64
Roland, 39
S.M., 135
⁎ Silas, 44
Taylor, 64
William, 64
Clay
Matilda x, 70
Clendenin
Anna, 95
⁎Ballard, 95
Eliza, 95
Close
Allen x, 113
Cocke
John x, 31
Cohen
Rodolph x, 71

Collins
Adam, 17
Addison, 28
Andrew, 95
Celicia, 95
Charles, 17
⁎Charles G., 17
Christopher, 17
Clarrissa, 28
⁎Elias, 95
Elijah, 95
Enoch, 17
Greenville, 22
Henry A., 17
Hester, 17
Hester Ann, 17
Hezekiah, 28
⁎Isaac, 89
Jennie, 28
⁎John, 28
Lafayette, 17
Mary, 17
Mary J., 22
Mary x, 10
Merritt, 95
Mortimer, 17
Nancy, 28
Nathan, 17
⁎ Nathaniel, 22
Patience, 17
Permelia x, 17
Salome, 17
Sarah, 89
Thomas, 28
Timothy, 95
Vincent, 95
⁎ William, 17
William R., 95
William x, 10, 66
Zedic x, 66
Zitthia, 17
Colvin
Elizabeth, 20
⁎ Jackson, 20
Rachel, 20
Solomon, 20
⁎William, 20
Conley
Adaline, 90
⁎Bayley, 90
Ira, 90
Isadora, 90
Laura, 90
Mary, 90
Connell
Jane x, 66
Malaria x, 66
Conner
Abagail, 123
⁎Addison, 123

Amanda x, 4
Amasetta x, 23
America x, 23
Amy, 119
⁎Andrew, 132
Charles, 23
Conwesley, 132
Emaretta, 123
Hetty, 5
⁎James, 123
John M., 123
John W., 23
Joseph, 132
Levina, 123
Lewis x, 129
Louisa, 23
Michael, 119
Mildred, 132
Permelia, 132
Samanthia, 123
Susan, 118
⁎William, 118
⁎William W., 23
Cook
Abner, 64
Abner x, 59
Catherine, 64
Eliza, 64
Eliza x, 1
Elizabeth, 64
Florence, 65
Frances, 65
George, 64
Henry, 64
Henry J., 64
⁎James, 24
Jennie, 64
John W., 64
Julius, 24
Louisa, 13
Martha, 13
Mary, 24, 64
⁎Mathew, 65
Nancy, 64
Peter x, 118
⁎Solomon, 64
Susan, 24
⁎Thomas, 13, 24
Cooper
⁎Catherine, 91
Floyd, 91
Francis, 91
Henderson, 94
Lucinda, 94
Mildred, 91
Nancy, 91
Phoebe, 91
⁎Polly, 91
Rebecca x, 105
Sally, 91

158

Cooper (continued)
Samuel, 91
Sarah, 91
*Silas, 94
Thomas, 91
Cornell
Amy M., 20
Louisa, 20
*Martin, 20
Cotton
*Charles, 97
Holland, 97
James, 97
Julia, 97
Richard, 97
Susan, 97
William, 97
Cowan
Alexander, 73
Henrietta, 73
Hester, 73
*James, 10, 73
Levina, 73
Mary, 73
Mary S., 10
Sarah, 10
*Thomas, 73
Thomas J., 10
Walter, 73
Willis, 73
Cox
*A.J., 18
Adala, 18
Albert E., 18
America M., 18
Cora S., 14
Eliza, 18
Elizabeth, 18
Emily x, 8
Geneva C., 14
Georgia A., 14
Henrietta H., 18
James A., 18
*James O., 14
Jennette, 18
*John A., 18
Joseph, 18
Margaret, 14
Mary A., 18
Sarah, 18
Sarah x, 8
*William, 18
Crabtree
Pricy, 78
*Rachel, 78
Cremeans
*Amasa, 66
Burton, 71
Catherine, 71
David, 66

*Durgan, 31
Edith, 71
*Elizabeth, 36, 66, 71, 122
George x, 67
Isaac, 71
*James, 31, 66, 71
*John, 122
Joseph, 71
Joycey, 71
Julia, 71, 122
Julia x, 130
Luther x, 4
Margaret, 66
Martha S., 122
Mary, 122
Miama x, 31
Michael, 71
Nancy x, 67
*Nathan, 122
Paulina, 71
Polly, 36
Richard, 71
Rose, 31
*Sanders, 71
Sarah, 31, 71
Sarah C., 122
Sarah x, 115
Susan x, 67
Thomas, 71
Wilson x, 67
*Winchester, 71
Crooks
Abraham x, 16
Crumb
*Daniel, 70
Elizia, 70
George W., 70
Maria, 70
Polly, 70
Rhoda, 70
Crumby
Elizabeth x, 2
Crump
Elizabeth, 61
*Isaac, 61
Martha, 61
Mary A., 61
Nancy, 61
Cummings
Adaline, 111
Angeline, 111
*Charles, 111
Ellender, 111
John, 111
Mary, 111
Minerva, 111
Syndey, 111
Cunningham
Elizabeth, 48

Georgia A., 48
Harriett, 48
*Isaac, 48
Kate, 48
Curry
Alfred H., 102
Barbary, 102
Benjamin, 102
Blackburn, 102
Elmira, 102
Emily, 102
*Franklin, 119
George, 102
Granville, 102
*Harrison, 121, 124
*Hiram, 102
John, 124
John C., 119
Joseph, 119
Laura, 119
Margaret, 95
Martha, 102, 121, 124
Mary, 124
Mayberry x, 124
Permelia, 102
Sarah A., 119
Sophia, 119, 124
*Timothy, 124
Washington, 95
*William, 95
Curtis
Eliza x, 75
Mary x, 75
Mathew x, 75
Custis
*Mary, 26
Cyrus
*Elijah, 16
James N., 16
James x, 92
John E., 16
*Joseph, 9
Joseph W., 16
Lucinda, 16
Margaret, 16
Mary, 13
Mary E., 16
Matilda, 13
*Sarah, 13
Sarah A., 16
Sarah E., 9
William H., 13
William T., 16
Davidson
Alex x, 46
Davis
Adaline, 85
Addison, 132

Albert, 58
Albert G., 12
Albion, 63
Allen, 131
*Alvin, 85
America, 131
Artenus, 70
*Benjamin S., 12
Charles, 132
Christopher, 63
Cortez x, 24
Cynthia, 63
Daniel, 85
Drucilla, 63
Edny x, 24
Eliza, 70
Elizabeth, 12, 61, 132
Elizabeth x, 116
Eugenia, 70
Florence, 58
George, 125
Georgia, 58
*Greenville, 58
Harriett, 12
*Harrison, 63
Henderson, 63
Isabella, 58
*J.M.C., 70
Jessee, 132
*John, 125
John S., 12
John x, 69
Joseph, 131
Josphine, 63
Lewellyn, 58
Licia, 131
*Lockie, 63
Louisa, 63
Marcellus, 70
Martha, 132
*Mary, 61, 132
Mary A., 63
Mary H., 12
Mary x, 38
Matilda x, 24
Milton J., 85
Missoura, 63
Nancy, 131
Nephrenus, 70
Oscar, 63
Paul, 63
Paulina, 24
*Samuel H., 131
Sarah, 125, 132
Sarah x, 70
*Sterling, 132
Thomas, 131
Victor, 58
*Wesley, 63

159

William, 63
✶William G., 24
William H., 63
William W., 12
Willie x, 24
Deacon
✶Andrew, 84
Elizabeth, 84
Henry C. x, 84
Laura, 84
Mary J., 84
Deal
Cadmus, 124
Ebenzer, 124
Henry H., 124
✶Henry H., 124
John, 124
Lucy, 124
Martha, 124
Dean
Catherine, 34
✶George, 34
Margaret, 34
Samuel, 34
Samuel x, 12, 35
Sarah, 34
Stephen, 34
Deboy
Elizabeth, 32
✶John, 32
Julia, 32
Mahala, 32
Margaret, 32
Polly, 32
Defoe
Albert, 88
Charles L., 88
Elizabeth, 87
James, 88
John, 87
Martha, 87
Rachel, 88
Sarah, 88
✶William, 87
William M., 88
Defor
Rachel x, 127
Deihl
Catherine x, 131
Deitz
Allen, 47
Charles, 44
Charlotte, 44
Elizabeth, 44
George, 44
Henry, 44
✶Hugo, 44
✶John R., 44
Levina, 44
Lewellyn, 44

Maria, 47
Mary, 47
Mary E., 44
Minerva, 44
Ola, 47
✶Otto, 44
✶Rodolphus, 47
Rosanna, 44
William C., 44
Dennison
George, 130
Jane, 130
Jennetta, 130
✶John, 130
Mahala, 130
Margaret, 130
Mary, 130
Derton
Ann, 5
Charles, 6
Eliza J., 3
✶Elizabeth, 4
✶Harrison, 5
Henry J., 3
Isabella, 5
✶John, 3
Louisa, 3
Louisa A., 3
Mary, 6
Mary A., 5
Philip, 3
Thomas, 3
✶William, 6
William D., 3
Dial
Caroline, 69
Catherine, 69
Edward, 69
✶Elisha, 14
Elizabeth, 69
James, 69
✶John, 14, 69
Juda, 69
✶Lucinda, 76
Mary, 69
Mary A., 76
Mary A.x, 69
Nancy, 15
Nancy Jr., 15
Panthea, 76
William, 69
Dick
✶A.J., 9
Anna E., 9
Ballard, 74
Benjamin, 74
Catherine, 74
Cynthia, 9
Francis, 74
Henry, 9

Henry J., 74
✶Joseph, 74
Margaret, 74
Mary x, 37
Morris F., 9
Rhoda, 74
Spurlock, 74
Diehl
Albert, 36
Catherine x, 131
✶Lewis, 35(2)
Robert, 36
Rosa, 35
Dillon
Adalaid, 23
Arinda, 9
Benjamin x, 61
Elizabeth, 61
George, 61
✶John L., 9
Julia, 61
Julius, 9
Lucy, 61
Lucy x, 23
Luvender, 9
Marlin x, 23
Mary J., 9
✶Rece W., 23
Ruth, 9
Sarah, 23
Squire x, 52
William F. x, 53
✶William J., 61
Diome
Delsey x, 47
Dolan
Jeanna x, 8
Joann x, 8
Dolen
Daniel, 37
Eliza, 37
Elletha, 8
Frances, 37
✶George, 8
James x, 37
✶John, 37
John x, 37
Julia, 37
Martha, 8
Rebecca, 8
Sarah x, 37
Doolittle
Alice, 131
Amanda, 131
Ambrose, 131
Cedora, 131
✶Luther , 131
Virginia, 131
Doran
Mary x, 115

Dotson
Amanda, 43
Charles, 43
Elizabeth, 44
Henry, 43
✶Jessie, 43
Lucetta, 43
Mary A., 43
Milton, 43
Sarah, 44
✶Thomas, 44
William E., 43
Douglas
Mary, 129
Rachel, 129
✶William H., 129
Douthit
Charlotte, 39
Clarence, 39
Columbia, 39
Edward, 39
John L., 39
Mary A., 39
Richard H., 39
✶William, 39
Drake
Amasetta, 90
Blackburn, 90
Elizabeth x, 90
Frances x, 63
Guy F., 90
✶Henderson, 90
Osborn, 90
Paulina, 90
Penelope, 90
Draper
John, 108
Mary, 108
Nancy, 180
Sarah, 108
Solomon, 108
Thomas, 108
✶William, 108
Drown
Benjamin, 31
Elizabeth, 31
George A., 31
Henry, 31
John, 31
Luke, 31
Martha, 31
Rufus, 31
Sarah, 31
Dudding
✶B.A., 55
Martha A., 55
Duffy
John B., 129
Martha, 129
Mary, 129

162

165

William H., 95
Holstein
  Addison, 108
  Arabella, 108
  Calbert, 108
  Cynthia, 108
  Elizabeth, 108
  Emma M., 108
  James R., 108
  John, 108
  Mary, 108
  ✻William A., 108
Holt
  Ida x, 87
  James x, 72
  Minerva x, 70
  Rebecca x, 94
  Sally x, 94
Holten
  ✻A.J., 97
  Albert G.J., 98
  ✻Allen, 94
  Anna x, 99
  Arisba, 96
  Calvin, 94
  Charles x, 96
  Cynthia x, 98
  Eliza, 98
  Elizabeth, 108
  Elizabeth x, 129
  Emily, 94
  Frances, 97, 98
  George, 108
  ✻George A., 96
  Harison, 94
  Jane, 94
  John, 97
  John H., 96
  ✦Joseph, 98
  ✦Joseph Jr., 98
  Julia, 94
  Louisa, 96
  Lucinda, 98
  Martha x, 100
  Mary, 97
  Mary A. x, 95
  Mary E., 98
  Mary x, 80
  Nancy, 94, 96, 98
  Nancy x, 117
  Nelson, 98
  Priscilla, 96
  Rachel x, 117
  Rebecca, 108
  Rebecca x, 98
  Ruth, 94
  Sally, 94
  Sarah, 98
  Sarah x, 110
  Thornton, 96

R

Toliver, 98
✦William, 94, 98
Holton
  Calvery, 94
Hotchkiss
  Mary x, 50
Houchins
  ✻Clarissa, 36
  ✻Frances, 114
  James H., 114
  Mary A., 114
  Rebecca, 114
  Rebecca x, 32
  William, 36
  William F., 114
Howard
  ✻Aaron, 62
  Daniel, 62
  David, 62
  Edward, 62
  Francis J., 62
  Hugh, 62
  John x, 18
  Lydia, 62
  Margaret, 62
  Susan, 62
  William, 62
Howell
  ✻A.B. , 131
  Francis, 131
  ✦John H., 15
  Mary E. x, 15
Hudson
  Mary x, 126
Huffman
  Andrew, 54
  Catherine, 54
  James, 54
  Thomas, 54
  ✻William, 54
Hughes
  Cora S., 55
  DeKalb x, 113
  James D., 55
  Jane x, 61
  Jeremiah x, 24
  Julia, 55
  Lorenzo x, 24
  Margaret x, 24
  Mary x, 24
  ✻R.B., 55
  Ralph x, 24
Hull
  Ann, 54
  Anna P., 55
  Bartholomew, 54
  Columbus, 54
  Eliza, 54
  Harriett, 54
  ✦John, 55

✦Martin, 54
  Matilda, 54
  Salome, 55
  Virginia, 55
  William M., 55
Hunter
  Charles, 92
  ✻Elizabeth, 92
  Margaret, 69
  Margaret x, 38
  ✻Samuel, 69
  William, 92
Huxom
  Charlotte, 45
  Elizabeth, 45
  Florence, 45
  ✻Henry, 45
  Sarah, 45
Imanion
  Emily x, 62
Insco
  James x, 54
Irving
  Amanda, 85
  James, 85
  Martha, 85
  ✦Robert, 85
  Samantha, 85
  Sarah, 85
  William T., 85
Ize
  Elizabeth x, 61
Jack
  ✻John, 68
  Levina, 68
  Mary E., 68
Jarrett
  Martha x, 121
Jarrold
  ✻Ambrose, 57
  Mary E., 57
Jefferson
  Albert G., 11
  America, 19
  Angelina, 11
  Elizabeth, 19, 21
  German, 117
  ✻Henry, 19
  ✻Henry Sr., 19
  Jackson, 19
  ✻John W., 11
  Joseph x, 22
  Louis, 21
  Louisa, 117
  Mahala, 19
  Malinda, 19, 21
  Marinda L., 19
  Mary, 21
  Mary A., 19
  Mary E., 19

Nancy, 21
  Rhoda, 117
  Samuel W., 19
  Thenia, 21
  ✻Thomas, 21
  ✻William, 117
  William H., 19
  William R., 11
Jenkins
  ✻A.G., 112
  ✻Anderson, 65
  Bailey, 65
  Eliza, 65
  Emily, 65
  Jennetta, 112
  Jennie S., 112
  John, 65
  Julia, 112
  Julia M., 112
  Laura, 112
  Susan, 112
  ✻T.J., 112
  Telitha, 65
  William, 65
  ✻William A., 112
  William G., 112
Jennings
  Mary, 115
  ✦Samuel R., 115
Jewell
  Abagail x, 33
  ✻Benjamin R., 36
  Catherine x, 42
  Gottier x, 32
  Helen x, 42
  Matt x, 33
  Puses, 36
Jimeson
  Benjamin, 28
  Hannah, 28
  James, 28
  ✻Joseph, 28
  Malinda, 28
  Susan, 28
Johnson
  Abner, 52
  Ailsey, 81
  Albert, 52
  ✻Alex, 53
  Almedia, 119
  America, 81, 102
  ✦Andrew, 81(3)
  Angeline, 102
  Ann, 118
  Anna, 53
  Armstead, 53
  Benjamin, 52, 94
  Betsy, 81
  ✦Burwell, 81, 82
  Caledoria, 109

167

Kennison
- Griffin, 87
- Malinda, 87
- Nancy, 87
- Victoria, 87

Ketcham
- Alonzo, 71
- Eliza, 71
- Hugh, 71
- John W., 71
- Margaret, 71
- Mary F., 71
- Vanilla, 71

Keyser
- Albert, 12
- David, 12
- Eliza, 12
- Emeline, 12
- Ephraim, 12
- George, 12
- George x, 12
- Hugh, 12
- John, 12
- Malinda, 12
- Oscar, 12
- Patrick H., 12
- Thomas, 12
- Valeria, 12
- William, 12
- William W., 12

Keyser/Kayser

Keyton
- Adaline, 118
- Amanda, 118
- Armilda, 118
- Harriett x, 22
- Henry, 118
- John L., 118
- John W., 118
- John x, 103
- Lucinda, 118
- Mary, 118
- Preston, 118
- Roland, 118
- William, 118

Killgore
- Charles, 126
- George, 125
- James, 125
- John, 126
- Joseph, 126
- Marshall, 126
- Mary, 126
- Nancy, 125, 126, 136
- Rachel, 125
- Thomas, 126
- Thomas W., 136
- William, 125

Kincaid

- Clarrissa, 72
- Cynthia, 72
- Henry, 72
- Malinda, 72
- Sarah, 72
- Wesley, 72
- William, 72

Kinder
- Elizabeth, 92
- Frances, 92
- Jackson x, 92
- Jasper, 92
- Julia, 92
- Mary, 92
- Nancy, 92
- Samantha, 92
- Samuel, 92

King
- Elizabeth, 28
- Emma, 107
- Frances, 107
- Jesse, 100
- John A., 107
- Juda, 100
- Martha, 28
- Mary, 28
- Mary x, 100
- Sampson, 28
- Sarah x, 100
- William H., 28

Kinnard
- Ann, 125
- Ephraim, 125
- George R., 125
- Harriett, 125
- Howard, 125
- Jane, 125
- Joseph, 125
- Margaret, 125
- Nancy, 125
- William H., 125

Kirk
- Andrew, 110
- Emerine, 28
- James, 28
- Jeremiah, 28
- Jessee, 110
- John, 28
- John E., 110
- Jordan, 111
- Julia, 111
- Leander, 110
- Manderville, 111
- Martha, 28
- Martin, 111
- Mary, 28, 110
- Nancy, 110
- Preston, 110
- Sarah, 28
- William, 28

- William J., 110

Kise
- Harriett x, 42

Knight
- Abagail, 114
- Abner, 20, 21
- Abner P., 20
- Alvin, 21
- Alvin S., 24
- Amasetta, 22
- Anna, 21
- Anselom, 20
- Carolina, 20
- Catherine, 20, 22
- Eliza, 21, 114
- Ellen x, 43
- Frances J., 7
- George, 21
- Harriett, 20, 21
- Henrietta, 22
- Henry, 22
- James, 21, 24
- John, 7, 21
- Lafayette, 22
- Leonard, 20
- Margaret, 7, 21, 22
- Mary, 20, 21, 24
- Mary x, 43
- Mathew, 24
- Matilda, 20
- Nancy, 24
- Nimrod, 22
- Parthenia, 21, 22
- Sarah, 20, 21, 22
- Sarah x, 43
- Susan, 114
- Wayne, 24
- William, 22, 24
- William A., 20
- William H., 20

Korn
- David, 36

Kraus
- Anna x, 10
- Walter x, 3

Kyle
- Adaline, 11
- Anna, 18
- Edgar, 3
- Eliza x, 53
- George, 11
- John, 18
- Margaret, 11
- Margaret x, 19
- Melitta, 3
- Missouri, 11
- Peter, 11
- Rebecca, 18
- Samuel, 11

- Sarah, 3, 18
- Teresa, 3
- Thomas, 3
- William H. x, 53

Lacy
- David, 136
- David R., 113
- Eustacia, 113

Laidley
- Albert, 2
- Alberta, 2
- Eliza, 48
- George, 48
- Helen, 48
- John, 2, 48
- Mary, 48
- Vesta, 2
- William S., 48

Lakeman
- Jane x, 121

Landrum
- James, 91
- John, 91
- Mary, 91
- Sarah, 91
- William, 91

Larkin
- Thomas x, 39

Latimore
- James M., 14
- Olive, 14
- Robert, 14
- Sarah J., 14
- Simeon, 14
- Thompson A., 14

Lattin
- Charles, 4
- Charles A., 4
- David C.S., 4
- Jane A., 4

Lavender
- Emily x, 92
- John W., 97
- Joseph, 97
- Nancy, 97

Lawrence
- Arabella, 105
- Charles, 94, 105
- Elizabeth, 94, 108
- Emily, 95
- George M., 94
- John, 108
- Joseph, 94
- Julia, 108
- Michael, 108
- Parthenia, 105
- Permelia, 95
- Preston, 94
- Rachel, 94

Lawrence (continued)
  Samuel, 94
  Sarah, 105, 108
  Theodore T., 95
 ✗William H., 95
Lawson
 ✱David, 100, 105
  Henry E., 105
  James, 105
 ✗ John, 105
 ✗ Jospeh, 105
  Julia, 105
  Kesine, 100
  Lucinda, 105
  Lucretia, 105
  Lucy, 105
  Mary, 105
  Mary A., 105
  Mason, 105
  Sarilda, 105
  Scott, 105
 ✱William, 105
  Zach, 105
Lawter
  Michael x, 15
Legg
  Addison, 122
  Allen, 122
  Charles, 122
  Eli, 122
  Elizabeth, 122
  John H., 122
  Rebecca, 122
 ✱Thomas, 122
  Vileta x, 122
 ✗Willis, 122
Leonard
  Mary, 36
 ✗Rufus, 36
Lesage
 ✱Frances, 21
  Henrietta, 21
  Joseph, 21
 ✗Julius, 21
  Mary, 21
  Zelia, 21
Letcher
  John x, 9
Letulle
  James L., 44
  Josephine, 44
  Lenora, 44
  Lewis, 44
 ✗Nancy, 44
  Sarah, 44
  Victora, 44
Libby
 ✱A.H., 74
  Charles, 74
  Ellen, 74

Linkfield
  Alice x, 112
  Frances x, 112
  Ida x, 112
  Riley x, 112
Lloyd
  Elizabeth, 25
  Fidelia, 2
  George, 25
  Jane A., 2
 ✗ John, 2, 25
 ✱R.J., 25
  Robert, 25
  Sarah, 25
  Susan, 25
  Urania, 2
  William, 25
Long
  Betsey, 14
  Charles x, 3
  Emily J., 14
  James S., 14
  Sarah B, 14
 ✱ William H., 14
  William M., 14
Louchine
  Sol x, 46
Love
  Ann, 25
  Charles, 25
  Conwesley, 25
  Cynthia, 131
  Daniel, 136
  Daniel ✱, 131
  John, 25
  Leonidas, 131
  Margaret x, 32
 ✱ P.E., 25
  Theodosius, 131
 ✱William, 128, 136
Lovejoy
 ✱Daniel, 51
  Jennetta, 51
  John, 51
Lucas
  Amanda, 88
  Andrew, 88
  Calvin, 73
  Chloe, 67, 73
  Cynthia A. x, 11
 ✱David, 67
  Emily, 88
 ✱George, 11
  Gordon, 11
  James J., 11
 ✗John, 68, 88
  John M., 73
  Leonard, 88
  Letta, 88
  Malvina, 73

  Marion, 68
  Martha, 68
  Mary, 67, 68, 88
  Minerva, 88
  Moses, 88
  Nancy, 88
  Paris, 88
 ✱Parker, 73
  Pheobe, 11
 ✱Price, 88
  Ralph, 88
 ✱Rebecca, 68, 73
  Samuel, 68
  Sarah, 67, 73, 88
  Sarah x, 11
  Susan x, 90
  William, 11, 68,
    88
Lunceford
  Calvery, 34
  Elijah, 34
  Elijah Sr.x, 34
  Emily, 34
  George W., 123
  Hugh M., 123
  John, 123
  John H., 34
 ✱ Joshua, 123
  Mary, 34
  Mary E., 123
  Nancy, 34
  Peter, 123
 ✗Richard, 34
  Sarah, 123
  Susan, 123
  William T., 123
Lusher
  Alice, 73
  Charles, 73
  Cynthia x, 73
  Elizabeth x, 68
  Frances x, 68
  George, 3
  Henry, 73
  Henry J., 3
 ✱Irving, 73
  James M., 15
  Jane, 73
  John, 73
 ✗Johnson, 3
  Lewis x, 73
  Lucy, 3
 ✱Margaret, 15
  Mary, 73
  Mary L., 15
  Matthew J., 15
  R.M., 73
  Sarah J., 15
  Scott, 3
  Toliver, 15

Lykins
  Andrew, 96
  Erasonus, 96
  Frances M.x, 96
  Herod, 96
  James, 96
 ✱John, 96
  Littleberry, 96
  Mary, 96
  Nancy x, 96
  Peter, 96
  Rebecca, 96
  William, 96
McCallister
  Adaline x, 130
  Albert, 85
 ✗Alexander, 85
  Allen, 120
  America, 84
  Ann, 80
  Catherine x, 111
  Cynthia, 80
  Dasen, 80
  Dicey, 80
  Edgar, 120
  Edney, 120
  Eliza, 120
  Elizabeth, 120
  Emma, 85
  Eveline, 85
  Hamilton, 120
  Harrison, 85
  Helen, 85
  Henry, 85, 120
 ✗Isaac, 120
  Isaac H., 85
  Isabella, 84
  Jackson, 120
 ✗James, 80, 84
 ✱John, 85, 120
 ✱Joseph, 85, 120
  Lafayette, 84
  Louisa, 85
  Lucinda x, 130
 ✱Malcom, 120, 136
  Malinda, 85
  Margery, 120
  Maria, 85
  Martha, 85
  Mary, 84, 120
  Nancy, 111, 120
 ✱Olivia, 120
  Parthenea, 111
  Patrick, 120
 ✱Perry, 111
  Polly, 80
 ✗Preston, 84, 85
 ✗Richard, 80, 111
  Sarah, 85, 111,
    120

169

Sarah x, 111
Senith x, 111
Susannan, 85
Thomas, 80
Wesley, 80
William, 80
William S., 80
McCarty
Sarah x, 2
McClure
*Allen, 109
Asberry, 109
James, 109
John, 109
Julia, 109
Nancy A., 109
Rhoda, 109
*William , 109
McCoggle
John x, 80
McComas
Adaline, 82
*Alexander, 67, 78
Alonzo, 72
America, 82
Andrew, 67
Andrew x, 26
*Aquilla, 90
Arminda, 72
Ballard x, 71
Benjamin, 72, 127
Billington S., 82
Blackburn, 72, 82
Blackburn x, 75
Catherine, 72, 82
Charles x, 103
Chloe, 72
Cynthia, 72, 74,
78
*David, 72, 78, 79
Docia, 72
Dyke, 72
Edney x, 103
*Elisha, 66, 72,
83
Elisha x, 69, 112
Eliza, 12, 67,
121
*Elizabeth, 78,
83, 90
Elizabeth x, 91,
117
Elvira x, 82
Emberson, 90
Emily, 79, 82, 90
Francis, 74
George, 72
H.A.W., 74
*Harrison, 72
*Henderson, 72

Herbert, 79
Hester, 72
Irene O., 7
*Isaac, 71
Isabella, 71
Jackson, 71
*James, 67, 78,
79, 90
*James M., 90
Jefferson, 71, 72
*Jesse, 74
Job. 127
*John, 12, 67, 83,
127
John M.B., 82
John x, 112
Juda, 67
Julia, 67, 82,
127
Julia x, 112
Lelia F., 12
*Lewis, 72
Lucinda, 127
Martha, 72
*Mary, 66, 67, 74,
82, 90, 127
Mary J.x, 75
Mary x, 75
Milton, 90
Minerva, 66, 67,
72
Moses, 90
Nancy, 71, 72
Paulina, 82
Perry x, 16
Peyton x, 25
Rocksalina, 66
Rush, 72
Sally x, 102
Sarah, 7, 79, 82,
90
Susan. 67
Thomas, 83, 90
*Thomas J., 82
Thomas S. x, 82
*Thomas Sr. , 83
Valeria, 90
Victoria, 90
Vitura, 67
*William, 7, 72,
134
William H., 127
William P., 90
William x, 112
Wirt, 79
McConnell
Albert T., 52
Eliza C., 52
James R., 52
Letitia, 52

Mary A., 52
*William, 52
McCorkle
*A.M., 31, 134
Ariana, 59
Catherine, 59
Effie, 31
Elleanor, 31
Frederick, 59
G.W.S., 31
George, 29
Ida, 31
*James, 59
Lafayette, 59
Louisa, 59
Mary J., 59
Olive, 59
Phoebe, 31
Sarah, 59
McCormick
Walstein x, 54
McCoy
Ailsey, 88
Dicy, 88
James, 88
Malinda, 88
Meredith, 88
*Robert, 88
McCullough
Bob, 50
Emma, 50
Frank, 50
Isadora, 50
Julius, 50
*P.H., 50
Rachel, 50
McCune
*Benjamin, 22
Charles, 22
Frank, 22
John, 22
Julia, 22
Lawrence, 22
Sarah, 22
McDonie
Charles B., 131
*James, 131
Mary, 131
William C., 131
McFarland
James x, 57
McGinnis
*A.A., 49
*A.B., 45, 135
*Achilles, 64
Allen, 64
Charlotte, 36
Eliza, 49
Elizabeth, 45
Henry H., 49

Ira x, 1
Joan, 36
*John B., 36
John W., 49
Lucian, 64
Miriam, 64
Sarah, 49
McKannon
*Matthew, 7
Rebecca, 7
McKeand
Alexander, 79
America, 79
Eleanor, 79
Eliza, 79
Emily, 79
*John, 79
Mary, 79
Sarah, 79
William, 79
McKendree
*A.F., 15
*Ariana, 3
Catherine, 15
Charles, 15
Elvira, 3
Emily, 15
Frances, 15
Lucinda, 3
Mary M., 3
Melitta, 15
Rebecca, 15
Robert, 15
Samuel, 15
Susan, 15
William, 15
McKibby
Harriet x, 33
McKinley
M.M. x, 45
McLary
Alice, 53
Barbary, 53
*David, 53
Jane, 53
Mary, 53
Nancy, 53
McLeary
*Alexander, 80
Catherine, 80
Charles, 80
Frances, 25
Isaac, 25
James, 25
Lucretia, 80
Mary, 25
*Robert, 25
McLeese
Mary Ann, 7
*Patrick, 7

171

Polly, 113	Gebring, 66	William H., 47	Bula, 84
Sarah, 113	George, 2	Molesworth	*Charles, 33, 134
*William, 113	*George F., 2	Cecelia R., 43	Charles x, 119
Midkiff	George H., 6	Cicero, 43	*Eaton, 62
*Abraham, 77	Georgia, 61	*W.W., 43	Edney, 33, 120
Adaline, 67	*H.H., 40, 135	Monroe	Elizabeth x, 46
Albert, 66, 77	Hannah C., 2	Charles A., 46	Ellen, 33
Alexander, 77	*Henry, 6, 61, 75	James H., 46	Eugene J., 7
America, 86	Henry A.W., 105	John E., 46	Fanny, 62
Eliza, 82	Henry H., 134	Margaret, 46	Frances, 7
Elizabeth, 67, 82	Isabella, 35	Sarah E., 46	Gensia, 96
Emily, 82, 86	*Jacob, 66, 105	*Thomas H., 46	George, 62
Emma, 77	*James, 66, 128	Watson, 46	Helen, 120
*Gordon, 82	James T., 127	William M., 46	Helen M., 7
Harriett, 67	Jane, 127	Montgomery	Henry, 62
Harvey, 82	*John G., 6, 133	Alexander x, 7	Ida, 33
Henry, 86	*John M., 127, 136	Moore	James, 96
Isabella, 77	John W., 6	Albert G., 39	James B., 134
Ivy, 77	Joseph, 6	*Alexander, 70	*James R., 7
James, 67	*Joycey, 66	Alice, 39, 109	James x, 53, 62
*John, 67, 77	Lenora, 35	Amanda, 39	*John, 33, 96,
Josephine, 67	Leonora, 40	Anderson, 109	119, 120, 133
Julia, 66	Margaret, 61	Charles, 4	*Joseph W., 7, 120
Lewis, 86	Martha, 105, 127	Corbin, 70	Lucetta, 62
*Louis, 67	Mary, 2, 99, 105,	Cyrus S., 43	Lucy, 62
Mary, 67, 77	128	Eliza, 4	Mahlon, 84
Sarah, 67, 77	*Moses, 99	Elizabeth, 70,	Martha, 33
*Solomon, 67, 82,	Polly x, 17	109	Mary, 119, 120
86	Rhoda, 75	Elizabeth x, 64	Nancy, 62
*Spencer, 66, 77,	Rosamond, 35	Emerine, 70	Rebecca, 96
137	Ruth, 99	*F.M., 39	Sarah, 7, 62, 120
Victuria, 77	Sigsmund x, 6	Frank B., 43	Thomas, 33, 62
Walden, 77	Susan, 61, 99	George, 4	Walter T., 7
Miles	Thomas, 99	Harriet, 39	*William, 62, 96
Elizabeth x, 78	Valeria, 105	James, 39	Morrison
Miller	*William, 99	John, 39	Albert, 86
Abagail, 61	William C., 6,	John Thomas, 4	Allen, 16
ALice, 105	135	Margaret, 70	Anna, 24
Atha, 105	*Wm.C., 2	*Mary, 4, 135	Benjamin, 117
Belle, 40	Mills	Nancy, 109	Calvery, 86
Burwell, 105	*John, 3	*Orren, 43	Calvin, 86
Caroline, 35	Mary, 3	Rachel, 70	Catherine, 83
Catherine, 99	William, 3	Salina, 39	117
Charles, 99	Mitchell	Sarah, 39, 43,	Charles, 24
Charles H., 6	Absolum, 75	109	David H. x, 13
*Charles W., 35	Charles W., 75	Susan, 109	David x, 121
Christian S., 2	Eliza, 75	*W.B., 4, 135	Eliza, 117
Claudius, 6	Elizabeth, 46	*William, 109	Elizabeth, 24, 86
Cora, 40	Fanny x, 75	Morey	Emily, 117
Dollie, 99	John, 46	Anna, 5	*Frances, 16
Edney, 105	John L., 75	Cynthia, 5	Frank, 24
Edward, 40	*Joseph, 84	Eliza, 5	George W. x, 13
Eliza, 6, 40, 127	Lucy, 47	Frances, 5	*Henry, 16, 24, 86
Emily E., 127	Nancy, 84	*Frank, 5	James, 83
Eugenia, 6	Nancy J., 47	Julia, 5	James L., 117
Eveline, 6	Pleasant G.x, 75	Morris	John, 86, 117
Florence, 6	*Samuel, 75	Albert A., 7	*John E., 83, 136
Frances, 6	Samuel x, 75	Armstead x, 119	John S., 86
Frank, 6	Susan, 75	*Benjamin, 84	*John T., 86
Frederick, 66	*William, 46	Betsey, 84	Malinda, 24

173

Cynthia x, 42
~~Parsely~~ PARSLEY
Parsley
Bridget, 122
Parsley
Daniel, 122
Franklin, 122
John, 122
Mary, 122
Nathaniel G., 122
∗Richard, 122
Sarah, 122
Parsons
Cynthia, 89
Edward, 70
Francis, 70
∗George W., 70
James, 70
James x, 30
John, 70, 89
Julia, 70
Lorenza, 70
Margaret, 89
Nancy, 77
∗Samuel, 89
Sarah, 70, 89
Susan, 77
Theresa, 89
Patterson
∗Berry, 56
John D., 56
Nancy, 56
Robert T., 56
Sarah M., 56
Patton
Harriett, 103
∗Robinson, 103
Pearson
Frances x, 54
Lewis x, 95
Nancy x, 92
Sarah x, 94
Simon x, 94
Pedro
S.M. x, 119
Perry
Albert, 114
Anna, 19
∗Benjamin, 79
Bula, 84
Charles, 84
Cynthia, 84
David, 80
∗Elijah, 84
Eliza, 114
Hannah x, 19
∗John, 79, 114
John H., 114
Julia, 79
Lucy, 114
Malachi x, 22

Margaret x, 5
Martha, 79, 84
Mary, 80
Peter, 79
∗Richard, 19
∗S.B., 84
Sarah, 84
Susan, 114
Telitha x, 19
Thomas H., 79
∗William, 115
∗William B., 80
William W., 114
Peterman
Frances, 44
Isadore, 44
Jacob, 44
∗Ralph, 44
William, 44
Peters
Elizabeth, 39
James, 39
∗Lewis, 39
Mary, 39
Richard, 39
Virginia, 39
Peterson
Frances x, 20
Petit
Durasia, 45
Frances, 45
∗Hugh B., 45
John A., 45
Julia, 45
Noah C., 45
William E., 45
Petrey
George, 76
John, 76
Maria, 76
Marion, 76
Martha, 76
∗Martin, 76
Mary, 76
Robert, 76
Peyton
∗Alexander, 17
Allen x, 34
Alvin, 85
Amanda, 85
Amasetta, 85
∗Archibald, 128
Betsey, 85
Catlett x, 85
Charles x, 85
Clara x, 85
Cynthia, 74
Daniel, 4
∗Elisha, 29
Eliza, 85

Elizabeth, 74, 85
Emma, 85, 128
Fianna, 17
Frances x, 128
Francis x, 15
Frank, 15, 85
∗Harrison, 85
Henrietta, 85
Henry, 74
Isabella, 17
Jennetta, 85
∗John, 29, 67
John W., 15
John x, 90
Juda, 67
L.M., 15
Lewis x, 29
Louis, 74
Louisa, 67
Lucinda x, 29
Margaret, 74
Margaret x, 74
Marietta, 85
Mary, 128
Mary J.x, 34
Mary x, 34
Mildred, 29
Nancy, 85
Pelina, 17
Perry x, 26
Randolph x, 85
S.M., 15
Sarah, 128
Susan, 128
Thomas, 15
∗William, 85
William H., 67,
   74
Pigg
John C.x, 52
Louisa x, 52
William x, 52
Pinchen
Elizabeth x, 115
Pine
∗Alex, 53
Chloe, 53
Elizabeth, 53
Emma, 54
∗Floyd, 53
Hester Ann, 53
James E., 54
John x, 103
Julia A., 53
Louisa A., 53
Martha F., 53
Mary, 53
Nancy E., 53
∗Overton, 53
Rufus, 53

Victoria x, 103
Virginia, 53
Washington x, 93
William x, 3
Plybon
Alfred, 57
Calvery, 57
Eliza, 48
Elizabeth, 48, 57
Emily, 58
Evermont, 58
Irene, 57
∗Jacob, 47
∗James C., 58
∗John, 48, 57
Louis, 57
Lucien, 58
Mary, 57
Polly, 47
Poage
Alberta x, 53
Anna M., 50
∗James, 50
James H., 136
John B., 50
Marcella x, 53
Sarah, 50
Poindexter
James x, 32
Pollard
J.C.x, 50
Polly
Amos E. x, 111
Mary A. x, 111
William x, 111
Poor
Alfred, 127
Allen, 127
∗David, 128
Elias, 127
∗Elisha, 127
Eliza, 128
Francis M., 128
Francis x, 126
George W., 128
Joseph L., 128
Mary J.x, 128
Sarah, 128
Stephen, 127
Susan x, 25
Tasey, 127
Porter
Adaline, 86
Albert, 117
∗Alexander, 28, 77
Alonzo, 55
∗Anna, 55
Benjamin F., 56
Catherine, 55
∗Cummings, 49

174

Porter (continued)
Cynthia, 28
*David, 102
Edney, 117
Elijah, 70
Elisha, 28
Eliza, 68
Elvira, 28
Emily, 117
Francis, 28
Harriett, 28
Jackson x, 69
Jacob, 86
*James, 69, 86
James H., 86, 102
James x, 68
*Jernel, 86
Jessee, 117
John, 28, 68, 77
John J., 86
John L. x, 69
John W., 102
John x, 69
Joseph, 55, 102
Juda, 86
Letha, 77
Levina x, 69
*Lewis, 68
Louisa, 86
Lucinda, 69
Malinda, 77
Margaret, 69
Martha, 117
Martha J., 102
Mary, 55, 102
Mary C., 56
Mary J., 56
Matilda, 117
Mildred, 77
Nancy, 56, 70, 86, 117
Nelsina, 86
Patrick, 28
Polly x, 69
Priscilla, 49
Rolin, 86
*Samuel, 69, 77
Sarah, 55, 77, 86, 117, 136
Sarah x, 69, 86
Tabitha, 28
*William, 69, 117
William x, 69
*Zephemiah, 56

Poteet
Amanda, 17
Clementine, 63
Frances B., 17
*H.C., 17
James, 63

James x, 128
John L., 63
Martha, 63
*Skelton, 63
Susan, 63
William A., 17

Powell
*Andrew, 96
Henry, 97
Mary, 97
Mary A., 96
Nancy, 96
*Phillip, 97, 136
Rebecca, 96

Powers
Thomas x, 49

Preble
Ulysus x, 42

Price
Evin x, 128
George L., 41
James A.x, 24
*Joseph, 41
Minerva, 41

Pridemore
Jeremiah, 105
*Joseph, 105
Nancy, 105
Rhoda, 105

Pritchard
Clarissa, 76
Eveline, 76
*Lewis, 76
Nancy, 76

Proctor
Agnes, 4
Ellen, 4
*George, 4, 5
James, 4
John, 5
Margaret, 4
Mary, 5(2)

Puckett
*John, 52
Nancy E., 52
Patsey, 52

Pugh
Jesse x, 62

Pullen
Andrew, 96
Charles, 96
Danville, 96
Elizabeth x, 96
James, 96
John B., 96
Martha, 96
Melissa, 96
Rebecca x, 96
Susan, 96
*William, 96

Pulley
*David, 19
John, 19
Julia A., 19
Lemanda, 19
Melissa, 19
Rebecca, 19
*William, 19

Quintin
Ahaz, 115
Calpherona, 115
Caroline x, 115
Elizabeth, 115
Frances x, 115
*James M, 115
Mahala, 115
Mary, 115

Rains
Albert, 25
Eliza, 25
James, 25
*Lewis, 25
Mary, 25
William x, 27

Ramsey
*Allen, 101
Bula, 101
Edward, 101
Ellen, 101
Nancy, 101
Nicholas, 101
William, 101

Rardon
Araminta, 112
*Lyman, 112

Ratcliff
Alice, 55
Ephrain, 55
George, 55
James, 55
*Jane, 55
Matilda, 55
Nancy, 55
Squire, 55
William, 55

Ray
Albert, 58
America, 58
Andrew, 85
Benjamin, 58
Blackburn, 83
*Catherine, 83
Eglantine, 58
Eliza, 58
Emily, 58
Greenville, 83
*Isaiah, 58
Jefferson, 58
John, 85
Joseph, 58

Julia, 85
Lemuel, 58
Lemuel x, 23
Levina x, 50
Lucy, 58
Marcellus, 58
Mary A., 58
Millard, 58
Morris, 85
Sarah, 58
Susan, 58
Ulysses, 83
Virginia, 58
*William, 58, 85
William W., 83

Ray/Roy

Rece
*Abia, 121, 134
*Addison, 121
Alice, 122
Amelia, 121
Andrew G., 49
Calvin, 121
*Edmund, 122, 136
Elizabeth, 121
Elizabeth x, 26
Emma V., 49
Georgia, 121
James, 121, 126
*James H., 126
*John B., 26
*John C., 49, 135
*John M., 121, 136
Joseph L., 121
Leonard, 121
Madera, 121
Margaret, 49
Martha, 121, 126
Mary, 121, 126
Mary x. 26
Miram, 121
Rebecca, 126
Sophia, 122
Theodore, 122
*Thomas H., 121, 126
Warren P., 121

Reed
Judson x, 54
Sophia x, 40

Reynolds
Alfred, 103
Amy, 103
*Archibald, 83, 136
Eliza, 53
Elizabeth, 126
*Ezekiel, 103
Frances, 52
*Griffin B., 126

George W.x, 93
Lucinda x, 93
Maria x, 93

Shipe
✶Charles. 5
Ellen, 5
Mary E., 5
William A., 5

Shoemaker
Charles x, 32
George, 49
✶James H., 49
Joanna, 49
Martha, 49
Sarah, 49

Shomburg
George, 45
✶John B., 45
Mary, 45

Short
Catherine x, 94
Ellen, 94
Emily, 94
Jeremiah x, 94
✶Robert, 94
Samuel, 94
Shelton x, 99
Sophia x, 94

Showans
✶Abagail, 62
Mary M., 62
Presley x, 26
Sally x, 81
Samuel. 62

Showater
Christiana, 36
✶Frank, 36

Shy
Abagail, 50
✶Benjamin, 48
Cenna, 50
Edgar, 48
Edney, 50
✶Edward, 47, 50
Elizabeth, 47
Eutassis, 50
Franklin, 50
✶H.W., 50
Henry, 50
Josephine, 50
Mahala, 47
Marcellue B., 50
Mary, 48
Mary E., 48

Sidebottom
John C. x, 115

Simmons
✶Adam, 56
✶Conwesley, 32
Deliah, 56

Elizabeth, 32
Henry A., 56
Joel, 56
Joseph, 56
Mary F., 32
Nathaniel, 56
Robert, 56
Sampson S., 32

Simpson
Catherine, 75
✶Charles, 75

Smallridge
Elizabeth, 120
James, 120
John, 120
✶John W., 120
Mary x, 35
Sampson x, 120

Smith
✶A.J., 80
Abraham, 43
Alexander, 97
Alfred, 111
Allen, 110
Almina x, 97
Amanda, 45
✶Ambrose, 27
America, 91
Anderson, 111
Andrew, 98
Angelina, 27
Anna, 36
Asinth, 111
✶Austin. 45
✶Ballard, 89
Barbary x, 124
Benjamin, 66
Betsey, 98
Burwell, 27
Catherine, 34,
   125
✶Charles, 22, 34,
   125
Charles E., 45
Columbus, 111
Crosby, 89
Cynthia, 98
Cynthia x, 30
✶D.D., 43
Daniel, 56
✶Daniel P., 125
David, 89
David F. x, 25
Dudley J., 43
✶E.A., 38
Edward E., 38
Eleanor, 89
Eleanor C., 43
Elijah, 125
Eliza, 31, 34

Eliza A., 125
Elizabeth, 22,
   27, 98, 88
Elizabeth x, 26
Elliza, 27
Emily x, 97
Emma, 27, 66
✶Eveline, 25
Frances, 89
Francis, 25
✶Frank, 36
Georgia, 43
Harriett, 88, 121
✶Harvey, 25, 97
✶Henry, 27, 31
Henry S., 45
Hulda, 89
Isaac, 88
Isadore x, 124
Jackson, 66
✶Jacob, 115
✶Jacob M., 27
Jacob x, 27
✶James, 27, 66,
   98, 121
James H., 34
James x, 88
Jane x, 26
✶Jessee D., 91
Jo Anna, 27
✶John, 25, 34, 66,
   97, 115
John C., 125
John C.x. 26
John J., 56
✶John W., 123
Joseph, 98
Joseph M., 80
Joseph x, 41, 80
Josephine, 38
Joshua, 125
✶Juda, 91
Julia, 111
Lafayette, 97
Lawrence, 115
Lewellyn, 45
Lewis, 89
Lewis H., 80
Lewis x, 95, 99
Louisa, 110
Lourana, 89
Lucy, 56, 97
Lucy x, 32
Luke x, 90
Mahala, 97, 110
Marcus, 25
Margaret, 123
Margaret x, 79
Martha, 27, 98
Martha x, 131

Martin, 34
Mary, 25, 27, 36,
   43. 91. 115.
   123. 124
Mary A., 34, 42
Mary A. x, 3
Mary J., 80
Mary P., 38
Mary x, 26, 80
Matilda, 115
Matilda x, 88
Nancy, 45, 97
nancy, 98
Nancy, 111
Nathan, 91
Nathaniel x, 80
Noah, 31
P.S., 135
Patsey, 66
Paulina, 125
✶Percival, 42
Percival S., 42
✶Peter, 111
Phoebe, 98
Polly, 124
✶Ralph, 110
Randolph, 27
Rebecca, 43, 123
Rebecca x, 88
Richard P., 42
Robert, 56
Samanthia, 98
✶Samuel, 97
Sarah, 22, 25, 27
sarah, 89
Sarah, 98, 111,
   125
Sarah J., 43
Sarah M., 80
Senia, 31
Sina, 89
Sinate, 91
Susan x, 85
Telitha, 27, 110
✶Thomas, 56, 98,
   124
Thomas x, 59
✶Traverse, 121
Victoria, 123
✶Viola, 27
Virginia x, 124
W.W. x, 8
Whitcomb, 43
✶William, 22, 27,
   43, 56, 98
William H., 66,
   111, 123
William x, 12
Zachariah, 31

Snapp

179

Ella, 54
⨯Jacob, 54
Sarah A., 54
Sasmuel, 54
Tennessee, 54
Sullivan
  Alonzo C., 51
  Amanda, 60
  Catherine, 51
  Daniel, 51
  David, 60
  Elizabeth, 51, 55
  Ellen x, 60
  *Henry, 51
  ⨯Jacob, 60
  ⨯James, 55
  Louisa, 60
  Martha, 51
  Mary, 55
  Mary J., 51
  Melissa, 51
Summers
  Constantine, 124
  Edgar, 124
  ⨯George W., 124,
    136
  Matthew, 124
  Sarah, 124
  Sylvester, 124
  Thomas, 137
  Thomas B., 124
  Tyre C., 124
Summerson
  ⨯Charles, 39
  Emma, 39
  Richard, 39
Swann
  Ballard, 83
  ⨯Benjamin, 25, 34
  ⨯Calvary, 33
  Catherine, 83
  Charlotte, 25
  Cynthia, 12, 33
  Daniel W., 34
  Edith, 34
  Elizabeth, 33
  Emanuel, 12
  Emily, 25, 33
  Enoch, 33
  Francis, 25
  George, 33
  *H.C., 83
  Henry C., 33
  Hester, 33
  *Hezekiah, 83
  James H., 12
  Jasper, 33
  Jerome S., 34
  ⨯John, 34
  John K., 33

John R., 12
Joseph, 33
Joseph W., 12
*Josiah, 33
*Levin, 11
Louisa, 25
Martha, 12
Mary, 33, 83
Mary A.x, 83
McHearston, 33
Nancy, 33, 83
Nancy B., 33
Patrick, 83
Rachel, 33
Reason, 33
Richard A., 34
Sarah, 33
Shelby, 12
Susan, 11
Thomas, 33
William, 33
Sweatland
  Anna, 16
  Carolina, 16
  *I.V., 16
  John S., 16
  Louis, 16
  Margaret, 16
  Martha, 16
  Mary, 16
  William x, 37
Switzer
  E.C.R., 15
  Ellen, 15
  *Jonathan, 15
  Rufus P., 15
  Vara A., 15
Tasson
  Cynthia, 30
  *John, 30
  Mary, 30
  Rebecca, 30
Taylor
  ⨯Allen, 129
  Catherine, 35
  Esther, 129
  Eveline, 132
  Frances x, 46
  *George, 132
  *Henry, 35
  Margaret, 129
  Susan, 129
  William, 35
  William x, 7
Teal
  Adam, 30
  Elizabeth, 30
  Jacob, 30
  John W., 30
  Lori, 30

Philip, 30
*Samuel, 30
Terissa, 30
William J., 30
Telginer
  Emile x, 10
Templeton
  Addison, 119
  Anna, 119
  Charles, 119, 122
  Esom, 119
  Frances, 122
  *Harvey, 119
  Isaac, 119
  ⨯James, 119
  ⨯Jesse, 122
  John, 119, 122
  Julia, 122
  Lucinda, 119
  Martin, 122
  Mary, 119
  Mary A., 119
  Matilda x, 16
  Ransom, 119
  Sarah, 122
  Thomas, 122
  William, 119
  William H., 122
Terry
  Elizabeth, 76
  Elizabeth x, 69
  ⨯Emily, 76
  James, 76
  Parker, 77
  Polly, 77
  Sarilda, 77
Thacketon
  B.H.x, 6
Thomas
  David, 128
  Joseph x, 102
  Mary, 128
  Nancy, 128
  Nelson, 128
  ⨯Susan, 128
  William M., 128
Thompson
  A.J. x, 62
  Adaline, 64
  ⨯Ahart O., 64
  Andrew, 104
  Angeline, 104
  *Carrie, 29
  Charles x, 57
  Elizabeth, 2, 29,
    93
  Ellender, 104
  Elsey, 104
  Emily, 64, 93
  Fountain x, 104

*Gilmore, 57
Harriett, 64
*Hasting, 104
Henry, 93
Isaac, 29
*James, 29, 64,
  93, 105
Jeremiah, 29
John, 29
*John ', 105
John x, 46
Julia, 105
Lawson, 29
Lucetta, 57
Lucinda, 57
Maria, 57
Martha, 29
Martha J.x, 56
Mary, 29, 104,
  113
Mary J. x, 57
Mary M., 105
Mary P.x, 56
*Matthew, 2
Milton, 64
Nancy A., 29
⨯Robert, 104
Stanhope, 29
Thomas, 57
⨯Virginia, 57, 104
⨯William, 29, 113
Winnie, 113
Thornburg
  Anna, 23
  Barbary, 38
  Benton, 38
  Caroline, 131
  Charles, 53
  Claudius, 23
  *David W., 52
  Elizabeth, 131
  Ellen, 6
  Emily, 23
  Emma, 23
  George E., 6
  *H.M, 38
  Isabella, 38
  James, 135
  ⨯James L., 53
  Joanna, 52
  John S., 6
  *John W., 23, 134
  John x, 38
  Maggie L., 6
  Mary, 4, 23
  Mary L., 6
  Mary M. x, 23
  Moses, 4
  ⨯Moses , 131
  Rachel, 52

181

Mary, 22
Mary F., 7
Patrick, 7
Rundle x, 50
*Thomas, 7
Walter, 7
William, 7, 22, 49
Warren
  Angelina, 40
  Caroline, 40
  Chancey, 40
  G.D., 40
  *George W., 40
Warrick
  Elizabeth, 88
  *Fielding, 88
  James, 88
  Mary, 88
  Nancy, 88
  Rhoda, 88
  Robert, 88(2)
  Thomas, 88
  Wesley, 88
  William W., 88
Watson
  *Alexander, 69
  E.H., 135
  Mary A., 69
  Mary x, 15
  Nancy J., 69
  Sarah, 69
  Virginia, 134
  Virginia x, 15
  William L., 69
Waugh
  *Charles, 67
  Hiram, 67
  Louara, 67
Webb
  *Alexander Jr., 34
  *Alexander Sr., 35
  Ann E.x, 93
  Cynthia, 104
  David, 35
  Eliza, 93
  Elizabeth x, 93
  Emogene, 93
  George, 26
  Hannah, 100
  Helen, 100
  Isabella x, 93
  James, 34, 93
  Jane, 100
  Jane x, 93
  John, 26, 100
  John B.x, 93
  Julia, 26
  Lowis, 93
  Margaret, 35

Marinda, 03
Mary, 104
Nancy, 35, 104
Peggy, 35
Roxana, 34
Samuel x, 93
Sarah, 35, 93
*Stephen, 35
Theodere x, 93
Therisa, 100
William, 34
*William W., 100
Weiger
  Frank, 35
  Frank x, 90
  Joseph x, 90
  *Lewis, 35
  Mary, 35
  Susan, 35
Wellington
  Charlotte, 41
  Elizabeth, 41
  *Erastus, 41
  *Erastus Jr., 41
  Frances, 41
  James W., 41
  Lucinda, 41
  Nathaniel, 41
  *Noadiah, 41
  Sarah, 41
  Zach.Taylor, 41
Westhoff
  Anna, 5
  *Arnold, 5, 135
  Edward, 5
  Joseph, 5
  Josephine, 5
Wheeler
  Hansley, 117
  John, 117
  Joseph B. x, 7
  Louisa, 117
  Lucinda, 117
  Mary, 117
  Matilda x, 109
  Peggy, 116
  *Reason, 117
  Vernila x, 109
  *William, 116
  *Zach, 117
White
  *Albert, 45
  Alice J., 46
  Caroline C.x, 40
  Catherine, 115
  Emma, 131
  Eustacia, 115
  *James H., 115
  Jane, 132
  *John, 45, 115

Lucy, 45, 132
Martha M., 45
Mary, 45, 131, 132
Moses, 132
Nimrod, 115
Peter *, 131
Sarah, 115
Susan G., 45
Theresa, 132
*Zach, 132
Whitten
  Cire, 4
  Elizabeth, 4
  Emeline, 4
  Hetty, 4
  *L.T., 4
  Mary M., 4
  Thomas M., 4
  William W., 4
Wikoss
  Lucinda x, 109
Wilkenson
  Barbary, 92
  David, 92
  George, 92
  Ira, 92
  *John, 92
  Mary F., 92
  Permelia, 92
  Wilber, 92
Wilkes
  Albert, 56
  Alexander, 56
  Barbary, 56
  *Burwell, 56
  George W., 56
  Henry, 56
  James, 56
  James x, 55
  Mary, 56
  Mary x, 127
  Nathan, 56
  Sarah, 56
Wilkinson
  Anna, 102
  Augustan, 102
  Barbary, 92
  *Benjamin, 102
  David, 92
  Eli, 102
  George, 92
  Ira, 92
  *JOhn *, 92
  John H., 96
  Martha, 102
  Mary T., 92
  Permelia, 92
  *Stephen, 96
  Wilbur, 92

William G., 102
William W., 96
Williams
  *A.W., 81
  America, 25
  Arthur x, 54
  Austin, 108
  Cynthia, 26
  David, 26, 81
  Eliza x, 54
  Elizabeth, 25, 26
  Felix, 108
  Frances B.x, 54
  *George W., 26
  James, 81
  Jane x, 13
  John, 108
  John x, 3
  Lily, 26
  Lucy, 108
  Mariam, 26
  Mary, 25, 81
  *Matilda, 75
  *Matthew, 108
  *Mourning, 117
  Nancy, 25, 117
  Patrick, 81
  Rebecca, 54
  Samuel, 108
  Samuel x, 116
  Sarah, 81, 108
  Spencer x, 12
  Thomas, 81
  Walter, 81
  *William, 25, 54, 133
Williamson
  Emma, 113
  *John, 113
  S.O., 113
Wilson
  *A.L., 31
  Charles, 62
  Eliza, 31
  Elizabeth, 31, 62
  Ellen, 31
  Emily, 31
  Frances, 31
  George x, 50
  Georgia, 31
  Harvey x, 31
  Hester, 31
  *James, 62, 134
  John, 31
  John T., 62
  Lemuel, 31
  Malinda, 31
  Mary, 31
  Nancy, 62
  Sarah, 62

www.ingramcontent.com/pod-product-compliance
Lightning Source LLC
Chambersburg PA
CBHW080238270326
41926CB00020B/4287